Charlotte M. M Lain
1995

MUSIC RESEARCH AND INFORMATION GUIDES
VOL. 18

TUDOR MUSIC

GARLAND REFERENCE LIBRARY
OF THE HUMANITIES
VOL. 1122

Music Research and Information Guides

TUDOR MUSIC

*A Research and
Information Guide*

With an appendix
updating *William Byrd:
A Guide to Research*

Richard Turbet

GARLAND PUBLISHING, Inc.
New York & London / 1994

Library of Congress Cataloging-in-Publication Data

Turbet, Richard.
    Tudor music : a research and information guide /
by Richard Turbet.
        p.   cm. — (Music research and information
guides ; vol. 18) (Garland reference library of the
humanities ; vol. 1122)
    "William Byrd, a guide to research since 1986"—P.
Includes index.
    ISBN 0–8240–4296–4
    1. Music—England—16th century—History and
criticism—Bibliography. 2. Music—England—17th
century—History and criticism—Bibliography.
3. Byrd, William, 1542 or 3–1623—Bibliography.
I. Title. II. Series.   III. Series: Garland reference
library of the humanities ; vol. 1122.
ML114.T
780'.942'09031—dc20   93–38771
                                    CIP
                                    MN

Printed on acid-free, 250-year-life paper
Manufactured in the United States of America

To My Godparents:

William Smart, and in memory of James H. Colsell
and Maisie Griffiths.

Also remembering with gratitude my late aunts,
Vera Colsell and Winifred Turbet.

CONTENTS

ACKNOWLEDGEMENTS

Without the grant I was offered by the Hinrichsen Foundation this project could not have been completed. To the Trustees and to their secretary, Lesley Adamson, my most profound gratitude.

Also I am immensely grateful to the British Academy for a Small Personal Research Grant for the preparation of camera-ready copy.

My third debt of institutional gratitude, no less keenly felt, is to the Research Committee of the University of Aberdeen for approving a period of Research Leave.

Personal thanks go to Reginald Pringle and Angela Carr, respectively University Librarian and Head of Learning Resources at Aberdeen University Library, for their unhesitating and constructive support; also to other colleagues whose assistance was valuable: Margaret Coutts, Katharina McCurdy, Sheona Farquhar, Carla Leslie, Lesley Hendry, Jennifer Beavan, Fred Murray, Gilian Johnston, Ann Milne, Margaret Ladwiniec, Michael Craig, Caroline Gilbert, Gordon Stables and Mary Murray. Elsewhere in the University I am glad to acknowledge the help of Roger Witts and Grant Simpson. Also I wish to pay tribute to the memories of Margaret Thomson, Maryon Buchan and Ronald C. Miller.

Fellow Librarians and archivists who have also been helpful include Malcolm Turner (British Library), John Wagstaff (Faculty of Music, University of Oxford), Peter Ward Jones (Bodleian), David Griffiths (University of York), Brian Dyson (University of Hull), Adrian and Ann Yardley (Guildhall School of Music and Drama), Helen Mason (Lincolnshire), David Cook (London Borough of Bromley), Paul Andrews (Bedford), Jeremy Upton (Edinburgh University) and Douglas Johnson (Staffordshire Record Society). I am also obliged to

Timothy Brown (Director of Music, Clare College, Cambridge), Alan Brown (University of Sheffield), Philip Brett (University of California), The Carver Choir, John Rutter, Donald Hunt, Harry Christophers, William Hunt, Anthony Scull and David Pears.

In my final year as an undergraduate at University College London, my tutor was the late A.G. Petti. Later I became his Research Assistant when he was Head of the Department of English at the University of Calgary, and I transcribed the Bagot Letters for his edition entitled *Roman Catholicism in Elizabethan and Jacobean Staffordshire* (Stafford: Staffordshire Record Society, 1979). It is a pleasure to acknowledge the early stimulus this gave me, leading indirectly and elsewhere to my work on Byrd, and more directly to an abiding love of secretary hand. He was one of very few people whom I have encountered who were equally at home academically in English Literature, his official subject, and Music, for which discipline he made some fine editions of Renaissance, including Tudor, works. I am glad to include, on merit, an essay of his on the recusant composer and pupil of Byrd, Peter Philips, and one by Christopher Harrison on Byrd and Staffordshire, discovered thanks to my earlier collaboration with Tony.

I owe a substantial debt of gratitude to Marjorie Leith who took over the typesetting when, just for a change, disaster stared me in the face. Her professionalism has been magnificent.

I thank my mother for her continuing interest and encouragement.

Finally, my family - wife Lynda and "The Young Ones" William and Rory - were "completely brilliant." God bless you.

INTRODUCTION

The penchant of the British for understatement is stretched to its limit in propagating their literature in general and the works of Shakespeare in particular. A casualty of this process is the nation's music, notably that of its finest period, the age of Shakespeare. His works are seldom described as originating during the age of Byrd. Yet in reading about, and listening to, the music produced in England and Scotland during the Tudor period, one becomes intoxicated by its high quality, huge quantity and wide variety. Thanks to recordings, broadcasts and concerts even the most obscure sacred music can be performed and heard. There will always be some who cannot find it within themselves to respond to music of this period, but for many it has changed their lives not only for the better, but for a "better" they had never anticipated. What makes Tudor music so interesting is that, like that of Spain, another country with a glorious heritage of music from this period, it tended to develop a little behind the pacesetters in Italy and the Low Countries, and in so doing retained many older insular traits that were adapted to suit new styles: the In nomine and the relationship of the consort song to the madrigal are cases in point. If the present *Guide* brings someone to Tudor music for the first time, or enables someone already familiar with it to develop their appreciation, it will have served a worthwhile purpose. But these are all words. The important thing is the music itself, and for that music to be performed and heard. The rewards of participation as exponent or audience are immeasurable. It is towards these rewards that the present book seeks to be a guide.

The apparently simple term Tudor proved troublesome to define. For the present *Guide* it covers music from the time of the Eton Choirbook to that of Adrian Batten, born in 1591, whose stylistically conservative anthems are often included in modern collections of Tudor sacred music.

Items have been positively selected for inclusion: the *Guide* is not an attempt to list every piece of writing on Tudor music. Therefore it is not necessary for the abstracts to recommend particular items as this is implicit in their inclusion. Abstracts certainly do not correspond to the length of the items to which they refer. Some items require little comment if their titles are self-explanatory. The length of an abstract is dictated by how much needs to be written to convey the gist of an item. Some short items are about knotty problems that need plenteous explanation. Some long items can be characterized briefly. A few items have been selected for one quirky or revelatory detail. Many were deliberately excluded because other writings deal with the same topic as capably or better. Warnings are posted where otherwise acceptable items contain information or opinions now superseded or plainly wrong. With one exception theses are not included because their information that is appropriate for abstracting in this *Guide* is recycled in monographic form or as articles. Those theses that might contain material of use to advanced researchers are all cited in items included in this *Guide*.

The entries are arranged into twelve broad subject categories, each category given a chapter, each entry given an italicized running number. Many entries are on more than one topic. For this reason, at the end of each chapter there is a list of entries that partly deal with the topic in hand but that are in other chapters. These are items that mention two or exceptionally three topics in some detail. Items that cover three or more topics are allocated to the general chapters I, II or XII. Where a particular item relates to another, a reference to the other item is included in the abstract except usually for items about the same composer. The musician index is intended for researchers wishing to construct bibliographies or reading lists for specific composers; this facility prevents the text from becoming choked with "see" and "see also" references. The names are taken from the titles of entries, but in the case of an article about a composer whose name does not appear in the title, the composer's name is italicized in the abstract and is included in the index. Names of authors are given as in the original items, but are made consistent (or corrected) for the author index. Pagination is not given for books unless they are entirely about Tudor music. Inverted commas are avoided wherever possible in the abstracts. If any authors successfuly abstract their own articles by way of introduction or summary, their wording is unhesitatingly adapted if it cannot be bettered, but is not extensively quoted verbatim. Citation is by running number. Items published up to the end of 1991 are included. The ordering is chronological by year and alphabetical by author within years except in chapter XII where the latter is alphabetical by composer.

It will be noted that Byrd is excluded from the main narrative, except for a few items that discuss him beside other composers. This is because my Composer Resource Manual *William Byrd: a Guide to Research* (New York: Garland, 1987) deals with every aspect of information about him and as this volume is easily accessible, there is no point in duplicating its contents. For some items readers are referred to the abstracts in the Manual on Byrd. The present *Guide* includes a substantial Appendix updating the Manual. As explained in the introduction to the Appendix, its numerical sequences and format continue those of the original Manual, but for the purposes of the present *Guide*, its running numbers, whether from the Manual or the Appendix, are prefixed *WB*: so, the Manual itself is numbered *WB153*. In the Appendix, running numbers referring to the rest of the *Guide* are prefixed *TM* (for Tudor Music) to avoid any confusion with *WB* numbers. It has been found possible to include items relevant to the Appendix that have been published up to the end of 1992. Of particular importance is the inclusion, in section A-X of the Appendix, of reproductions of hitherto unpublished fragments of pieces by or attributed to Byrd. A further guide to Byrd research, to cover the 450th anniversary year 1993, with supplementary material from 1992 (itself a possible but less likely anniversary year), is to be published in *Brio* during 1994 or 1995.

"I guess that covers everything."
(Groucho Marx: *Horse Feathers*)

I REFERENCE WORKS

This unavoidably miscellaneous chapter contains dictionaries, encyclopaedias, histories, catalogues including early printed music, and guide to periodicals. These items are too general to be confined within subsequent categories, and tend to cover a chronological or geographical range beyond what is defined as Tudor. Library catalogues are discussed in the introduction to chapter X: Source Materials.

1. Abraham, Gerald, ed. *The Age of Humanism 1540-1630*. The New Oxford History of Music, 4. London: Oxford University Press, 1968. ML160.N44.

    Several essays in this now rather dated survey contain sections on Tudor music. In chapter 2, "The Sixteenth-Century Madrigal," Edward J. Dent devotes the last eight of thirty sections to the madrigal in England and various specific composers in a clear-sighted though brisk survey. Nigel Fortune devotes six sections in chapter 4, "Solo Song and Cantata," to consort songs and ayres from mid-century to Rosseter. Frank Ll. Harrison is given the whole of chapter 9 for "Church Music in England" but in only fifty pages tries to impart too much information in insufficient space. The sections on English music in the chapters by Meyer and Apel on consort and solo instrumental (mainly keyboard) music are of little account beside their own monographs (see *341* and *271*).

2. Brown, Howard Meyer. *Music in the Renaissance*. Prentice-Hall History of Music Series. Englewood Cliffs: Prentice-Hall, 1976. 0136085059. ML172.B86.

The outstanding general introduction to the music of the period within which the Tudors functioned. Brown devotes a section to England within the chapter on national styles 1520-60, and Tudor composers are mentioned in further chapters on instrumental music and the Reformation, though in the latter Brown deals with psalters and not Anglican liturgical music. He devotes a quarter of his penultimate chapter to an appreciation of Byrd.

3. Caldwell, John. *The Oxford History of English Music.* Vol. 1: From the Beginnings to c.1715. Oxford: Clarendon, 1991. 0198161298. ML286.C28.

Supersedes all previous histories of English music. Chapters 4-8 deal comprehensively with all aspects of the Tudor period, and it is valuable to be able to appreciate, from surrounding chapters, the continuum within which Tudor music evolved, and what it in turn became. Illustrations are good, the bibliography less so. Caldwell's judgements are judicious throughout. He endeavours to mention as many significant musicians as possible without allowing his narrative to degenerate into a mere list. Unfortunately he accepts the existence of the specious category of "great " Services: see *WB163* and *WB183.*

4. Fidler, Linda M. *and* James, Richard S., *eds. International Music Journals.* Historical Guides to the World's Periodicals and Newspapers. Westport: Greenwood, 1990. 0313250049. ML128.P2416.

Lists alphabetically. Short essays encapsulate the ethos of each journal. The only drawback in the case of Tudor music is that in Appendix E, "Subject listing of periodicals by title," there are no headings for early music nor authenticity. The content is not limited to current journals.

5. Gooch, Bryan N.S. *and* Thatcher, David. *A Shakespeare Music Catalogue.* Oxford: Clarendon, 1991. 5v. 0198129416/24/32/ 40/59. ML134.5.S52G6.

In the first three volumes lists all music related to the

authenticated and apocryphal works of Shakespeare. Of particular interest are the lists of musical stage directions for each play. Very few Tudor composers feature in these volumes, and although volume four includes an alphabetical index of composers, a chronological listing would have been useful. Of most value to students of Tudor music is the final volume, a selective and annotated bibliography, divided into sections on topics such as theatre music in Shakespeare's England, his knowledge and use of music and song, Shakespeare and composers, Shakespeare and musical performance, and lists of Shakespearean music. As another poet wrote, "that is all Ye know on earth, and all ye need to know" about Shakespeare and music. The *terminus ad quem* is the end of 1987.

6. Heyer, Anna Harriet. *Historical Sets, Collected Editions, and Monuments of Music: A Guide to Their Contents.* 3rd ed. Chicago: American Library Association, 1980 2v. 083890288X. ML113.H52.

   Lists volume titles within the complete works of specific composers, series such as *Musica Britannica* and *Early English Church Music* and titles of individual works in sets such as those of the Musical Antiquarian and Motett Societies important early in the Tudor revival. Also gives full catalogue entries for published editions of such "monuments" as the Fitzwilliam Virginal Book. Scheduled for publication in December 1992 is *Collected Editions, Historical Series & Sets, & Monuments of Music: a Bibliography* by George R. Hill and Norris L. Stephens (Berkeley, CA: Fallen Leaf).

7. Hodges, Anthony, *comp., and* McGill, Raymond, *ed. The British Union Catalogue of Music Periodicals.* London: Library Association, 1985. 0853655170. ML128.P24.

   Lists British locations of all music periodicals taken by libraries in the United Kingdom and Republic of Ireland.

8. Lesure, Francois. *Recueils imprimes XVIe-XVIIe siecles. I: Liste chronologique.* Repertoire international des Sources musicales. München: Henle, 1960. ML113.I6.

Chronological list of all anthologies published during the sixteenth and seventeenth centuries, with contributing locations. Index of composers and compilers. Companion to *13*. No sign of II.

9. Penney, Barbara. *Music in British Libraries*. 3rd ed. London: Library Association, 1981. 0853659818. ML21.G7.

Lists all libraries in the United Kingdom that contain musical collections. Provides addresses, hours of opening, telephone numbers, names of music librarians, services, special collections and publications. Since the majority of Tudor music manuscripts are in British libraries, besides many early printed editions, this is an indispensable practical resource. A new edition was scheduled under the same imprint early in 1992.

10. Reese, Gustave. *Music in the Renaissance*. Rev. ed. New York: Norton; London: Dent, 1959. ML172.R47.

The two final chapters of this *magnum opus* are devoted to England: chapter 15 from c.1450 to c.1531 and sacred music to c.1635; chapter 16, secular music c.1535 to 1635. Reese subdivides his chapters into specific topics, such as music for instrumental ensemble, and in the course of each he reviews its development chronologically, mentioning as many composers and works as appropriately possible, supported by copious illustrations. A particular strength is the way Reese places English circumstances within the context of those of continental Europe.

11. Roche, Jerome *and* Roche, Elizabeth. *A Dictionary of Early Music from the Troubadours to Monteverdi*. London: Faber, 1981. 0195202554. ML100.R695.

The only dictionary in English devoted to early music. Includes proper names.

12. Sadie, Stanley, *ed. The New Grove Dictionary of Music and Musicians*. London: Macmillan, 1980. 20v. 0333231112. ML 100.N48.

Best musical dictionary in English. Contains entries for c.150 Tudor composers, for many of whom this is the only reference of any substance. This should be the first port of call for anyone researching even the most obscure Tudor composer, followed by *303* and *91*.

13. Schlager, Karlheinz *et al, eds. Einzeldrücke vor 1800.* Repertoire international des Sources musicales. Kassel: Bärenreiter, 1971. 12v. ML113.I6.

List of all publications from before 1800 devoted to a single composer. Provides locations. Awaiting completion. Companion to *8*. Alphabetical by composer.

14. Schnapper, Edith B., *ed. The British Union-Catalogue of Early Music, Printed Before the Year 1801: a Record of Holdings of Over One Hundred Libraries Throughout the British Isles.* London: Butterworth, 1957. 2v. ML116.B7.

Attempted listing of all known pre-1801 printed music in British libraries, though some were unable to supply full holdings. Entries by composer (or keyword where anonymous). Gives locations. Superseded by *8* and *13*, and though less accurate, provides fuller entries, still having its uses for some aspects of bibliographical checking. Includes alphabetical index of titles.

See also WB141, WB142, WB150.

II GENERAL WORKS

This chapter includes items that deal with the Tudor period but not with any specific aspect. Items dealing, however broadly, with specific aspects of Tudor music will be found in the appropriate succeeding chapters.

15. Austern, Linda Phyllis. "'Sing againe syren': the Female Musician and Sexual Enchantment in Elizabethan Life and Literature." *Renaissance Quarterly* 42 (1989): 420-48.

Explains the Renaissance attitudes to women and to music. By quoting contemporary literary texts that refer to women, the author is able to delineate the role expected of females in making music at this time in England. There was much fear of inflaming male sexual awareness through the juxtaposing of music and femininity, so although musical females were encouraged in their musical accomplishments, they were generally required to keep them private, though many did not do so.

16. Buxton, John. *Elizabethan Taste*. London: Macmillan, 1963; rev. repr. 1965. N6765.B87.

Chapter V is devoted to music. The author details what is known of Queen Elizabeth's own accomplishments and tastes, and goes on to discuss sacred music, the musical education and tastes of courtiers and the nobility, and the role of music in the home and the theatre. Copious background information helps to place music in the contemporary context of religious controversy, patronage and overseas influences. This study emphasizes the extent to which music permeated late Tudor society. The author clarifies the various contemporary attitudes to music, but these attitudes all reflect a unified comprehension of music's purpose. Explaining this is his most substantial achievement.

17. Hollander, John. *The Untuning of the Sky: Ideas of Music in English Poetry, 1500-1700*. Princeton: Princeton University Press, 1961; repr. ed. New York: Norton, 1970. ML3849.H54.

Concerns certain beliefs about music rather than music itself. These beliefs were changing during the centuries in question from a mediaevel view of the function of music as reflecting universal order, to one regarding it as decorative metaphor, duly reflected in contemporary poetry. By 1603, strictly the end of the Tudor period, little advance seems to have been made, allusions to music remaining traditional.

18. Hughes, Andrew. "Continuity, Tradition and Change in English Music up to 1600." *Music & Letters* 46 (1965): 306-15.

Much of this article describes the techniques of pre-Tudor English composers, but in the final pages the author suggests that composers of Byrd's generation continued to use mediaeval techniques such as troping, variation, melisma and altermatim, adapted to new circumstances. In view of the verse anthem's perceived relationship with altermatim settings of the Magnificat and mass, the author feels that the Reformation had little effect on some aspects of music, as traditional means were adapted rather than discarded.

19. Johnson, Paula. *Form and Transformation in Music and Poetry of the English Renaissance.* Yale Studies in English, 179. New Haven: Yale University Press, 1972. 0300015445. ML286.2.J6.

Compares music and poetry as arts in "serial" form. In the case of a piece of music, "the listener ... cannot choose to have its sounds presented to him in any order other than that in which they are in fact presented." In the case of literature, "the convention of reading from left to right will inevitably affect the order of a reader's experience, whether or not he begins a book at the beginning, goes on to the end, and then stops." The author takes her musical examples from the Tudors, utilizing madrigals, keyboard music and motets. Despite my somewhat hostile comments in *WB123*, this is an interesting study, culminating in a chapter on "The Emergence of the Climactic Progression" which points the way to Defoe and beyond.

20. Monson, Craig. "Elizabethan London." In *The Renaissance: from the 1470s to the End of the Sixteenth Century*, ed. by Iain Fenlon. Man & Music, 2. Basingstoke: Macmillan, 1989, pp. 304-40.

Describes the musical life of the capital. Referring to the Church, the author differentiates between the ethos of the Chapel Royal at one extreme and puritanical parish churches at the other. As to secular music, Monson deals with the Court whose musicians were often imported from abroad; the professional musicians and minstrels catering to the remaining musical needs of the city; and musical amateurs, whether royalty, nobility or gentry. The author underscores his narrative throughout with quotations from literature or from observers, often foreign. The structure of this chapter makes clear the increasing musical literacy of the amateurs.

21. Shire, Helena Mennie. *Song, Dance and Poetry of the Court of Scotland under King James VI.* Cambridge: Cambridge University Press, 1969. 052107181X. ML288.2.S49.

Traces the development and decline of the court-song, or "musik fyne," in Scotland. The author considers the various influences of ballads, contemporary religious and political circumstances, and Scotland's geographical location. She pays particular attention to the role of poetry, and explains the existence of the Castalian band, the King's name for his poets at Court, one of whose preoccupations was the kinship between poetry and music. Musical illustrations of court-song were edited by Kenneth Elliott.

22. Wulstan, David. *Tudor Music.* London: Dent, 1985; Iowa City: University of Iowa Press, 1986. 378pp. 0460044125. 0877451354. ML286.2.W8.

As I wrote in *WB35*, this is less a coherent monograph than a collection of essays. The sort of vagaries and extravagances mentioned in that review apropos Byrd may be extended to cover Wulstan's attitude to other composers: for instance his subjective dislike of the sonorous and effective Services for men's voices by William Mundy, and his derisive remarks about one of Orlando Gibbons's most glorious verse anthems *Behold Thou Hast Made My Days.* Despite their whimsical titles, each of the book's thirteen chapters constitutes a substantial essay. After an introductory initial chapter, the second, "The Silver Swanne," observes the new poetry of Thomas Wyatt and his successors that was available to be set to music. Chapter 3, "Small and Popular Musickes," covers street and ministrel music, while chapter 4, "Private Musick," reviews Court and household music and discusses some performance problems. Chapter 5, "With Fingers and with Penne," and 6, "Graces in Play," are respectively about keyboard music and its interpretation. Chapter 7, "The Meaning of the Author," is about editing and its ramifications for performance. Arguably most important is chapter 8, "A High Clear Voice," in which the author gives the fullest (though not final: see *WB187*) account of his view, previously propagated in articles in 1966/7 and 1979, that Tudor music should be sung a minor third higher than written in contemporary texts (disputed by Bowers: see *397* and especially *398*). The remaining chapters, nine to thirteen, deal chronologically with sacred music: "Ad Usum Ecclesiae Anglicanae" with the rite of Sarum under Kings Henry VII and VIII; "A Playn and Distincte Note" with the Prayer Books of Edward VI; "The Lighte of Candelles" with Latin music under Mary and Elizabeth I; "The Chauncels as in Tymes Past" with the Church of England under Elizabeth and James I; and "Distracted Tymes" with Thomas Tomkins, most prolific and longest lived of Anglican Tudor composers. For a book of this importance the references and index are seriously inadequate. Some biographical assumptions are rectified in *434*.

See also 290, 368, 448, 600, WB160, WB165, WB168.

III SACRED VOCAL MUSIC

Bibliographical studies of sources are in chapter X.

23. Allenson, Stephen. "The Inverness Fragments: Music from a pre-Reformation Scottish Parish Church and School." *Music & Letters* 70 (1989): 1-45.

Describes fragments of polyphonic music surviving in the archives of Fort Augustus Abbey, Scotland, but thought by the author to have originated in the parish church and school at nearby Inverness around the middle of the sixteenth century. He gives an introduction to the history and general contents (not all of which are musical) of the fragments, with some remarks on palaeography. Tables provide a summary of contents of fragments, chants and the distribution of fragments of one of the psalms. The narrative concludes with a discussion of date and provenance, debating the possibility of English origins. Appendices comprise an inventory and transcription of the music.

24. Aplin, John. "Anglican Versions of two Sarum Invitatory Tones." *Music Review* 42 (1981): 182-92.

Explains how early Anglican composers incorporated excerpts of Sarum plainsong into vernacular liturgical, for structural reasons: in the absence of a musical tradition for the new Church of England, composers borrowed suitable material from the now defunct Roman liturgy. The author finds two pieces, both settings of the Venite for Mattins, which incorporate different Sarum invitatory tones. One is anonymous, the other by Robert Adams. He suspects a second piece by Adams, a setting of the Nunc dimittis for Evensong, may provide an example of the use of a third tone, as yet unidentified.

25. Aplin, John. "Cyclic Techniques in the Earliest Anglican Services." *Journal of the American Musicological Society* 35 (1982): 409-35.

Analyses attempts by the first Anglican composers to provide a unity in their works entirely musical in its origins, not arising from the liturgical necessity of the Prayer Book of 1552. The author concentrates on Sheppard, Robert Parsons, William Mundy and Tallis. He detects, after the best of the mature Elizabethan style, a period of retrospection in the early seventeenth century.

26. Aplin, John. "'The Fourth Kind of Faburden': the Identity of an English Four-Part Style." *Music & Letters* 61 (1980): 245-65.

Suggests that even after the Reformation in England some pre-Reformation techniques were perpetuated. One such was called the "Fourth Kind" by Scottish Anonymous (see *426*), characterized by four-part texture with the plainsong in the tenor. The plainsong was that of the psalm tones, and was used in vernacular polyphony. The author cites other early theorists who described or referred to this kind of faburden, and he provides illustrations of contemporary Anglican works that seem to comply with it. He notes Latin precedents in the *Plainsong Masses* of Taverner and Sheppard, and in Tallis's untitled Mass à 4. Finally he traces the dissemination of the style as an influence and aspect of technique in many substantial Anglican liturgical works, and wonders whether the Fourth Kind was a decisive factor in establishing the standard four-part texture of the mid-sixteenth century. There is an appendix of mid-century works based on psalm tones.

27. Aplin, John. "A Group of English Magnificats 'Upon the Faburden'." *Soundings* 7 (1978): 85-100.

Announces discovery of six pieces probably composed before 1553 which show that the old faburden melodies had more than a casual influence on the earliest music composed for the new Church of England. The author discusses and compares each item in detail, and outlines musical differences between English and Latin Magnificats against the contemporary theoretical background. Well illustrated.

28. Aplin, John. "The Survival of Plainsong in Anglican Music: Some Early English Te-Deum Settings." *Journal of the American Musicological Society* 32 (1979): 247-75.

In the aftermath of the Reformation many composers continued for a short time to use pre-existing plainsongs as the main means of structural organization for their liturgical works in the vernacular. The author dwells on the Te Deum, and describes the several settings of the vernacular text in which plainsong plays a part. He suggests that most subsequent settings, from Tallis to Gibbons and on to the Commonwealth, justify further consideration of the chant's role in evolving tonal design, so that in this context the meaning of "freely composed" may need careful definition.

29. Baillie, Hugh. "A London Church in Early Tudor Times."*Music & Letters* 36 (1955): 55-64.

History of musical activities at St Mary-at-Hill, 1478-1559, including names of organists and layclerks, and a note of its books of polyphony. Tallis and William Mundy were associated with the church.

30. Baillie, Hugh. "Some Biographical Notes on English Church Musicians, Chiefly Working in London (1485-1569)." *Research Chronicle* 2 (1962): 18-57.

List compiled from churchwardens' accounts, manuscripts and printed sources.

31. Baillie, Hugh. "Squares." *Acta Musicologica* 32 (1960): 178-93.

Assembles all known evidence in an attempt to define the term "squares" for which no contemporary definition or description exists. The author describes the origin of the problem, lists the repertory of fifteen Kyrie tenors known as squares and used as canti firmi in the mid-Tudor period, and gives all known occurrences of the term. He then comments on the three masses *Upon the Square* and their canti firmi, one by William Mundy and two by Whitbroke, and provides copious notes on the eight sources in which squares have been found. Finally he attempts some general conclusions concerning the origins and technique of this elusive but important term.

32. Baillie, Hugh *and* Oboussier, Philippe. "The York Masses." *Music & Letters* 35 (1954): 19-30.

Describes a reconstructed choirbook, and its six masses and four Kyries, from a manuscript in the Borthwick Institute, York. The only named composers are Willliam Horwood and John Cuk. The manuscript is dated c.1515. No concordances were known when the article was written and none have since emerged (see *82*).

33. Beechey, Gwilym. "Morley's Church Music". *Musical Times* 122 (1981): 625-9.

Summary of both the Anglican and Latin music, with notes on editions and writings about them. The author speculates about the models for some of the Latin works, usually amongst the Byrd canon. Subsequent articles reveal more about Morley's debts to other composers in his sacred music (*118, 119, WB158 and WB176*).

34. Benham, Hugh. "The Formal Design and Construction of Taverner's Works." *Musica Disciplina* 26 (1972): 189-209.

Considers the masses and antiphons, dealing with texture, cantus firmus statements, head-motif and parody techniques. Special reference is made to the Mass *Mater Christi.*

35. Benham, Hugh. *Latin Church Music in England, c.1460-1575.* London: Barrie and Jenkins, 1977. 247pp. 0214200590. ML3031.B46.

Aims to study in detail the body of elaborate large-scale music composed for the Latin rite of Sarum between 1475 and the Reformation. The author describes copiously the daily ecclesiastical routine, the structure of services and place of music within them. By taking individual major composers in turn, devoting half a chapter to some, he is able to give a comprehensive account of the scope of the repertory and how it developed stylistically. This is an essential work for the understanding of Tudor music.

36. Benham, Hugh. "Latin Church Music under Edward VI." *Musical Times* 116 (1975): 477-80.

Puts forward grounds for supposing that, despite the abandonment of a Latin liturgy in favour of vernacular services during the reign of Edward VI, some Latin works were composed. The author lists four works - one by Robert Johnson and three by Tye - and gives reasons for dating them from Edward's reign.

37. Benham, Hugh. "The Music of Taverner: a Liturgical Study." *Music Review* 33 (1972): 251-74.

Endeavours to establish as closely as possible in what circumstances each piece of Taverner's church music was used, both masses and motets, from the liturgical point of view. In a carefully tabulated and illustrated presentation, the author offers incidental suggestions about chronology and Taverner's compositional style and technique.

38. Bergsagel, J.D. "On the Performance of Ludford's Altermatim Masses." *Musica Disciplina* 16 (1962): 35-55.

Seven of Ludford's masses constitute the complete system of daily votive masses of the Virgin remaining in English music. The term altermatim indicates a type of mass in which sections for a soloist alternate in performance with sections of (in this case) three-part harmony, and the author investigates the practical problems in performing these masses.

39. Blezzard, Judith. *Borrowings in English Church Music, 1550-1950.* London: Stainer & Bell, 1990. 0852497849.

Deals both with borrowings by Tudor composers and with borrowings from the Tudors by later composers. The three parts of this study cover music borrowed from sacred sources, from secular sources, and borrowings of musical style.

40. Blezzard, Judith. "Christopher Tye: a Quatercentenary Note." *Musical Times* 114 (1973): 1051-5.

Study of anthem *O God be Merciful unto Us* which survives in several different versions in twelve manuscript sources dating from 1548 to 1844.

41. Blezzard, Judith. "A Note on Robert Whyte." *Musical Times* 115 (1974): 977-9.

Brief review of his life and reputation, both contemporary and subsequent, followed by a discussion of his small Anglican corpus, especially the anthem *Lord Who Shall Dwell in Thy Tabernacle*. The author comments on contrafacta and adaptations involving the use of instruments.

42. Brett, Philip. "Facing the Music." *Early Music* 10 (1982): 347-50.

Contribution to the debate about *Tallis's Spem in alium* and Striggio's *Ecce beatam lucem,* contemporary works in forty parts. The author compares the compositional methods of the composers, and the musical content and effect of the pieces. Provocatively, he complains of critical emphasis on what he regards as peripheral matters such as dates of composition and performance, with no words being exchanged on the subject of content.

See *140*.

43. Brett, Philip. "Homage to Taverner in Byrd's Masses." *Early Music* 9 (1981): 169-76.

See *WB99*.

44. Brothers, Lester D. "Avery Burton and his Hexachord Mass." *Musica Disciplina* 28 (1974): 153-76.

After copious biographical introduction, provides a tabulated and illustrated analysis of the mass, assuming it to be for five voices. This problem, with its 6-4 cadences in train, dominates the latter part of the article, which should only be read for its biographical content. The author's subsequent article, *45*, is an emendation of the analytical content, but it is worth keeping the present article to hand as, together with its successor, it illustrates the problems posed by the survival of fragmentary texts.

45. Brothers, Lester D. "New Light on an Early Tudor Mass: Avery Burton's *Missa Ut re mi fa sol la*". *Musica Disciplina* 32 (1978): 111-26.

Emendation of *44*, adding to its biography and incorporating John Bergsagel's suggestion that the mass is in six, not five, parts as originally thought, the missing part being the lowest. The author also argues, with illustration, that Burton's is a parody, or derived, mass.

46. Brown, David. "The Anthems of Thomas Weelkes." *Proceedings of the Royal Musical Association* 91 (1964-5): 61-72.

Begins with a cogent chronological review of Weelkes's

madrigals, noting various influences and the composer's originality, before discussing the anthems themselves. First the author deals with some structural issues amongst the full anthems. Proceeding to the verse anthems, he notes that over three-quarters survive incomplete, but draws attention to Weelkes's tendency to self-quotation.

47. Brown, David. "The Styles and Chronology of Thomas Morley's Motets." *Music & Letters* 41 (1960): 216-22.

    Perceives they were composed in two styles: the earlier ones under the influence of Byrd's *Cantiones*, the later ones more madrigalian. The author uses both bibliographical and biographical information in suggesting the sequence of their composition. See also *118* and *119*.

48. Byard, Herbert. "Farewell to Merbecke?" *Musical Times* 114 (1973): 300-3

    Despite the title, this is an introduction to Merbecke's music. Initially the author concentrates on his unison setting for the new Anglican liturgy, *The Booke of Common Praier Noted,* 1550, and the "farewell" refers to the possibility of its falling out of use by the Church of England because of modern luturgical innovations (though it was only revived during the nineteenth century by Tractarians). This the author would welcome if it would lead to attention being directed towards Merbecke's few surviving polyphonic works - a mass, two motets and a carol - about which he writes briefly and respectfully.

49. Caldwell, John. "The 'Te Deum' in Late Medieval England." *Early Music* 6 (1978): 188-94.

    Describes how the Te Deum became associated with several specialized conventions which cast interesting light not only on performance practice but also compositional attitudes to areas such as cantus firmus and tonality. The author compares compositional procedures with those of faburden, and he places much emphasis on the question of transposition. Both organ and vocal settings are discussed.

50. Charteris, Richard. "'Fuerunt mihi lacrymae': Alfonso Ferrabosco
    the Elder or the Younger?" *Essays on Italian Music in the
    Cinquecento,* ed. by Richard Charteris. Altro Polo. Sydney:
    Frederick May Foundation for Italian Studies, 1990, pp.113-
    30.

    Recent research has enabled scholars to differentiate the
    works of father and son where uncertain attributions exist,
    leaving the ascription of only the present work still to be resolved.
    The author disagrees with the opinions of other modern scholars,
    and favours the attribution to the elder Ferrabosco first put
    forward by Francis Tregian between 1609 and 1619, and
    supported here by formidable bibliographical and stylistic
    evidence.

51. Charteris, Richard. "The Motets of Alfonso Ferrabosco the Elder
    (1543-1588)." *Consort* 38 (1982): 445-60.

    Comprehensive and illustrated introductory account with lists
    of motets and sources. Includes references to contemporary
    composers and problems of dating, the latter exemplified by nine
    specified comparisons with the works of Lassus.

52. Collins, H.B. "John Taverner's Masses." *Music & Letters* 5 (1924):
    322-34.

    Review article concerning volume I of *Tudor Church Music*
    (London: Oxford University Press, 1922) but with perceptive
    comments about some of the more doubtful and difficult
    passages in the musical texts. See also *53.*

53. Collins, H.B. "John Taverner - Part II." *Music & Letters* 6 (1925):
    314-29.

    Review article concerning volume III of *Tudor Church Music*
    (1923: see *52*). The author's criticisms of its editorial procedures
    illuminate Taverner's own compositional procedures, and he
    provides historical contexts for his comments. See also *684.*

54. Collins, H.B. "Latin Church Music by Early English Composers." *Proceedings of the Musical Association* 39 (1912-13): 55-83.

Factually outdated in parts, but an admirable introductory survey of music from Taverner to Dering. The comments are illuminating and perceptive, such as his suggestion that Byrd's *Christus resurgens* is modelled on that of John Redford, though Kerman is sceptical in *WB100* (p.65) and le Huray ignores the idea in *WB175*. See also *55*.

55. Collins, H.B. "Latin Church Music by Early English composers. - Part II." *Proceedings of the Musical Association* 43 (1916-17): 97-121.

Discusses composers omitted from *54*, with some supplementary comments on Byrd, especially his *Exsurge Domine*.

56. Collins, H.B. "Thomas Tallis." *Music & Letters* 10 (1929): 152-66.

Review article concerning volume VI of *Tudor Church Music* (1928: see *52)*. Contains some textual criticism and comments on many individual items, especially concerning musical structure.

57. Collins, Walter S. "The Reconstruction of the Evening Service for Seven Voices by Thomas Weelkes." In *Five Centuries of Choral Music: Essays in Honor of Howard Swan*, ed. by Gordon Paine. Festschrift Series, 6. Stuyvesant: Pendragon, 1988, pp.93-126.

Describes the author's approach to reconstructing Weelkes's fragmentary *Ninth Service*. Having listed surviving sources and previous attempts at reconstruction, the author gives five principles of reconstruction and applies these to various aspects of the *Ninth Service* such as the nature of the surviving vocal parts, whether there is any need for verse and full markings and for organ accompaniment, how to reconstruct missing voices, how to underlay the text, and how to present a modern score. His agonizings about the title are faintly risible, and instead of "cantor" he should use the proper Anglican designation Precentor. He makes frequent reference to Weelkes's anthem *O Lord Grant the King a Long Life* which has passages of music in common with the *Ninth Service.*

58. Daniel, R.T. "Contrafacta and Polyglot Texts in the Early English Anthem." In *Essays in Musicology: a Birthday Offering for Willi Apel,* ed. by Hans Tischler. Bloomington: Indiana University, School of Music, 1968, pp.101-6.

Notes that there were surprisingly few contrafacta (Latin works fitted with English words) in the repertory of the early Anglican anthem. A small number date from the beginnings of the new Church of England, while most appeared for the first time during the seventeenth century. Having offered some reasons for this, the author devotes the rest of the article to a chronological survey of contrafacta, concluding with a note of some problems and two observations: the practice continued well after those early years of Anglicanism when there really was a dearth of suitable music, and most of the works subsequently adapted had been composed by recognized masters. See also *WB178.*

59. Daniel, Ralph T. *and* le Huray, Peter. *The Sources of English Church Music 1549-1660.* Early English Church Music Supplementary Volumes, 1. London: Stainer and Bell, 1972. 1v. in 2. ML120.E5D3.

Lists sources both manuscript and printed (including selected modern editions) for all known surviving sacred music composed to English words between the Reformation and Restoration. The compilers provide incipits for anonymous works. Part I contains abbreviations and symbols, including the key to modern publishers; the keys to manuscript and printed sources; musical incipits of anonymous compositions; and first-line index of anthems. Part II contains lists of anonymous compositions with sources and editions, and anthems and Services listed alphabetically by composer with sources and editions. A second edition is in preparation.

60. Dart, Thurston. "Music and Musicians at Chichester Cathedral, 1545-1642." *Music & Letters* 42 (1961): 221-6.

> Provides information about activities and size of the choir, duties of the organist and choirmaster, the music and the lives, as they relate to Chichester, of John Cooper (alias Coprario), Thomas Ravenscroft, Thomas Weelkes and Clement Woodcock amongst others.

61. Davison, Nigel. "Structure and Unity in Four Free-Composed Tudor Masses." *Music Review* 34 (1973): 328-38

> The four works are Taverner's *Meane Mass,* Tye's Mass à 5, Sheppard's *French Mass* and Tallis's *Mass à 4.* Begins by warning that just because a mass has no title in its source it should not be assumed that it is not based on a plainsong. The author traces the development of sectional structure in the composition of masses during the sixteenth century both in England and on the continent. After his discussion of the four masses, the last three of which are based structurally on Taverner's, he warns that neither Appleby's nor Sheppard's *Meane Masses* were based on it. See *43* for an account of Byrd's debt to Taverner's mass.

62. Davison, Nigel. "Tye's Mass 'Euge Bone'." *Musical Times* 121 (1980): 727-30.

> Seeks to establish by close analysis that this mass is derived from Tye's own motet *Quaesumus omnipotens*. The author credits Jason Smart with the original discovery, and suggests why Tye may have "leant" on a mass based on such a plainsong for a motet whose text is quite different, a solution as much to do with Tye's psychology as with his musicality.

63. Davison, Nigel. "The *Western Wind* Masses." *Musical Quarterly* 57 (1971): 427-43.

> Detailed discussion of the three masses by Taverner, Tye and Sheppard on the same tune, noting points of similarity and dissimilarity, and making comparisons with contemporary

continental practice. In addition the author notes omissions from the verbal text. He considers the origin of the tune as it survives independently of the masses, the relationship of the tune to its form used in the masses, and why the composers chose this tune.

64. Dimsdale, Verna L. "English Sacred Music with Broken Consort." *Lute Society Journal* 16 (1974): 39-64.

Concentrates on Richard Alison's *The Psalmes of David*, William Leighton's *The Teares or Lamentacions of a Sorrowfull Soule* and Robert Tailour's *Sacred Hymns*. The author discusses not only the contents of each volume including such matters as clefs and layout, but also the role and use of the instruments, specifying, where there is uncertainty, which instruments.

65. Doe, Paul. "Latin Polyphony under Henry VIII." *Proceedings of the Royal Musical Association* 95 (1968-9): 81-96.

Seeks to draw attention to the influence on late Henrician music of Thomas Cranmer, archbishop of Canterbury, who was influenced in his student days by Lutheranism. This leads the author to postulate a link between German compositional techniques and those of Taverner, Tye, Tallis and Sheppard in some of their masses. He also suggests some reasons for change in the repertory and style of polyphony, most of which he thinks took place during Henry's reign, rather than during that of his Roman Catholic daughter Mary I, who only succeeded him after the brief, austerely Protestant reign of his son and her half-brother Edward VI.

66. Doe, Paul. "Tallis's 'Spem in alium' and the Elizabethan Respond-Motet." *Music & Letters* 51 (1970): 1-14.

Notes that three of Tallis's works are of a scale beyond the routine liturgy: *Missa Puer natus, Gaude gloriosa* and *Spem in alium*. After briefly commenting on Tallis's likely purposes in composing the first two, the author concentrates on *Spem in alium*. Stylistically he dates it towards the end of Tallis's life, as a respond divorced, in Elizabeth's Protestant reign, from its Roman

Catholic liturgical origins. Having suggested that it was performed in Elizabeth's chapel before or after services, or that it may have been part of a Renaissance theatrical spectacle, he concludes that it was probably composed for the Queen's fortieth birthday in 1573, at the instigation of Byrd who entrusted the actual composition to Tallis. But his parting shot is that since the earliest sources date from the reign of James I, there is no conclusive evidence that it is by Tallis at all, and he suggests Morley. See *140* and *42* for the latest words on this saga.

67. Doe, Paul. "The Tudor Workshop: a Note on Thomas Tallis (died 23rd November 1585)." *NEMA Journal* (January 1986): 2-5.

Looks at Tallis as a member of a contemporary workshop: a group of composers producing music for a specific purpose, such as the new Anglican daily liturgy. Most of their manuscript sources are anonymous, indicating that at the time it did not matter who composed the music, the purpose for which it was written being more important. The author proceeds to some provocative questions. Is it necessary to celebrate anniversaries, to have collected editions by composer rather than by source, to know the publishing history of a certain work? Should such music not be exhibited in a glass case in a museum? Unable to recreate the original circumstances of this music's composition we listen to it for recreation, but some of Tallis's works are so striking they must be special commissions, so far unidentified. "But are there seriously any musicians who would not *like* to know more, rather than just gaze into a glass case?".

68. Ellinwood, Leonard. "Tallis' Tunes and Tudor Psalmody." *Musica Discipline* 2 (1948): 189-203.

Introduction to Parker's psalter of 1567, for which Tallis wrote and harmonized nine tunes, with a note of metres and song forms used by Tallis. Gives all nine tunes in Tallis's own harmonizations, the eighth also as arranged in Ravenscroft's psalter of 1621, and a Lamentation Tallis composed for Day's psalter of 1563.

69. Ellis, Mark *and* Pilgrim, Jack. *Gibbons: Anthems (i) This is the*

Record of John (ii) Hosanna to the Son of David. Mayflower Study Guides, 6. Leeds: Mayflower Enterprises, 1984. 35pp. 0946896100.

The first chapter, "Analysis and Commentary," is the only important one, as the remaining five are better covered elsewhere, in *648* and *91.* The analyses, which divide the pieces into constituent sections of 5-17 bars, are thorough and despite the school provenance of this booklet, others will find the analyses worthwhile and rewarding.

70. Evans, D.R.A. "Thomas Tomkins and the Prince of Wales." *Welsh Music* 7 (Summer 1983): 57-69.

Provides evidence that Tomkins's remarkable and advanced verse anthem *Know You Not,* which does not appear in *Musica Deo sacra,* was composed for the funeral of Henry, Prince of Wales in 1612. The article includes analysis and illustrations, with a note of a modern reconstruction and edition.

71. Fellowes, Edmund H. *English Cathedral Music.* 5th ed., rev. by J.A. Westrup. London: Methuen, 1969. O416148506. ML3131.F3.

Thanks to judicious updating and adjustment by Westrup this has remained a useable introduction. The first nine (of nineteen) chapters impinge on the Tudor period, the first three providing background material. Those who wish to savour Fellowes's original will find themselves rewarded when referring to the first edition of 1941. It contains not only some interesting service-lists from the nineteenth century, but also some of Fellowes's salty prejudices subsequently watered down by Westrup, though this implies no criticism of Westrup.

72. Flanagan, David. "Some Aspects of the Sixteenth-Century Parody Mass in England." *Music Review* 48 (1988): 1-11.

Discusses parody techniques as manifested in three English Masses whose models are known to survive: Fayrfax's *O bone Jesu,* Taverner's *Mater Christi* and Tallis's *Salve intemerata.* The author refers to continental practice and mentions two other masses by Taverner: *Sancte Wilhelme* or *Small Devotion,* which is less parodic than *Mater Christi,* and the "Strene" or *Plainsong Mass* which may parody either itself or a lost mode. He tabulates his contention that the antiphonal approach exhibited in *Mater Christi* is the technical model for Sheppard's *Cantate* and Tye's *Euge bone,* both of which may be parody masses. In support he recalls that all three composed *Western Wind* masses, and that Tye's "Meane" Mass à 5 and Sheppard's *Frences* or *French Mass* resemble Taverner's own *Meane Mass.* This mass also influenced Byrd (see *43*) and the author notes a similarity between the openings of the Glorias of Byrd's Mass à 4 and Taverner's *Mater Christi* mass. He concludes that parody technique itself was not influential in England, but that Taverner's antiphonal scoring in his parody masses was influential in certain cases.

73. Ford, Robert. "Clement Woodcock's Appointment at Canterbury Cathedral." *Chelys* 16 (1987): 36-43.

   Produces evidence that Woodcock was a Substitute or Conduct (lay songman) in the choir from 1565 to 1570, and draws attention to the irregularity of his being a layman in such an appointment.

74. Ford, Wyn K. "Chichester Cathedral and Thomas Weelkes." *Sussex Archaeological Collections* 100 (1962): 156-72.

   Comprehensive account of Weelkes's relationship with Chichester Cathedral, where he was employed for over twenty years. The author refers not only to contemporary documents concerning Weelkes, but also to other documents which illustrate how the cathedral itself functioned during Weelkes's organistship.

75. Frost, Maurice. *English & Scottish Psalm & Hymn Tunes, c.1543-1677.* London: S.P.C.K., 1953. M2136.F85E5.

   The main section of this monograph consists of a bibliography (with musical contents) of Old Version psalters followed by the tunes associated with each psalm. To this section are appended a group of Scottish common tunes unattached to particular psalms, and those tunes from Ravenscroft's 1621 psalter not encountered in earlier publications. The second section provides earlier tunes associated with versions of the psalms other than the English and Scottish editions of the Old Version.

76. Fuller-Maitland, J.A. "A Scottish Composer of the 16th Century." In *Gedenkboek aangeboden aan Dr D.F. Scheurleer op zijn 70sten Verjaardag, bijdragen van Vrienden en Vereerders op het Gebied der Muziek.* 's-Gravenhage: Nijhoff, 1925, pp.119-22.

Introduction to the motet *O bone Jesu* in nineteen parts composed by *Robert Carver.* The biographical information has been superseded by *630.* Correctly the author's surname should be unhyphenated.

77. Gill, Louis A. "The Anthems of Thomas Tomkins: an Introduction." *Musica Disciplina* 11 (1957): 153-88.

Based on twelve anthems selected for their variety of compositional technique. Discusses the contemporary musical background and Tomkins's technique in relation to this, as to what he owed to his predecessors and successors and in what ways he was original.

78. Hannas, Ruth. "Concerning Deletions in the Polyphonic Mass Credo." *Journal of the American Musicological Society* 5 (1952): 155-86.

Attributes such deletions in English masses to insecurity occasioned by vacillating policies during the reigns of Henry VIII and Edward VI. Various charts indicate the nature of the deletions. See also *35,* pp.12-13.

79. Harrison, Frank Llewellyn. "An English 'Caput'." *Music & Letters* 33 (1952): 203-14.

Musical analysis of *Salve Regina* by *Richard Hygons,*

composed late in the fifteenth century. This work has a tenor cantus firmus based on the melisma on the word "caput" in the antiphon *Venit ad Petrum* as found in a fourteenth-century Sarum processional in England. In an earlier article (outside the scope of the present guide) it had been suggested that the cantus firmus on which certain masses by Dufay and other continental composers was based was of English provenance. Although Hygons's work was composed after these masses, the author feels it supports the argument in favour of such a provenance.

80. Harrison, Frank Llewellyn. "The Eton Choirbook: its Background and Contents (Eton College Library ms. 178)." *Annales musicologiques* 1 (1953): 151-75.

    Comprehensive introduction, describing character of Henry VI and his motive for founding Eton College, its early history and routines, the Choirbook itself and, summarily, its composers. There is a full catalogue which includes missing items and concordances.

81. Harrison, Frank Ll. "The Repertory of an English Parish Church in the Early Sixteenth Century." In *Renaissance-Muziek, 1400-1600: Donum Natalicium René Bernard Lenaerts*, ed. by Jozef Robijns. Musicologica Lovaniensia, 1. Leuven: Katholieke Universiteit, Seminarie voor Muziekwetenschap, 1969, pp.143-7.

    Transcribes an inventory dated 1524 from the Church of All Saints, Bristol. It provides evidence of a comprehensive repertory of music which bears comparison with that of King's College, Cambridge in the same decade, with which All Saints' list seems to have much in common liturgically. The author also transcribes another inventory dated 1535-6 from All Saints. Polyphonic music in up to five parts by composers such as Fayrfax was sung there throughout the year.

82. Hofman, May *and* Morehen, John, *comps. Latin Music in British Sources c1485-c1610*. Early English Church Music Supplementary Volumes, 2. London: Stainer and Bell, 1987. 176pp. 0852496737. ML120.G7H63.

Indispensable research tool listing manuscript sources, printed sources, Latin compositions alphabetically by composer with sources and editions, Latin compositions by foreign composers in British sources alphabetically with sources, anonymous compositions with sources and editions, incipits of anonymous compositions, and first-line index of compositions. The entry for each piece of music also includes its liturgical status and the clefs of each vocal part from the copy text which, where there is a choice, is asterisked among the list of sources. Manuscript sources until as late as the nineteenth century are listed.

83. Howard, Michael. "Orlando Gibbons." *Musical Times* 92 (1951): 160-4.

Durable introduction to life and work. Confines remarks on latter to the church music with appreciative and illuminating comments about the verse anthems and Service, particularly *Behold Thou Hast Made My Days as it Were a Span Long*.

84. Illing, Robert H. "Tallis's Psalm Tunes." *Miscellanea Musicologica* 2 (1967): 21-74.

Comprehensive analysis of the nine psalm tunes composed by Tallis for Parker's 1567 psalter, with a general introduction to the published psalter itself, remarks on contemporary editorial methods, and features of typographical and notational interest. The author provides facsimiles of the tunes in the original edition and a keyboard reduction, plus exhaustive commentaries on each of the nine tunes including details of modern editorial and bibliographical problems.

85. James, Peter. "Thomas Tomkins: Sacred Music Omitted from Musica Deo sacra." *Soundings* 2 (1971-2): 29-45.

Lists and discusses 25 such items, some incomplete. Important for announcing discovery of Byrd's *Exalt Thyself O Lord* disguised in its source as "Set up Thyself O God" attributed to Tomkins.

86. Jeans, Susi. "Musical Life at Exeter Cathedral." *Quarterly Record of the Incorporated Association of Organists* 43 (1958): 103-5

Useful biographical sketches of John Lugge, Edward Gibbons, Hugh Facy and Robert Parsons II. Works are listed and, where appropriate, commented upon illuminatingly.

87. Kerman, Joseph. "The Elizabethan Motet: a Study of Texts for Music." *Studies in the Renaissance* 9 (1962): 273-308.

Investigates significance of composers' choice of texts after the Elizabethan Settlement. An historic and seminal article, expanded and updated by Kerman in chapter 1 of *WB100*.

88. Langdon, John. "Tye and his Church Music". *Musical Times* 113 (1972): 1011-15.

After a summary of Tye's anthems and motets, analyses his three surviving masses.

89. Leaver, Robin. *'Goostly Psalmes and Spirituall Songes': English and Dutch Metrical Psalms from Coverdale to Utenhove, 1535-1566.* Oxford Studies in British Church Music. Oxford: Clarendon, 1991. 0198161689. ML3186.L45.

Investigates origins and parallel development of metrical psalmody in English and Dutch, and its use within the vernacular liturgies. The author explains the impact of the Reformation, and of committed Protestantism in particular, on music in worship, and he traces the continuum of pre-Reformation hymnody and post-Reformation Protestant psalmody. The latter was stimulated by greater desire for the vernacular in worship and the rise of printing (see *481*). Thereafter he traces the sources and contents of mid-century English psalters, noting which congregations or denominations used them. There was a wish for sung congregational worship, and some influence from stranger churches, those of displaced continental Protestants exiled in England. All this was disrupted during the Roman Catholic reign of Mary, when committed English Protestants had themselves to flee abroad. Leaver's final chapter before his Conclusion gives an account of such worship back in England after the death of Mary and the accession of her moderate Protestant sister Elizabeth.

90. le Huray, Peter. "The English Anthem 1580-1640." *Proceedings of the Royal Musical Association* 86 (1959-60): 1-13.

From his study of surviving manuscript sources, to whose paucity he draws attention, the author notes the contemporary popularity of a very few specific composers, and indicates how such manuscripts circulated. He assesses the contemporary state of the conduct of cathedral music, predominantly dire except in the cases of the two royal foundations: the Chapel Royal and St George's Chapel, Windsor Castle. He attempts to differentiate between the church anthem and sacred madrigal, and to define the use of instruments in divine Service. After a section on provincial cathedral organists and their compositions, he closes with a consideration of the three most popular Chapel Royal composers after Byrd, Tomkins and Gibbons: Hooper, Giles and Child. This paper focuses on material that is subsequently developed in *91*.

91. le Huray, Peter. *Music and the Reformation in England, 1549-1660*. Studies in Church Music. London: Jenkins; New York: Oxford University Press, 1967; repr. ed. Cambridge Studies in Music. Cambridge: Cambridge University Press, 1978. 0521219582. ML3131.L44.

This is, and shows every sign of remaining for the forseeable future, the standard text on the composers and music of the early Church of England. Only the penultimate of its eleven chapters does not impinge directly on Tudor music. The first six describe the historical, theological and legal background to the Reformation. The rest look in detail at the liturgical pieces and anthems, and at the men who composed them. The chronological treatment assists a sense of development, though it is clear that stylistically the music in question remained conservative for reasons of decorum and doctrine. The author lists in the appropriate chapters all the composers who wrote any

Anglican music, and tabulates the outputs of the more significant musicians. His comments on the status of the various composers are informative and judicious, as are his observations about the roles and development of the genres in which they composed. Most of all, his analyses of notable pieces of music are observant, penetrating and cogent. In chapters 7-9 he mentions several composers not even present in 12. See also 93 and WB163.

92. le Huray, Peter. "Music in a Provincial Cathedral: Chichester from Reformation to Restoration." Musical Times 128 (1987): 161-5.

Information about personnel and duties, including a table showing the family backgrounds of choristers.

93. le Huray, Peter. "Towards a Definitive Study of Pre-Restoration Anglican Service Music." Musica Disciplina 14 (1960): 167-95.

Based on a thematic catalogue of pre-Restoration Services and anthems compiled from a collation of all sources of music known at the time of writing. The catalogue does not appear in the article, which consists of a copious commentary on those sources. The extent of the loss of such material is brought home by a listing of the 41 establishments where daily services were sung, the sizes of their choirs, and the minute number of surviving partbooks. The article deals primarily with pre-Restoration liturgical sources, but includes annotated lists of pre-Restoration secular sources plus a few Restoration sources rich in pre-Restoration Anglican music. See also 91 and 502.

94. Leech-Wilkinson, Daniel. "An Elizabethan Motet from Longleat." Musical Times 121 (1980): 438-49.

Announces discovery in the Old Library, Longleat, of a motet in eight parts in honour of Queen Elizabeth. The author describes the source bibliographically, its likely provenance, and the music, which seems stylistically continental. It is reproduced on pages 448-9.

95. Long, Kenneth R. *Music of the English Church*. London: Hodder and Stoughton, 1971; New York: St. Martin's Press, 1972. 0340149620. ML3131.L6.

Although the serious researcher is better served by other scholars, particularly in *91,* the first eight (of nineteen) chapters can be used selectively. The monograph is written from a practical, Anglican perspective which, Anglican music being as eclectic as it is, involves discussion of many peripheral matters, such as Byrd's *Gradualia*. The author also deals with contemporary traditions of music in worship, sources and style, providing a thorough historical and liturgical background. Although beginning rather abruptly at the Reformation, he sets the Tudors within the continuum of the history of the music in question, devoting part of his final chapter to the Tudor revival in the twentieth century.

96. Messenger, Thomas. "John Lloyd and his *Missa 'O quam suavis'.*" *Welsh Music* 6 (Summer 1980): 33-41.

Analysis of Lloyd's only surviving large-scale composition. Illustrated with biographical introduction. See also *97.*

97. Messenger, Thomas. "Number Symbolism in John Lloyd's Mass." *Welsh Music* 6 (Spring 1982): 51-3.

Numerological postscript to *96.*

98. Messenger, Thomas. "Texture and Form in the Masses of Fayrfax." *Journal of the American Musicological Society* 24 (1971): 282-6.

Analysis of how Fayrfax planned his units of texture within the four-movement structure of the masses. Illustrated with tables.

99. Milsom, John. "The Date of Ludford's Lady Masses: a Cautionary Note." *Music & Letters* 66 (1985): 367-8.

Uses bibliographical evidence to suggest that the previously assumed date of Ludford's manuscript, c.1510-25, is too early. By comparing the printed paper, on which it is written, with the apparently identical paper used for the *XX Songes* published in 1530, the original estimation for the date of the copying, though not the composition, of Ludford's masses must be moved onwards by several years.

100. Milsom, John. "A New Tallis Contrafactum." *Musical Times* 123 (1982): 429-31.

Announces discovery of the earliest surviving fragment of *Gaude gloriosa* in which English words have been set to the music. See also *103.*

101. Milsom, John. "Songs, Carols and Contrafacta in the Early History of the Tudor Anthem." *Proceedings of the Royal Musical Association* 107 (1980-1): 34-45.

Estimates the influence of songs, carols and contrafacta on the emerging Tudor anthem, especially from formal and structural viewpoints. Contrafacta seem to have had little influence, but that of carols seems to have been more durable, though neither of the two late Tudor works mentioned in this context were intended for Divine Service.

102. Milsom, John. "A Tallis Fantasia." *Musical Times* 126 (1985): 658-62.

Offers evidence that Tallis's motet *O sacrum convivium* was originally conceived as a consort fantasia which included elements from what became the motet *Absterge Domine*. See also *103.*

103. Milsom, John. "Tallis's First and Second Thoughts." *Journal of the Royal Musical Association* 113 (1988): 203-22.

Comprehensive review of Tallis's compositional procedures, with reference to his vocal works. The author supplements, but does not repeat, information in *100* and *102*, and gives fresh information about *Salvator mundi* (second setting), *O salutaris hostia, When Shall My Sorrowful Sighing Slack* and *Remember Not O Lord God.* He concludes that Tallis usually tinkered with the inner parts of his contrapuntal vocal works, tending to leave the outer shell alone, throughout the compositional process. Some surviving versions may provide Tallis's first or interim thoughts. In some cases it is hard to discern a final version, unless it is published in the 1575 *Cantiones.* Tallis's insecurity may be due to his having to adapt to new, imitative compositional techniques in mid-career.

104. Monson, Craig. "The Preces, Psalms and Litanies of Byrd and Tallis: Another 'Virtuous Contention in Love'." *Music Review* 40 (1979): 257-71.

   See *WB96.*

105. Morehen, John. "The English Consort and Verse Anthems." *Early Music* 6 (1978): 381-5.

   Describes likely origins of the consort anthem as a form, and sees the verse anthem as a separate genre. Maintains that where consort and verse forms exist for a single anthem, these forms are mutually exclusive, being for secular and sacred performance respectively.

106. Morehen, John. "The Gibbons-Loosemore Mystery." *Musical Times* 112 (1971): 959-60.

   Establishes that the composer of the popular anthem *O Lord Increase Our Faith* (and another, lesser known) was Henry Loosemore, not Orlando Gibbons as usually ascribed until this time.

107. Noske, Frits. "John Bull's Dutch Carol." *Music & Letters* 44 (1963): 326-33.

   Full discussion of *Den Lustelijcken,* including publishing history, provenance of tune, historical significance and full transcription.

108. Palmer, William. "Gibbons's Verse Anthems." *Music & Letters* 35 (1954): 107-13.

Notes how Gibbons developed the form from Byrd's lead, and comments on aspects of Gibbons's style, such as word-setting, use of embellishment, treatment of solo voice, exploitation of verse passages, accompaniments and choruses.

109. Parrott, Andrew. "Grett and Solompne Singing: Instruments in English Church Music Before the Civil War." *Early Music* 6 (1978): 182-7.

Provides documentary evidence of involvement of instruments, of what those instruments were, and of payments made to the players. About a quarter of the article is devoted to the years up to 1603, but many practices detailed only after that date may reflect procedures initiated during the Tudor period.

110. Patrick, Millar. *Four Centuries of Scottish Psalmody*. London: Oxford University Press, 1949. BS1440.A1P3.

Explains the origins of metrical psalmody, its development in England and continental Europe, the composition of the psalter, and the circumstances giving rise to the publication of the first Scottish psalter in 1564. The discussion of subsequent Scottish psalters is of interest in respect of what tunes were preserved from, in English terminology, the Tudor period. The author elucidates the names of various tunes and their status, and provides appropriate information about composers, arrangers and compilers.

111. Payne, Ian. "Music at Jesus College, Cambridge, c.1557-1679." *Proceedings of the Cambridge Antiquarian Society* 76 (1986): 98-103.

Describes the development of the musical establishment, including details of personnel and expenditure. The regime during the Elizabethan period seems to have been puritanical.

112. Payne, Ian. "The Musical Establishment at Trinity College, Cambridge, 1546-1644." *Proceedings of the Cambridge Antiquarian Society* 75 (1985): 53-69.

     Copious account of an important musical foundation. Notes responses to political and religious developments of the times and includes lists of musicians and payments, with appropriate information about the musicians themselves. The author speculates authoritatively on the nature of the choir's repertory throughout this volatile period.

113. Payne, Ian. "The Sacred Music of Thomas Ravenscroft." *Early Music* 10 (1982): 309-15.

     Well-illustrated survey, with complete list including incipit, scoring, source, type of anthem, missing parts and date. Considers the anthems' provenances, Ravenscroft's technique, his debt to older composers, and problems of reconstructing inner parts.

114. Payne, Ian. "Two Early Organists of Exeter Cathedral: Matthew Godwin and Arthur Cocke." *Devon and Cornwall Notes and Queries* 35 (1983): 133-42.

     Biographical details, with transcription of Cocke's otherwise unpublished In Nomine à 5.

115. Payne, Ian. "The Vicars Choral of Exeter Cathedral: a Disciplinary Study, c.1540-c.1640." *Reports and Transactions of the Devonshire Association* 115 (1983): 101-22.

     Deals with the maintenance of discipline by the Cathedral authorities in the immediate post-Reformation era, in respect of the nature and punishment of misdemeanours.

116. Phillips, Peter. "A Commentary on Avery Burton's *Mass on the Hexachord*." *Early Music* 7 (1979): 218-21.

     Describes the provenance of the mass and the controversy over the probable missing part. The author comments on

Burton's compositional technique and style, and their relation to those of his contemporaries and later composers, and he enthuses about the impact of the mass in performance.

117. Phillips, Peter. *English Sacred Music, 1549-1649.* Oxford: Gimell, 1991. 0951578405.

Intended as an encyclopaedia or handbook for music with sacred words in English between the Reformation and the Commonwealth. Although the author concentrates on Anglican church music, he also refers to sacred vocal chamber music. In the first part of the monograph, after an historical introduction, he deals with the anthem, chronologically by those composers whose works survive, devoting complete chapters to Byrd and Tomkins, all of whose 102 anthems he surveys. Within these chapters he differentiates Anglican full and verse anthems from domestic full and consort anthems. He devotes the final chapter to Services, with which he deals generically. Unnecessarily his genres - short, middle, great and verse - are modern. As far as the Tudors categorized Services, they described them, if at all, as short or long. Terms such as full, whole, medio chori or "with verses" were not mutually exclusive of short or long, and there was certainly no such category as great (see *WB163* and *WB183*). Despite discussing so many works of all types, the author provides plenty of illustrations. The whole is well indexed but the bibliography is thin, ceasing six years before the date of the introduction. The author's opinions are clearly stated but not polemical, as he wishes to draw attention to a fine repertory rather than to flex his critical muscles. Some of his musicology is oldfashioned, such as his *unquestioning* acceptance of Byrd's augmented sixths (p.92) and some is current, such as his preference for Coste as composer of a setting of *Save Me O God* also ascribed to Byrd. His discussions of individual pieces involve both musical analysis and practical considerations such as vocal ranges.

118. Phillips, Peter. "'Laboravi in gemitu meo': Morley or Rogier?" *Music & Letters* 63 (1982): 85-90.

Produces evidence that suggests strongly that Morley

plagiarized a motet composed by Philippe Rogier and published by him in 1595.

119. Pike, Lionel. "'Gaude Maria Virgo': Morley or Philips?" *Music & Letters* 50 (1969): 127-35.

Suggests this work, originally taken to be by Morley, is his recomposition of a motet by Philips. (Both composers were pupils of Byrd.)

120. Pike, Lionel. "Marian Symbolism in Philips." *Musical Times* 125 (1984): 461-5.

Illustrates how in certain Marian motets Philips uses solmization as a device through which to symbolize the Virgin and her personal qualities. The author notes that Philips based the opening of one of his works, *Gaude Maria*, on a setting by Victoria. Also he points out Sheppard's use of solmization at the beginning of *Gaude gaude gaude Maria.*

121. Pike, Lionel. "Peter Philips' Les rossignols spirituels." *Consort* 27 (1971): 50-63.

Draws attention to the unusual circumstances of the book's publication, the only one of Philips's music not produced by his usual publisher. The author suggests for whom it was intended, describes the book itself bibliographically, and details the contents, with illustrations.

122. Pike, Lionel. "Philips's 'Salve Regina'." *Musical Times* 116 (1975): 737-9.

Discusses the structure of the piece and Philips's technique in view of its faulty source and in the light of the author's own attempts to reconstruct it. It was hitherto unpublished, and was reproduced as the issue's music supplement. He gives a full account of the source, a manuscript score without words after the first two, and ponders the nature of the copyist's own source. Finally he suggests when and where Philips composed it.

123. Pike, Lionel. "Tallis - Vaughan Williams - Howells: Reflections on Mode Three." *Tempo* 149 (1984): 2-13.

Howells experienced Vaughan Williams's *Fantasia on a Theme by Thomas Tallis* as a paradoxical combination of old and new which had a determining influence on his own music. The author seeks to introduce this topic to point the way to further investigation. To do so he begins by analysing musically Tallis's theme, from Parker's 1567 psalter. He surmises what Vaughan Williams found attractive about it, and illustrates copiously the use to which Vaughan Williams put it in his *Fantasia*, observing that the work is itself an analysis of Tallis's theme. He goes on to note several pieces by Howells that are indebted to Vaughan Williams, some personally but others showing the influence of Tudor music via that of Vaughan Williams. See also *578*.

124. Pilgrim, Jack. "Tallis' *Lamentations* and the English Cadence." *Music Review* 20 (1959): 1-6.

Notes the feeling for tonality, remarkable for its period, in Tallis's Lamentations, the most striking feature of which is the abundance and variety of English cadences.

125. Pine, Edward. "Westminster Abbey: Some Early Masters of the Choristers." *Musical Times* 94 (1953): 258-60.

Details from 1479 to 1560, when the list on the organ case commences.

126. Rimbault, Edward F., *ed. The Old Cheque-Book or Book of Remembrance of the Chapel Royal from 1561 to 1744*. London: Camden Society, 1872; repr. ed. Da Capo Press Music Titles. New York: Da Capo, 1966. ML286.8.L5S26.

Valuable source of information about church musicians of the Tudor period. The Chapel Royal was the monarch's own body of clergy and musicians. Amongst the latter the finest in the land were recruited. Chapters I and II are devoted to appointments and obituaries of the organists, Gentlemen and others, though the remaining sixteen chapters contain items concerning the activities of the Gentlemen of the Tudor period. The book is indifferently indexed but there is an interesting introduction by Rimbault to the original edition, and a further one by Elwyn A. Wienandt to the reprint. See also *133.*

127. Ross, D. James. "Robert Carver: A Quincentenary Celebration." *Brio* 24 (1987): 14-25.

Weighs conflicting biographical evidence, analyses all the surviving music with special attention to questions of performance, and suggests some additions to the canon. The author is keen to draw attention not only to Carver's uniqueness, but to his affinities with composers as varied as Dufay, Josquin, those of the Eton Choirbook, and his younger English contemporary Sheppard. The article is well illustrated. Similar content in *128* and *129.* Ross's monograph *Musick Fyne: Robert Carver and the Art of Music in Sixteenth Century Scotland* is scheduled to be published in Edinburgh by Mercat Press in 1993. See also *630.*

128. Ross, D. James. "Robert Carver: Quincentenary of a Neglected Genius." *Musical Opinion* 110 (1987): 358-60.

Based on *127.*

129. Ross, D. James. "Robert Carver (1487-1566) a Sixteenth Century Scottish Master of Polyphony." *Consort* 43 (1987): 1-12.

Condensed and illustrated version of *127.*

130. Sandon, Nick. "Another Mass by Hugh Aston?" *Early Music* 9 (1981): 184-91.

Considers Aston's biography, lists his compositions and the sources in which they appear, and suggests he is the composer of an anonymous and untitled mass of which only the bass part survives in its unique source. There are "Observations" on Sandon's attribution in subsequent issues: "Hugh Ashton's Maske" by Judith Blezzard, 9 (1981): 519-20, and "Hugh Aston's Variations on a Ground" by Oliver Neighbour, 10 (1982): 215-6.

131. Sandon, N.J. "Paired and Grouped Works for the Latin Rite by Tudor Composers." *Music Review* 44 (1983): 8-12.

Lists sixteen suggested groupings by ten composers, with reasoned introduction detailing the types of sacred composition involved, which were usually of festal proportions.

132. Shaw, Watkins. *From Tallis to Tomkins: a Survey of Church Music, c.1550-c.1650.* Church Music Society Occasional Papers, 22. London: Oxford University Press, 1954. 17pp. ML2931.S5.

Inquires how much music from the prescribed period was in use in English cathedrals 1950-1, draws attention to then neglected works available for performance, and offers guidance to modern choirmasters of parish churches about pieces within the range of a competent and balanced choir. Of particular interest is the appendix "List of 54 Latin Works by William Byrd available in Separate Form." See also *WB157* and *WB182.*

133. Shaw, Watkins. *The Succession of Organists of the Chapel Royal and the Cathedrals of England and Wales from c.1538, also of the Organists of the Collegiate Churches of Westminster and Windsor, Certain Academic Choral Foundations, and the Cathedrals of Armagh and Dublin.* Oxford Studies in British Church Music. Oxford: Clarendon, 1991. 0198161751.

As far as the Tudor period is concerned this book includes all relevant details of the organists' biographies from the 27 cathedrals of the Old and New Foundations; the Chapel Royal; St. George's Chapel, Windsor; Trinity College, Cambridge; Eton College; Magdalen and New Colleges, Oxford; Winchester College; plus Christ Church and St. Patrick's Cathedrals, Dublin. Much of the author's information is unavailable elsewhere, for instance concerning the year of Robert Parsons's death (p.3). It is organized alphabetically by cathedral, then chronologically by organist. The author provides a cogent introduction to the whole, and to individual establishments where appropriate. The entries give dates, circumstances of appointment and departure, musical qualifications and financial arrangements. This is a monumental and indispensable work.

134. Smith, Alan. "The Cultivation of Music in English Cathedrals in the Reign of Elizabeth." *Proceedings of the Royal Musical Association* 94 (1967-8): 37-49.

     Demonstrates that the idea of a golden age, at least in respect of the performance of music in cathedrals, must be treated with caution. Although the queen tried to give the lead in her own Chapel Royal, a combination of economic inflation and the hostility of the Puritan clergy led to low standards, poor morale and indiscipline amongst cathedral choirs, despite the high quality and quantity of music being written for the new Anglican church.

135. Smith, Alan. "Elizabethan Church Music at Ludlow." *Music & Letters* 49 (1968): 108-21.

     Account of musical establishment at Ludlow Parish Church, Shropshire, c.1567-81. Contemporary documents indicate activities comparable with those of a cathedral. The author provides details of numbers of singers, payments, conduct of services, purchases of manuscript and upkeep of the organ. He concludes with a commentary on the surviving manuscripts of music sung in Ludlow at this time, to which he appends a description and inventory of Ludlow church music manuscripts, c.1570-c.1660, valuable because they are the only surviving manuscripts which can definitely be said to have been used in Elizabethan church services.

136. Smith, Alan. "The Gentlemen and Children of the Chapel Royal of Elizabeth: an Annotated Register." *Research Chronicle* 5 (1965): 13-46.

     Chronological list by date of appointment with, where known, voice, where commissioned, dates of appointment and resignation or death, source of information, position, whether present at Elizabeth's funeral, plus comments. There is a comprehensive introduction. The register provides circumstantial evidence as to which voices specific Gentlemen sang: for instance Byrd was probably a countertenor (p.28).

137. Smith, Alan. "Parish Church Musicians in England in the Reign of Elizabeth (1558-1603): an Annotated Register." *Research Chronicle* 4 (1964): 42-92.

Introduction and bipartite list, by surname and by place. Principal sources are churchwardens' accounts. Includes all those engaged in musical activity down to organblowers, and excludes cathedrals and collegiate foundations.

138. Smith, Carleton Sprague. "Table Blessings Set to Music." In *The Commonwealth of Music*, ed. by Gustave Reese and Rose Brandel in honor of Curt Sachs. New York: Free Press; London: Collier-Macmillan, 1965, pp.236-82.

Contains several references to early English examples, pp.259ff., including texts of Hooper's *My God, O King* and Farmer's *We Praise O God* neither listed in *59*.

139. Stevens, Denis. "Robert Carver and his Motets." *Monthly Musical Record* 89 (1959): 170-5.

After a brief biographical sketch, provides an introduction to the texts and music of Carver's two surviving motets.

140. Stevens, Denis. "A Songe of Fortie Partes, Made by Mr. Tallys." *Early Music* 10 (1982): 171-81.

Suggests date, place and mode of first performance of *Spem in alium* and of English version, with review of other critics' opinions, emphasizing its relationship to Striggio's *Ecce beatam lucem* also in forty parts and composed around the same time. See also *42* and *66*.

141. Stevens, Denis. *Tudor Church Music*. 2nd ed. London: Faber; New York: Norton, 1966. 97pp. MS2931.S8.

Traces the stylistic changes and developments from 1485 to

1603 with special reference to the principal liturgical forms used by composers of the time. The five chapters cover history and liturgy, the ordinary of the mass, the motet, music for the English rite, and the role played by instruments. A fine introduction to the topic, it complements the more detailed studies *22, 35, 91* and *117.* It is well illustrated and comes with a 7" 45rpm EP.

142. Stulken, Marilyn Kay. "The Hymn Tunes of Orlando Gibbons." *Hymn* 33 (1982): 221-34.

Takes in turn each of Gibbons's contributions to George Wither's *Hymnes and Songs* and notes the modern hymnals, American, British and Australian, in which they appear. Each tune is analysed though, as in the case of Song 20, it is not always clear whether the author makes allowance for the fact that Gibbons only provided treble and bass parts. She notes the use to which part of one of Gibbons's anthems was put. By quoting the texts of the modern hymns to which Gibbons's tunes have been set, she sheds light on a neglected aspect of Tudor music in the twentieth century.

143. Terry, R.R. "John Merbecke (1523(?)-1585)." *Proceedings of the Musical Association* 45 (1918-19): 75-96.

Superseded factually, but interesting for analysis of mass *Per arma iusticie.*

144. Thurlow, Alan John. "The Latin Church Music of John Sheppard (Edition and Commentary)." Dissertation (referred and not resubmitted), Cambridge, 1979. 2v. 394pp., 497pp.

Seeks, by examination and analysis of the works, not only to assess the value of the contribution of Sheppard's Latin church music to early Tudor polyphony as a whole, but also to produce a complete edition of his Latin church music. The six chapters of volume I include an introduction and go on to deal with Sheppard's biography, the manuscript sources of the music, editorial procedures, the Latin church music itself and, by way of a summary, Sheppard's style. Three appendices provide a catalogue of works and sources, published eidtions of Sheppard's music including Anglican and instrumental music, and a list of the trancriptions of Sheppard's Latin church music made by Alexander Ramsbotham for the projected second series of *Tudor Church Music*. The analyses in chapter 5 benefit from the discussions of sources and editorial procedure in the preceding chapters and as in *WB100* each work benefits from individual attention. The editions in volume II offer interesting differences from subsequent editions, such as *Early English Church Music*, in the completions of fragmentary passages. This is the most substantial work on Sheppard but its provenance has prevented its having been included in any previous bibliography, and continues to restrict its availability. A copy has been placed by the author in the library of Chichester Cathedral for public consultation. It is an essential text for anyone researching Sheppard.

145. Tovey, Donald Francis. "Wilbye and Palestrina: Four Sixteenth-Century Motets." In *Essays in Musical Analysis*. Vol. 5: *Vocal Music*. London: Oxford University Press, 1937, pp.12-19.

Includes analysis of Wilbye's *O God the Rock of My Whole Strength.*

146. Uhler, John E. "Thomas Morley and the First Music for the English Burial Service." *Renaissance News* 9 (1956): 144-6.

Informed advocacy of Morley's Burial Service, describing the music of each of its four sections, and listing those occasions when it is known to have been used before having been supplanted by the later Service of William Croft. Concludes by suggesting reasons for its having fallen into disuse.

147. Vann, Stanley. "Tallis: Father of English Cathedral Music." *Organists Review* 70.4 (1985): 25-30.

Historically slanted view of Tallis's life and work, beginning with brief biography, followed by chronological accounts of his Latin and Anglican church music. In the former, the author isolates certain compositional techniques and comments on how Tallis uses them, especially in relation to the historical development of the motet. He also makes a practical observation about Tallis's ability to write for a resonant accoustic. The section on the Latin music is well illustrated. That on the Anglican music has only one illustration, but there are illuminating comments on individual anthems, and he makes a revealing comparison between two of Tallis's compositions, one for either denomination.

148. Vining, Paul. "Orlando Gibbons: an Index to the Full and Verse Anthems." *Early Music* 3 (1975): 379-81.

Marks 350th anniversary of the death of Gibbons, giving details of commemorative service. Annotations to the index itself describe the state in which each item has survived and indicate any problems of attribution.

149. Vining, Paul. "Orlando Gibbons: the Incomplete Verse Anthems." *Music & Letters* 55 (1974): 70-6.

Notes on provenance and structure of nine anthems (seven verse, two full) which survive only fragmentarily. Six of the verse anthems were subsequently reconstructed in volume 21 of *Early English Church Music* (only a bass part of the seventh survives, though this too is printed) along with the texts of the two full anthems. Characteristic of the helpfulness of the author's comments is his pointing out the similarity between Gibbons's *Thou God of Wisdom* and Byrd's *Thou God that Guid'st*.

150. Vining, Paul. "Wither and Gibbons: a Prelude to the First English Hymn Book." *Musical Times* 120 (1979): 245-6.

Ponders whether Gibbons provided any of the fourteen tunes, all of which are anonymous, in Wither's *The Songs of the Old Testament*, 1621, as a trial run for his famous *The Hymns and Songs of the Church* two years later, for which Gibbons provided several acknowledged tunes.

151. Weidner, Robert W. "Tye's *Actes of the Apostles:* a Reassessment." *Musical Quarterly* 58 (1972): 242-58.

Advances the case for treating the book on its merits, unlike previous critics who tended to dismiss it. The author comments on the verse and the music, with ample examples, and emphasizes the unpretentiousness of the conception.

152. Welch, C.E. *Two Cathedral Organists: Thomas Weelkes (1601-1623) and Thomas Kelway (1720-1744).* The Chichester Papers, 8. Chichester: Chichester City Council, 1957.

See pages 2-4. Reproduces on page 10 "A Catalogue of all the songe-bookes for the performance of Divine Service; appertaining to the Cathedral Church ... of Chichester ... 1621" and therefore during Weelkes's tenure of the post of Organist.

153. Wilkes, Roger. *English Cathedrals and Collegiate Churches and Chapels: their Music, Musicians and Musical Establishments: a Select Bibliography.* London: Friends of Cathedral Music, 1967. ML128.C54W54.

Useful annotated list containing some items which have general references to Tudor music, but which it is not appropriate to include in a specialized bibliography.

154. Williams, Carol J. "The Salve Regina Settings in the Eton Choirbook." *Miscellanea Musicologica* 10 (1979): 28-37.

Tabulates the fourteen surviving settings, an examination of which indicates that at least six identifiable conventions had developed within the settings, revealing substantial agreement among the composers of this group of works.

155. "By Whom?: a Favourite Miniature Re-examined." *Church Music Society Report* 76 (1981-2): 28-33.

Looks afresh at the sources and musical text of the anthem *Lord for Thy Tender Mercies' Sake* to try to gain any further insight as to whether it was composed by *Richard Farrant,* as originally thought, or *John Hilton,* more favoured subsequently. The author, himself anonymous, offers an eminently sensible and plausible solution to the problem.

See also 157, 304, 397, 398, 403, 413, 414, 415, 430, 459, 463, 465, 474, 475, 476, 483, 485, 490, 491, 494, 495, 496, 497, 502, 517, 523, 525, 543, 546, 547, 550, 551, 552, 559, 565, 573, 575, 576, 580, 582, 586, 593, 594, 598, 599, WB156, WB157, WB158, WB161, WB163, WB175, WB176, WB177, WB178, WB180, WB181, WB182, WB183, WB184, WB187.

IV SECULAR VOCAL MUSIC

This section includes writings about masques and music for the theatre. Bibliographical studies of sources are in chapter X.

156. Adams, Joseph Quincy. "A New Song by Robert Jones." *Modern Language Quarterly* 1 (1940): 45-8.

Announces the discovery of *The Love of Change,* a hitherto unknown song by Robert Jones, whose manuscript of which is reproduced in facsimile. The author argues that Jones took his text from the version published in Francis Davison's anthology *A Poetical Rapsodie* of 1602, and he provides a brief provenance of Jones's manuscript.

157. Arkwright, G.E.P. "Elizabethan Choirboy Plays and their Music." *Proceedings of the Musical Association* 40 (1913-14): 117-38.

Introductory account, with description of origins, the music, its composers, and developments such as the verse anthem.

158. Arnold, Denis. "Croce and the English Madrigal." *Music & Letters* 35 (1954): 309-19.

Evidence of Croce's popularity in England, and his influence on Morley and his contemporaries.

159. Arnold, Denis M. "Thomas Weelkes and the Madrigal." *Music & Letters* 31 (1950): 1-12.

Comprehensive study of Weelkes's corpus, commenting on his style, frame of musical reference, response to texts, sources of inspiration, and developing sense of structure, as well as placing his works in historical perspective.

160. Austern, Linda Phyllis. "'Art to Enchant': Musical Magic and its Practitioners in English Renaissance Drama." *Journal of the Royal Musical Association* 115 (1990): 191-206.

Identifies three types of practitioners in the occult - the enchanter, the witch and the magician - who are depicted in English drama of the Tudor period as exploiting music for their purposes. Contemporary theorists divided music into the speculative, for instance that "musical harmony ... both emblematic and productive of the greater universal order and concord," and the practical, which was performed and heard. Normally the two types were mutually exclusive, but the stage was one situation where they met, to further magical ends.

161. Austern, Linda Phyllis. "Thomas Ravenscroft: Musical Chronicler of an Elizabethan Theater Company." *Journal of the American Musicological Society* 38 (1985): 238-63.

Gives the provenances of Ravenscroft's eleven surviving theatre songs, and concentrates on his relationship with the Children of Paul's. The author demonstrates how his songs illustrate some musical conventions of the contemporary stage, shows what sort of music was performed by the company, and illustrates how each musical setting helped to integrate the song into a dramatic unity. She provides background information about children's plays and companies. Her analyses of the songs contain several illustrations. See also *241*.

162. Bernstein, Jane A. "An Index of Polyphonic Chansons in English Manuscript Sources, c.1530-1640." *Research Chronicle* 21 (1988): 21-36.

Of value as a reflection of Tudor taste, and for evidence of influences on English composers. Composer and first line indices.

163. Bernstein, Jane A. "Philip van Wilder and the Netherlandish Chanson in England." *Musical Disciplina* 33 (1979): 55-75.

   Consists of a comprehensive biography and a summary of his chanson technique, with a complete list of works. Wilder had some influence on younger English composers (see *705*) so the circumstances of his moving from his native Netherlands to settle in England, and his activities there once settled, are of importance and interest.

164. Brennecke, Ernest. "The *Country Cryes* of Richard Deering." *Musical Quarterly* 42 (1956): 366-76.

   Commentary on one of the only English sets of cries to exploit country rather than city tunes.

165. Brennecke, Ernest. "The Entertainment at Elvetham, 1591." In *Music in English Renaissance Dramas*, ed. by John H. Long. Lexington, KY: University of Kentucky Press, 1968, pp. 32-56.

   Account of the musical activities during the visit of Elizabeth I to the home of the Earl of Hertford, which involved Morley, Baldwin, Pilkington and Edward Johnson.

166. Brett, Philip. "The English Consort Song, 1570-1625." *Proceedings of the Royal Musical Association* 88 (1961-2): 73-88.

   Describes the emergence of the consort song as a distinct form, making the point that this native tradition was not eclipsed by the Italianate madrigal. The author draws attention to the role of instruments and to the place of choirboys and their plays in the development of the form. After a substantial consideration of Byrd's role in establishing the identity of the consort song (see *WB57*) he concludes with a review of the consort song in the hands of later composers such as Peerson and Gibbons, before its demise due to changes in contemporary musical taste.

167. Bridge, J. Frederick. "Country Cryes". *Proceedings of the Musical Association* 49 (1922-3): 21-8.

Introduction to cries by *Dering* and *Cobbold*.

168. Bridge, Frederick. "The Musical Cries of London in Shakespeare's Time." *Proceedings of the Musical Association* 46 (1919-20): 13-20.

Introduction to the cries of *Weelkes, Gibbons* and *Dering*, with comments on their origins and contents.

169. Brown, James Walter. "An Elizabethan Song-Cycle." *Cornhill Magazine*. New Series 48 (1920): 572-9.

Describes a group of eleven songs that conforms to the definition of a song-cycle. It occurs untitled in two partbooks from Carlisle Cathedral and was composed by *Richard Nicolson*. The author gives the words of eight of the songs, and an account of the provenance of the partbooks and of Roger Smith, whose name appears in the bass partbook.

170. Brown, Patricia A. "Influences on the Early Lute Songs of John Dowland." *Musicology* 3 (1968-9): 21-33.

Seeks to prove that Dowland's lute songs owe more to the English tradition, and particularly to the consort song, than to the likes of the French lute-accompanied air de coeur: in fact Dowland was bringing English practices up to date with those operating on the continent by providing lute-accompanied solo songs. The author discusses Dowland's songs in respect of the subjects of the poetry he chose to set, and she provides a table to demonstrate that he eschewed simple strophic settings, instead tailoring his music to the form of the individual poem. Having considered the influence on Dowland of French airs, popular songs and dances, and the English madrigal, she concludes that the prime influence on his ayres was the consort song tradition exemplified by the work of Byrd. Her second table indicates that Dowland's songs have more in common structurally with those of *Byrd* and *Whytehorne* than with the other potential influences she discusses.

171. Carpenter, Nan Cooke. "Christopher Tye and the Musical Dialogue in Samuel Rowley's *When You See Me, You Know Me.*" *Journal of Research in Music Education* 8 (1960): 85-90.

Provides all the appropriate quotations from Rowley's play, and relates them to the contemporary theory and teaching of music. The author also mentions other references to music in Tudor drama.

172. Charteris, Richard. "The English Songs of Alfonso Ferrabosco the Elder." *Studies in Music* 17 (1983): 79-86.

Discusses the two English songs ascribed to Ferrabosco in *12* plus three others subsequently discovered by the author. All five are for five voices, and he provides provenances, incipits and texts.

173. Charteris, Richard. "New Light on Ferrabosco's Chansons." *Consort* 38 (1982): 461-2.

Notes that two that have survived have English texts.

174. Charteris, Richard. "Newly Identified Italian Madrigals Englished." *Music & Letters* 63 (1982): 276-80.

Announces discovery of sixteen madrigals by *Alfonso Ferrabosco* with English translations surviving solely in manuscript, and 28 of *Dering's* canzonettas. In two appendices, one for either composer, the author gives the "englished" title, the Italian original, the published collection in which they originally apeared, and the manuscripts in which the "englished" works survive.

175. Cohen, Judith. "Thomas Weelkes's Borrowings from Salamone Rossi." *Music & Letters* 66 (1985): 110-17.

Establishes that Weelkes borrowed both texts and music of

six canzonettas from Rossi's *Primo libro delle canzonette a tre voci* of 1589, to form the entire group for five voices in his *Madrigals* of 1597.

176. Collet, Robert. "John Wilbye: Some Aspects of his Music." *Score* 4 (1951): 57-64.

    Worthwhile introduction to the subject-matter of Wilbye's texts and the formal character of his music.

177. Cutts, John P. "A Reconsideration of the *Willow Song.*" *Journal of the American Musicological Society* 10 (1957): 14-24.

    Provides a corrected and complete text of the famous anonymous song from Shakespeare's *Othello,* with a comparative analysis of the sources.

178. Dart, Thurston. "Purcell and Bull." *Musical Times* 104 (1963): 31.

    Account of Purcell's autograph transcription of a canon for ten voices by Bull.

179. Davie, Cedric Thorpe. "A Lost Morley Song Rediscovered." *Early Music* 9 (1981): 338-9.

    Announces discovery, in the Margaret Wemyss manuscript, of *White as Lilies*, number fifteen of Morley's *The First Booke of Ayres*, 1600, whose unique surviving copy is defective, containing only the first fourteen of 21 items indexed. See *93* for a study of the *Booke* that predates this discovery, and *564* for a study of the manuscript.

180. Doughtie, Edward. *English Renaissance Song.* Twayne's English Authors Series, 424. Boston, MA: Twayne, 1986. 185pp. 0805769153. ML3849.D7.

    Of nine chapters, the first two deal with music and poetry and with the historical context of the study. The next two are devoted to Whytehorne and Byrd. After a further two which look at Italian music "englished" and the English madrigal, the next pair are devoted to Dowland and Campion, before a summarizing "coda." The monograph is aimed primarily at literary readers. The author explores the reciprocal influences of music and poetry, and discusses the possible effect of music on the development of metrics. Little space is devoted to song in drama but a substantial bibliography, aided by the author's comments in his introduction, directs interested readers to relevant studies. See also *WB148*.

181. Doughtie, Edward. "George Handford's Ayres: Unpublished Jacobean Song Verse." *Anglia* 83 (1964): 474.

Biographical introduction to Handford, with a description of the manuscript containing his "Ayres" plus the texts of unpublished lyrics (subsequently reprinted in *186*). According to the author this is the only manuscript collection of lute songs that is a carefully prepared work by one man.

182. Doughtie, Edward. "Robert Southwell and Morley's *First Booke of Ayres.*" *Lute Society Journal* 4 (1962): 28-30.

Supporting the suggestion in *662* that Morley was a Roman Catholic in his youth, announces the discovery that the text of number four, *With my Love*, is adapted from the poem *Sith my Life* by the Jesuit martyr Southwell. The author ponders Morley's reasons for reordering those of Southwell's stanzas he chose to set, and the possible interpretation of those stanzas.

183. Einstein, Alfred. "The Elizabethan Madrigal and 'Musica Transalpina'." *Music & Letters* 25 (1944): 66-77.

See *WB42*.

184. Evans, Willa McClung. *Ben Jonson and Elizabethan Music.* Lancaster, PA: Lancaster Press, 1929; repr. ed. New York: Da Capo, 1970. ML80.J7E82.

Deals with songs in the miscellaneous collections of Jonson's verse (including songs not set to music and not intended for singing), in the plays and in the masques. The book is written from a literary perspective so the musical content is modest, but it attempts to be comprehensive and contains some worthwhile insights, notably in the general first chapter on song forms.

185. Fellowes, Edmund Horace. *The English Madrigal Composers.* 2nd ed. London: Oxford University Press, 1948. 364pp. ML2631.F46.

In its day an important book, it has been substantially superseded by *208*. Nevertheless it is still worth reading because the author had edited every work mentioned and he discusses, in more or less detail, thirty composers and their works, plus the *Oriana* and English lutenist composers. Subsequent research has made good some of his omissions and rendered some of his facts and interpretations inaccurate: Byrd was patently not the founder of the English madrigal school, Dowland was not born in Ireland, and so on. However, Fellowes occasionally provides interesting insights into the pieces he features, all of which he knows from inside, and unlike some selfconsciously scholarly critics is keen to point out salty chords or progressions merely for their savour rather than to analyse all the pleasure out of them. His three once-useful appendices have also been superseded: the biographical synopsis by *12*, the index of first lines by *197* and the references to original editions in principal libraries by *13* and *14*.

186. Fellowes, E.H. *English Madrigal Verse, 1588-1632.* 3rd ed. rev. and enl. by Frederick W. Sternfeld and David Greer. Oxford: Clarendon, 1967. 798pp. PR1195.M2F4.

Contains the poetic texts of the madrigal collections and songbooks printed in England. (The revisers include Handford's unpublished "Ayres" of 1609 because in their opinion the collection had been prepared for publication: see *181*). The book is in two parts, devoted respectively to madrigals and lute songs. Both parts consist of a list of publications followed by the poems themselves. For consistency, spellings have in the main been modernized. Nevertheless, in the lists of publications the wordings of the title-pages are reproduced as in the originals. Fellowes himself edited the first two editions, and the third represents a radical revision of his material, explained in detail in the introduction. There are copious notes, with addenda and indices of authors and translators, and of first lines.

187. Fellowes, Edmund H. "The Songs of Dowland." *Proceedings of the Musical Association* 56 (1929-30): 1-26.

Introduction to the songs, with emphasis on certain features such as form, rhythm and tempo. It is obvious from *637* that many of Fellowes's factual comments about Dowland are embarrassingly inaccurate, but his comments on the songs themselves are worthwhile as coming from one who not only edited them but who also performed them in public (see *585*).

188. Fellowes, E.H. "The Text of the Song-Books of Robert Jones." *Music & Letters* 8 (1957): 25-37.

Feels that Jones's accompaniments are almost certainly misrepresented in their original edition, and ponders the proper course for an editor to pursue by way of emendation. See *12* for details of Jones's five songbooks.

189. Fortune, Nigel. "Philip Rosseter and His Songs." *Lute Society Journal* 7 (1965): 7-14.

After a brief biographical introduction, reviews Rosseter's corpus of songs, summarizing its characteristics and providing examples from individual songs. The author is sceptical as to whether Campion provided the lyrics for Rosseter's section (part II) of their joint publication *A Booke of Ayres*, 1601. (See *240*).

190. Greer, David. "Campion the Musician." *Lute Society Journal* 9 (1967): 7-16.

Concentrates on the purely musical aspect of the songs, to the exclusion of any literary associations. The author discusses Campion's structure, particularly his consistent use of strophic form and the extent to which even different lines within the stanza are set to the same repeated passage of music. To maintain the integrity of his tunes, Campion also exploited rhythmic and sequential repetition, and, since his writings reveal his suspicion of contrapuntal methods, his textures are predominantly homophonic, though the author notes his few manifestations of polyphony and chromaticism. Other influences are popular melodies and some aspects of continental music, notably French and Italian, though even here Campion keeps himself on a tight rein, and the few looser exceptions are enumerated. Finally the author comments on those songs for which Campion provided alternative partsong versions for three or four voices.

191. Greer, David. "A Dowland Curiosity." *Lute* 27 (1987): 43-4.

Debates the authenticity of a setting of *Adieu Sweet Amaryllis* attributed to Dowland and only surviving in a modern arrangement by Hamilton Harty in a manuscript at Queen's University, Belfast.

192. Greer, David. "Five Variations on 'Farewel Dear Love'." In *The Well Enchanting Skill: Music, Poetry, and Drama in the Culture of the Renaissance: Essays in Honour of F.W. Sternfeld,* ed. by John Caldwell, Edward Olleson and Susan Wollenberg. Oxford: Clarendon, 1990, pp.213-29.

Examines five aspects of the history of *Robert Jones's* ayre, from his *The First Booke of Songes,* 1600: its progress to Scotland and the continent, parody by Jones himself, quotation by Shakespeare in *Twelfth Night* and similarities with popular tunes of the day. A list of musical sources is appended.

193. Greer, David. "The Lute Songs of Thomas Morley." *Lute Society Journal* 8 (1966): 25-37.

Focuses on *The First Booke of Ayres*, 1600, Morley's only publication devoted to lute songs. Before doing so, the author looks at the solo versions of the *Canzonets*, 1597, and arrangements of his part music that survive in manuscript. (In his paragraph on *O Mistress Mine* he wrongly states that the keyboard setting by Byrd is of this song: see *WB129*, p.145). He characterizes the collection as a whole, drawing examples from various songs, before dealing in more detail with seven individual items. He appends a list of contents (only one copy of the print survives and that is incomplete) and concordances (from which two of the seven missing songs can be identified). See *179* for a subsequent discovery.

194. Greer, David. "The Part-Songs of the English Lutenists." *Proceedings of the Royal Musical Association* 94 (1967-8): 97-110.

Examines the songs of the lutenists in their version as partsongs rather than as solos. The author analyses the processes by which such ayres became partsongs, or sometimes vice versa, to try to arrive at a deeper understanding of the nature of the ayre and of performance practices associated with it.

195. Greer, David. "Two Songs by William Corkine." *Early Music* 11 (1983): 346-9.

Announces the rediscovery of *What Booteth Love* (with edition of complete song) and discovery of hitherto unknown *Sad is the Time*, for which the author provides a literal transcription of the words. See also *530*.

196. Gross, Harvey. "Technique and *Episteme*: John Dowland's "Can She Excuse My Wrongs"." *Bulletin of Research in the Humanities* 86 (1983-5): 318-34.

Analyses Dowland's success in providing an apt musical setting of the text to produce a balanced, unified entity, in relation to contemporary épistémè, which is "concerned to denote a period's modes of acquiring and interpreting knowledge as revealed in the structure and function of signs." Includes the text of the poem, collated from editions of 1597 and 1613, and an edition of the song itself.

197. Hall, Alison. *E.H. Fellowes: an Index to The English Madrigalists and The English School of Lutenist Song Writers.* Music Library Association Index and Bibliography Series 23.

Boston, MA: Music Library Association, 1984. 091495430X. ML120.G7H34.

Comprises numerical list of volumes of both series, composer index and title index, with useful short introduction.

198. Harley, John. "Two Jacobean Songs: Ladlawe's 'In Sorrow's Drown'd' and Campion's 'Shall I Come, Sweet Love, to Thee?'" *Early Music* 6 (1978): 385-9.

Discussion and editions of the only Jacobean songs to survive in settings specifically for voice and keyboard.

199. Harper, John. "A New Way of Making Ayres? Thomas Campion: Towards a Revaluation." *Musical Times* 110 (1969): 262-3.

Considers Campion underrated as a musician. The author points out how he differs from Dowland as a composer of ayres and, though he acknowledges Campion to be only a minor composer, he notes and illustrates his merits.

200. Harris, Anne P. "'Touches of Sweet Harmony': Shakespeare's Music." *Brio* 25 (1988): 14-20.

Introductory account of references to music in Shakespeare's plays. Discusses what Shakespeare and his audience would expect from one another. The author remarks on his use of references to music as imagery, and on the use of music itself as transcending words, and he summarizes the contemporary philosophical attitude to music. She refers to Shakespeare's use of songs and to his stage directions requiring music, and suggests instrumentation. Finally she discusses Shakespeare's developing use of musical imagery.

201. Harwood, Ian. "John Maynard and *The XII Wonders of the World.*" *Lute Society Journal* 4 (1962): 7-16.

After a brief bibliographical note, proceeds with a biography of Maynard, followed by a summary of the contents of *The XII Wonders.* The author seeks to rectify the poor opinion in which the collection had hitherto been held, and discusses Maynard's compositional style and some problems of performance thrown up by the print. He does not deal with the music for lyra viol that completes the collection, but mentions the few other pieces that survive with ascriptions to Maynard.

202. Helm, Everett B. "Italian Traits in the English Madrigal." *Music Review* 7 (1946): 26-34.

After a brief introduction to the Italian Madrigal, notes the Italian influence as manifested in works by Morley, Weelkes and Wilbye, but also notes where Italian influence was small or non-existent, such as in the works of Byrd and Whytehorne.

203. Henning, Rudolf. "A Possible Source of *Lachrymae?*" *Lute Society Journal* 16 (1974): 65-7.

Suggests *Dowland* modelled his *Lachrymae* theme on Rore's madrigal *Quando lieta sperai.*

204. Hillebrand, Harold Newcomb. "The Child Actors: a Chapter in Elizabethan Stage History." *University of Illinois Studies in Language and Literature* 11 (1926): 7-355.

Comprehensive study in eleven chapters and three appendices, detailing from what, and how, the companies of child actors developed from the twelfth century onwards. The author delineates the prominent role of the Chapel Royal, and he describes what the boys acted, and what they did in addition to their acting.

205. Hudson, Frederick. "Robert White and his Contemporaries: Early Elizabethan Music and Drama." In *Festschrift fur Ernst Hermann Meyer zum sechzigsten Geburtstag,* ed. by Georg Knepler. Leipzig: VEB, 1973, pp.163-87.

Documentary biography, with copious quotation and illustration. The author provides full and unprecedented detail of Whyte's dramatic activities in respect of the Chester mistery play cycle in 1567 and 1568. His account of Whyte's works is summary, though he gives a full list of titles.

206. Johnson, Rose Marie. "A Comparison of "The Cries of London" by Gibbons and Weelkes." *Journal of the Viola da Gamba Society of America* 9 (1972): 38-43.

Lists cries used by either composer. The author also refers to Dering's *The Cries of London,* which she suggests predate Gibbons's, as the text of the latter appears to be a condensation of the former. She gives Dering's text with the analogous places in Gibbons's, plus Weelkes's complete text and a tabular analysis of its general structure. Also she provides a chart listing these three and all other English works known to the author which use street cries.

207. Joiner, Mary. "Another Campion Song?" *Music & Letters* 48 (1967): 138-9.

Suggests *Tarry Sweete Love,* an unascribed song in *GB-Och Mus.* 439 may be the work of Thomas Campion. Provides transcription.

208. Kerman, Joseph. *The Elizabethan Madrigal: a Comparative Study.* American Musicological Society Studies and Documents, 4. New York: American Musicological Society; London: Oxford University Press, 1962. ML2631.K47.

The outstanding monograph on its topic. Although the author pays his respects to Fellowes, he seeks to broaden the approach taken in *185*, to compare the various English composers among themselves and to compare the English composers with the Italians. He discusses English madrigal verse, Italian influence, the native song tradition, and various aspects of the Elizabethan madrigal itself. There is a judicious conclusion, and an appendix on Elizabethan music and publishing. The whole is well illustrated.

209. Kerman, Joseph. "Master Alfonso and the English Madrigal." *Musical Quarterly* 38 (1952): 222-44.

Enquires into career and reputation in Elizabethan times of *Alfonso Ferrabosco I,* the style of his madrigals and their possible influence on Morley and his contemporaries. The author suggests that Ferrabosco's congeniality to English composers was in "His unconscious bias towards the style of sacred music, his reserve before a literary text, his artisan interest in music for the sake of technique." See *643* for the dates of his sojourn in England.

210. Kerman, Joseph. "Morley and 'The Triumphs of Oriana'." *Music & Letters* 34 (1953): 185-91.

Introduction to the origins of the collection, and analysis of Morley's parody of the madrigal by Croce which probably inspired Morley to compile *The Triumphes.*

211. Leech-Wilkinson, Daniel. "My Lady's Tears: a Pair of Songs by John Dowland." *Early Music* 19 (1991): 227-33.

In Dowland's *Second Booke of Songs,* 1600, *Flow my Tears,* his texting of the *Lachrymae* pavan, is placed second to *I saw my Lady Weep.* The author investigates the reasons for this placing of the vocal version of Dowland's most famous work, albeit behind an outstanding song, when one would have expected it to head the collection. He concludes that the two songs form a pair, of which the former is an introduction to the latter and is possibly a musical continuation of the dedication to the Countess of Bedford. Certainly it cannot stand alone and requires *Flow My Teares* for completion, whereas the latter is self-contained. Morley also set the former text, as *I Saw My Lady Weeping,* and although the author concedes that Dowland could well have followed Morley's flawed setting, he concludes that Morley followed Dowland's, confirming Morley's reputation as an habitual borrower and arranger of other composers' music.

212. Lindley, David. "John Danyel's 'Eyes Looke No More'." *Lute Society Journal* 16 (1974): 9-16.

Danyel's song derives from his own solo lute pavan

Rosamond. In *242* and *371* it was suggested that Danyel's poet brother Samuel provided the text. The author disputes this, asserting that John wrote his own text. Also, *pace 242* he demonstrates that far from being the next step from the lute solo *Rosamond,* Danyel's song was structurally refined by reference to Dowland's *Flow My Teares.*

213. Long, John H. "Music for a Song in 'Damon and Pithias'." *Music & Letters* 48 (1967): 247-50.

Announces the discovery of a ballad tune which puzzled John Ward in *261.* The author establishes that the song, *Awake Ye Woful Wights,* was composed by *Richard Edwards* for his own play *Damon and Pithias* in 1564.

214. McCray, James. "The Canzonets of Giles Farnaby." *Choral Journal* 20 (May 1980): 13-16.

Devotes a paragraph to each of the works in Farnaby's *Canzonets,* 1598.

215. McCray, James E. "The Canzonets of Thomas Morley." *Choral Journal* 19 (September 1978): 28-35.

Based on survey of Morley's works in the canzonet style. Gives a brief account of the style itself, then devotes a paragraph to every item in Morley's collections entitled *Canzonets* of 1593 and 1597, excepting those pieces which the author does not define as canzonets. He attends in the same way to the canzonet in *A Plaine and Easie Introduction* (see *427*) and to two of Morley's own canzonets in his compilation *Canzonets, or little short songs to foure voyces: celected out of the best and approved Italian authors,* also 1597.

216. McGrady, Richard. "Campion and the Lute." *Music Review* 47 (1986/7): 1-15.

Considers Campion's inconsistent and idiosyncratic treatment of the lute in his accompaniments. The author identifies the questions raised by Campion's procedures but admits that they do not go very far towards any answers, though a developing refinement of detail is balanced by an increasingly unidiomatic use of the instrument in later publications.

217. McGrady, Richard. "'Chromatique tunes and measur'd accents': John Danyel's Can Dolefull Notes." *Music Review* 50 (1989): 79-92.

Analyses Danyel's song to demonstrate its important standing in the developing use of chromaticism in English music. The author suggests that its relatively complex construction is Danyel's response to the more measured form of song becoming more fashionable through the influence of Rosseter and Campion. He also notes in passing that John's brother Samuel Danyel, the poet, vigorously disagreed with Campion's opinions on the preferability of measure over rime in contemporary English poetry. The author concludes that John Danyel found a metaphor for his art in this poem, and suggests that the song is a statement of artistic faith.

218. McGrady, Richard. "Coprario's Funeral Teares." *Music Review* 38 (1977): 163-76.

Describes the circumstances in which the *Funeral Teares* were composed after the death of the Earl of Devonshire in 1606. The author relates the song-cycle to contemporary meditational techniques and discusses each song in detail, comparing them generally with the compositions of Ferrabosco, Morley, Danyel and particularly Dowland, who set one of the same texts, *In Darkness Let Me Dwell.*

219. McGrady, R.J. "Thomas Morley's *First Booke of Ayres*." *Music Review* 33 (1972): 171-6.

Published in 1600, Morley's book was the earliest volume of lute songs to appear in England without alternative polyphonic arrangements. The author restates Morley's importance to the development of English secular vocal music in the final decade of the sixteenth century by discussing the book's contents in the light of Morley's two major influences: Byrd's teaching and music, especially his conservative consort songs, and the Italian madrigal.

220. Manning, Rosemary J. "Lachrymae: a Study of Dowland." *Music & Letters* 25 (1944): 435-53.

Most information and comment overtaken by *637* but the last two pages contain some discussion of a few of the later songs.

221. Maynard, Winifred. *Elizabeth Lyric Poetry and its Music*. Oxford: Clarendon, 1986. 246pp. 0198128444. ML79.M4.

Attempts to explore and illustrate the ways in which lyric poetry and music interacted in Elizabethan England. The author devotes chapters to early and later songbooks and miscellanies, Sidney and Campion, ayres and masque songs, and to vocal music in Shakespeare's plays. Her touchstone is the question "What is the poem for?" Although not all Elizabethan lyrics were originally intended for singing, she uses this criterion to investigate not only the contexts in which lyrics were set to music, but also the nature of the alliance between the two. Here she refers to social matters such as popular taste and to technical matters such as coping with scansion or composing for dramatic effect.

222. Mellers, Wilfrid. *Harmonious Meeting: a Study of the Relationship Between English Music, Poetry and Theatre, c.1600-1900*. London: Dobson, 1965. ML3849.M5.

Explores the meeting in the title by way of detailed commentaries on specific pieces. In the first part of the book, about three quarters of which deals with composers who qualify as Tudor, the author traces the origins of the process whereby music became inherently dramatic. He devotes chapters to humanistic elements in *Byrd's* Latin church music, progressive elements in Anglican music, and various aspects of the contemporary madrigal and ayre. In addition he avers that since the pieces chosen for discussion were selected for their general significance as well as for their intrinsic merits, the book amounts to a history of part of the mind of England.

223. Milne, J.G.C. "On the identity of Weelkes' 'Fogo'." *Research Chronicle* 10 (1972): 98-100.

Offers alternative suggestion to that of Fellowes in *185* (p.203) concerning the enigmatic name in the madrigal *Thule, the Period of Cosmography.*

224. Milsom, John. "Cries of Durham." *Early Music* 18 (1989): 147-60.

Concerns frequently anthologized poem *The Maidens Came.* It is an anonymous Tudor lyric which, in its usual anthologized form, is an excerpt from a longer work, the text of which begins "Alone walking." Most significantly, in its unique source it is set to music in an isolated treble partbook explaining the disjointed nature of the text if the treble does not sing all the words in the lyric. The author provides musical and textual transcriptions with commentary. He suggests that the text refers to the great fair held in Durham on the feast of St Cuthbert's translation. Not only does he relate it to English cries such as those of Gibbons, Weelkes and Dering, but more closely to the anonymous Scottish *Pleugh Song.*

225. Mishkin, Henry G. "Irrational Dissonance in the English Madrigal." In *Essays on Music in Honor of Archibald Thompson Davison, by his Associates.* Cambridge, MA: Department of Music, Harvard University, 1957, pp.139-45.

Gives seven illustrated examples of certain "irrational" procedures, and ponders the unorthodoxy of certain radical English madrigalists such as Greaves, Cavendish, Jones and Carlton, suggesting it might be attributed in part to the rejection of scholasticism in England during the seventeenth century.

226. Monson, Craig. "George Kirbye and the English Madrigal." *Music & Letters* 59 (1978): 290-315.

Discusses eighteen unpublished madrigals by Kirbye additional to his *First Set*, 1597. With reference to the provenance of the manuscript in which they appear, Kirbye's own published collection, and the work of contemporary composers, the author provides an account of Kirbye's own status and technique as a madrigalist, and of his status in late Elizabethan musical life.

227. Monson, Craig. "Richard Nicolson: Madrigals from Jacobean Oxford." *Early Music* 6 (1978): 429-35.

Discusses several of Nicolson's madrigals, pondering his stylistic dilemma and the fact that he chose not to publish them.

228. Monson, Craig. "Thomas Weelkes: a New Fa-la." *Musical Times* 113 (1972): 133-5.

Announces discovery of Weelkes's three-part madrigal *Thus Sings My Dearest Jewel.* The author describes the provenance of the source and, having confirmed the attribution to Weelkes, he suggests that, judging by its placing in the source, Weelkes had intended publishing it among his *Ayres* of 1608 but for reasons unknown overlooked it. It was reproduced as the issue's music supplement.

229. Murphy, Catherine A. *Thomas Morley: Editions of Italian Canzonets and Madrigals, 1597-1598.* Florida State University Studies, 42. Tallahassee: Florida State University, 1964. MT110.M87.

Deals with two of Morley's compilations of works by other composers: the *Canzonets* of 1597 (see *215*) and *Madrigals to five voyces. Celected out of the best approved Italian authors,* 1598. Contents, sources, poets, texts and a note of editions of all works from either set are provided.

230. Pattison, Bruce. *Music and Poetry of the English Renaissance.* 2nd ed. London: Methuen, 1970. 222pp. 0416197507. ML286.2.P3.

Contains some outmoded lines of thought, but remains a usable introduction to the subject. The monograph consists of ten chapters, which cover music in sixteenth-century society, the singing of poetry, the literary and musical professions, the new poetry and music, musical and poetical forms, the madrigal, the ayre, musical influence on poetry, the ballad and dance, and a conclusion on the divergence of music and poetry from one another. Originally published in 1948, the publisher describes this new edition as a reissue, and the author admits to only minor revisions despite a good deal of relevant work having been published in the meantime. This includes *166* and *208*, none of which has impinged on the text. Doughtie covers less ground in *180* but responds to postwar research. Nevertheless Pattison's approach is unique in that he considers how the literary and musical approaches impinged on one another creatively and he suggests how a poet or a composer went about crafting their poem or song being mindful of the creative technique of his opposite number. According to the author, the composers emerge from this process slightly less well than the poets.

231. Payne, Ian. "George Kirbye (c.1565-1634): Two Important Repertories of English Secular Vocal Music Surviving Only in Manuscript." *Musical Quarterly* 73 (1989): 401-16.

Describes *GB-Ob* Mus. f.20-24 and *GB-Lrcm* 684, particularly from the viewpoint of reconstructing missing parts. The author emphazises the significance of clef dispositions in the surviving parts when working on the parts requiring reconstruction. He compares Kirbye's practice with that of *Byrd*, upon whose *Psalmes, Sonets and Songs* of 1588 the works in question were modelled. He also notes Kirbye's musical debt to Luca Marenzio.

232. Pilkington, Michael. *Campion, Dowland and the Lutenist Songwriters.* English Solo Song: Guides to the Repertoire. London: Duckworth, 1989. 179pp. 0715622730.

Lists composers alphabetically, then their published collections, then each song in order. Anonymous works are listed at the beginning of the sequence, and the anthology *A Musical Banquet* at the end. For each entry the author gives the title, poet, tonality, collection, range of voice part, meter, duration, level of difficulty, most suitable voice(s), subject, description of vocal line, description of piano accompaniment and further comments. It will be seen that this book is aimed at popularizing a repertory for which an authentic accompaniment may not be available to the potential performer, although he states that his comments on the piano accompaniment apply also if it is played on the lute.

233. Poulton, Diana. "The Black-Letter Broadside Ballad and its Music." *Early Music* 9 (1981): 427-37.

Describes the development of the ballad and its publishing history. The author discusses the various subjects in the ballads, the tunes that became attached to them and the provenances of those tunes, which were often set by leading musicians of the day.

234. Poulton, Diana. "The Favourite Singer of Queen Elizabeth I." *Consort* 14 (1957): 24-7.

Brief account of the life, and single surviving composition, of *Robert Hales.*

235. Rastall, Richard. "The Minstrels of the English Royal Households, 25 Edward I - 1 Henry VIII: an Inventory." *Research Chronicle* 4 (1964): 1-41.

Includes reigns of Henry VII and Henry VIII.

236. Ratcliffe, Stephen. *Campion: on Song.* Boston, MA: Routledge & Kegan Paul, 1981. 200pp. 0710008031. M6410.C3.

After an initial chapter in which the author endeavours to account for Campion's enduring reputation, the remaining four chapters are a prolonged aesthetic analysis of one song, *Now Winter Nights.* Respectively they deal with syntax and substance, phonetic structure, music and prosody. The author writes from a literary perspective, and promises the reader that though the analyses may seem dull, inhumane and myopic, patience will be rewarded by enlightenment. Viewing the fragile modesty of Campion's song beside the relentless and almost aggressive pursuit and justification of the analysis, it is interesting to discover on page xvi of the preface that one such as Philip Brett supported the project often "against his own better judgement."

237. Rooley, Anthony. "New Light on John Dowland's Songs of Darkness." *Early Music* 11 (1983): 6-21.

Contends that Dowland's musical melancholia was more apparent than real, and that he invented a persona to suit his artistic intentions. This he expressed through his *Lachrymae* epigram. The author uses Dowland's own words, those of sympathetic contemporaries and studies in other disciplines to endorse his opinion, making a point of placing Dowland in a European, as well as an English, context, with copious comparisons and illustrations throughout. See *263* for a refutation of the author's philosophical theories.

238. Ruff, Lillian M. *and* Wilson, D. Arnold. "Allusion to the Essex Downfall in Lute Song Lyrics." *Lute Society Journal* 12 (1970): 31-6.

Successor and supplement to *239*, aiming to overcome the scepticism of musicians who regarded the conjunction of events depicted therein as fortuitous.

239. Ruff, Lillian M. *and* Wilson, D. Arnold. "The Madrigal, the Lute Song and Elizabethan Politics." *Past & Present* 44 (1969): 3-51

Deals separately with either musical category. The Earl of Essex, Queen Elizabeth's favourite whom she subsequently imprisoned and executed, figures largely in the publishing history of the madrigal, and some sensitive publications were apparently suppressed until after his execution. Some madrigal verse was political, containing sentiments which were overtly or covertly sympathetic to him, and some composers were known to be well disposed towards him. The authors use such arguments to explain the contents and publication date of *The*

Triumphes of Oriana. As to the lute song, there was a tendency to set texts of a Roman Catholic provenance, as well as others that referred to the omnipresent Essex. After the execution of Essex, the Queen's death, the arrival of a new king and the Gunpowder Plot, the political momentum of these two forms waned, and although senior composers maintained the impetus and were joined by some junior ones, their textual sources were still those of the days before the death of Essex. See also *238*.

240. Ryding, Erik S. "Collaboration between Campion and Rosseter?" *Journal of the Lute Society of America* 19 (1986): 13-28.

Campion and Rosseter's joint collection *A Booke of Ayres* was published in 1601. It was divided into two parts, the first containing songs composed by Campion, the second, Rosseter. It is a matter of dispute as to whether Campion provided all the lyrics for the collection or merely those for his own songs (see *189*). The author argues that the work of Rosseter can be detected in the accompaniments to several songs in Campion's part of the *Booke*. He also cites articles that deal with the literary aspects of the compilation of the *Booke*.

241. Sabol, A.J. "Ravenscroft's 'Melismata' and the Children of Paul's." *Renaissance News* 12 (1959): 3-9.

Suggests that *Melismata*, hitherto overlooked as a source of information about Ravenscroft's association with the theatre, contains several stage songs identifiable with specific Paul's plays. See also *161*.

242. Scott, David. "John Danyel - His Life and Songs." *Lute Society Journal* 13 (1971): 7-17.

Biographical introduction, followed by commentary on each of the twelve songs in his only surviving collection *Songs for the Lute Viol and Voice*, 1606, of their time second only in quality to the songs of Dowland.

243. Scott, David. "Nicholas Yonge and his Transalpine Music." *Musical Times* 116 (1975): 875-6.

Brief biographical introduction to Yonge, first to publish Italian madrigals in England, followed by summaries of the contents of both sets of his *Musica transalpina*, 1588 and 1597.

244. Spearitt, Gordon. "The Consort Songs and Madrigals of Richard Nicolson." *Musicology* 2 (1965-7): 42-52.

After a brief biographical introduction, deals with either category in turn. The author ponders the questions of performance practice in respect of the consort songs, and when they were composed, paying particular attention to *GB-Lbl* Add. 17797 which contains most of Nicolson's secular vocal music. For both categories he prints the first stanza of verbal text, and on this bases his discussion of Nicolson's compositional procedures. Excluded are the two *Joan quoth John* songs which are the subject of *245*.

245. Spearitt, Gordon P. "Richard Nicolson and the 'Joan quoth John' Songs." *Studies in Music* 2 (1968): 33-42.

Supplement to *244*. After a biographical introduction, deals with both songs individually, and in either case the author discusses the respective manuscript sources, and describes how Nicolson set the texts, making comparisons where appropriate.

246. Spink, Ian. *English Song, Dowland to Purcell*. Paperback ed. London: Batsford, 1986. 0713451580. ML2831.S68.

Useful in the present context for indicating the manner in which late Elizabethan song developed and influenced English music beyond the Restoration. The appearance of Dowland's name in the title is significant, as little attention is paid to his own predecessors and their influence. This is a reissue of the original 1974 edition with corrections and an updated bibliography.

247. Sternfeld, Frederick W. "A Song from Campion's Lord's Masque." *Journal of the Warburg and Courtauld Institutes* 20 (1957): 373-5.

Summary of Campion's involvement with masques, for four of which he wrote the entire verbal text and also composed part of the music. The music and words of *Woo Her and Win Her* were published as part of an appendix to the *Somerset* masque of 1614, but the song is stated as belonging to *The Lords Maske*, 1613. The author provides a facsimile of the original text with accompaniment for lute (tablature) and basso, as well as his own transcription.

248. Stevens, John. *Music & Poetry in the Early Tudor Court.* London: Methuen; Lincoln, NE: University of Nebraska Press, 1961. ML286.2.S8.

Considers the entire surviving repertory of early Tudor song, and endeavours to provide an aid to understanding the contemporary attitudes of those setting words to music. Basing much of his evidence on the three surviving songbooks - the Fayrfax, Henry VIII and Ritson manuscripts - the author aims to display the relationship between words and music in an historical perspective up to the Reformation. In a part of the monograph devoted to literature, he reconstructs a social world of courtly versifying. In the third part he offers a social history of music-making in ceremonies, entertainments and plays, in the home, played by amateurs and by professionals. Finally in his epilogue he tries to elucidate that experience within the songs themselves that can bring the modern listener more closely to understand, or even actually to share, the feelings of the early Tudor court. Some biographical and historical assumptions are updated in *434*.

249. Stevens, John. "Sir Philip Sidney and 'versified music': Melodies for Courtly Songs." In *The Well Enchanting Skill* (see *192*), pp.153-69.

Analyses Sidney's thoughts about music in its relations to poetry. The author concentrates on the three practical issues raised by Sidney himself: the words of a good poem have in themselves a certain musical quality; they can be accompanied by music, that is, have tunes supplied that were not specifically composed for those words; or they can be "prepared for the well enchanting skill of music," that is, written with a view to musical setting.

250. Sullivan, William V. "Tobias Hume's First Part of Ayres (1605)." *Journal of the Viola da Gamba Society of America* 5 (1968): 5-15; 6 (1969): 13-33; 7 (1970): 92-111; 8 (1971): 64-93; 9 (1972): 16-37.

Consists of four chapters. The first deals with the importance of Hume's music (volume five, above) and the second (volume six) describes the 1605 edition. The third is spread over volumes seven and eight, the songs being discussed in the former and the instrumental music and Hume's musical directions in the latter. The fourth chapter, in volume nine, is a concluding summary. There are two appendices. The first reproduces the text of *The True Petition of Colonel Hume,* 1642, the second the texts of five songs.

251. Swanecamp, Joan. *English Ayres: a Selectively Annotated Bibliography and Discography.* Westport: Greenwood, 1984. 141pp. 0313234671. ML128.S359.

Alphabetical listing by composer, but beginning with general section. Lists are subdivided into literature, music and recordings. Annotations are sparing but full titles, *RISM* numbers and, where appropriate, contents are provided for the music, and contents for the recordings.

252. Teo, Kian-Seng. "John Wilbye's Second Set of Madrigals (1609) and the Influence of Marenzio and Monteverdi." *Studies in Music* 20 (1986): 1-11.

Wilbye's *Second Set* was published eleven years after his *First.* Although not departing in any radical way from the style of the *First Set,* to a greater extent Wilbye exploited the use of various kinds of sequences. The author seeks to show that contemporary Italian practice, most significantly as exemplified by Marenzio and Monteverdi, was responsible for two features that enrich Wilbye's writing in this later collection: pedal sequence, and treating an entire multivoice phrase as if it were a single melodic entity. The article is comprehensively illustrated.

253. Teo, Kian-Seng. *Chromaticism in the English Madrigal.* Outstanding Dissertations in Music from British Universities. New York: Garland, 1989. 343pp. 0824020448. ML2631.T46.

Defines the English attitude to chromaticism and reviews the sources in which it appears in England c.1550-1625. In the light of this, the author devotes the rest of the monograph to discussions of chromaticism in the work of specific composers, among whom Dowland and Weelkes are assigned separate chapters. He appends "A Checklist of the Content of San Marino, California, Huntington Library Ellesmere MSS EL 25A 46-51," an important English source of native and Italian madrigals, but which includes some English In nomines and sacred songs.

254. Teo, Kian Seng. "Thomas Whythorne's Songs for Three, Four and Five Voices (1571)." *Music Review* 51 (1990): 11-24.

Concentrates on Whytehorne's use of chromaticism, and whether this had some influence on contemporary English composers and on the development of chromaticism in England. In particular the author invokes Morley and Byrd, whom he feels rapidly outpaced Whytehorne in technique, and, from a later generation, Wilbye.

255. Teo, Kiang Seng. "Three Continental Chromatic Compositions in Mid-Sixteenth-Century England." *Music Review* 46 (1985): 1-11.

Notes the existence in England, in the Lumley Library (see *456*), of three highly chromatic works by Lassus, Rore and Caimo. The author endeavours to trace possible connections between leading English composers and the owners of the Lumley Library, and to relate the three foreign compositions in question to the chromatic practice of English composers. He notes the large quantity of music by Byrd in the Lumley Library, to the exlusion of most other English composers and, bearing in mind that Byrd dedicated his second *Cantiones* to Lord Lumley (1591), suggests that any continental influence on later English composers came personally or indirectly through Byrd, who was influenced, as far as it suited him, at first hand.

256. Teplow, Deborah. "Lyra Viol Accompaniment in Robert Jones' *Second Booke of Songs and Ayres* (1601)." *Journal of the Viola da Gamba Society of America* 23 (1986): 6-18.

Jones's collection of songs was the first in England to present music in the lyra viol style that matured under Jenkins and Simpson. Even here it is only suggested as an alternative form of accompaniment though it is the earliest in England to be written in tablature notation. The author discusses Jones's accompaniments in detail, seeking thereby to understand how an accompaniment style came to be created, and to establish the relationship between the lyra and lute accompaniments in the *Second Booke*. The article is copiously illustrated.

257. Toft, Robert. "Musicke a sister to poetrie: Rhetorical Artifice in the Passionate Airs of John Dowland." *Early Music* 12 (1984): 191-9.

Uses *Sorrow Stay* and *In Darkness Let Me Dwell* to illustrate how Dowland constructed his songs in the genre of passionate airs. He exploited various rhetorical devices aimed at lively description or counterfeit representation, for instance in the repeated setting of certain emotive words or phrases from the lyrics in question.

258. Tovey, Donald Francis. "Weelkes: Four Madrigals." In *Essays in Musical Analysis*. Vol. 5: *Vocal Music*. London: Oxford University Press, 1937, pp.3-12.

Musical analyses of *Three Virgin Nymphs* (1597), *Thule, the Period of Cosmography* (1600), *O Care, Wilt Thou Despatch Me* (1600) and *Like Two Proud Armies*(1600).

259. Uhler, John Earle. "Thomas Morley's Madrigals for Four Voices."

Music & Letters 36 (1955): 313-30.

Commentary on Morley's collection of 1594, emphasizing his dramatic response to the texts, but wrongly tries to associate him with Shakespeare (see *664*).

260. Waldo, Tommy Ruth. "Music and Musical Terms in Richard Edwards's 'Damon and Pithias'." *Music & Letters* 49 (1968): 229-35.

Discusses Edwards's use of incidental music in his play, especially the functional, structural and dramatic effect of the placing of the songs, with a brief consideration of the significance of the required instrumental music. The author also examines Edwards's use of musical terms in the text of the play, of which there are over fifty.

261. Ward, John. "Music for a Handefull of Pleasand Delites." *Journal of the American Musicological Society* 10 (1957): 151-80.

This poetical miscellany of 1584 contains 32 ballads, for 27 of which pre-existent tunes are specified to which the words can be sung. The author considers each item in turn, describes fully each prescribed tune, and outlines the historical content of the collection. See also *213*.

262. Wells, Robin Headlam. "Ars amatoria: Philip Rosseter and the Tudor Court Lyric." *Music & Letters* 70 (1989): 58-71.

Seeks to excuse the lyrics of lute songs from the accusation that they subordinate meaning to sound, basing his discussion on Rosseter's *A Booke of Ayres*, 1601. The author points out that the lutenists' songs are in collections conceived as units from which individual songs, themselves artefacts of words and music, should not be detached and analysed in isolation. He emphasizes the composer's relationship with his audience, who will have understood the nuances in apparently conventional lyrics. Frequently he returns to the idea of dissimulation: how the apparently guileless lyrics in fact convey a deeper meaning, how religious authorities disapproved of it, and how Castiglione commended it in his fashionable *Book of the Courtier*. Since both the artlessness and self-expression of these songs are deliberately illusory, it depends on the performer to give life to the song, to persuade the audience. Yet the final song in the collection ends stoically: "the world is but a play."

263. Wells, Robin Headlam. "John Dowland and Elizabethan Melancholy." *Early Music* 13 (1985): 514-28.

Rejects the suggestion in 237 that the roots of Dowland's melancholy were in Hermetic Neoplatonism. Instead he relates Dowland's songs to the increased interest among poets and composers in affective writing. This caused someone like Dowland to set in an emotional way lyrics conventional for their time. Melancholy was welcome as a subject in a lyric because it lent itself so well to such affective writing.

264. Wells, Robin Headlam. "The Ladder of Love: Verbal and Musical Rhetoric in the Elizabethan Lute-Song." *Early Music* 12 (1984): 173-89.

Deals with the paralleling of verbal patterns in musical terms. Judiciously selecting examples from the works of Dowland, Rosseter, Jones and Danyel, the author illustrates how the rhetoric of the lyrics was complemented by a metrical rhetoric, beginning with the composers' often scalic response to the contemporary icon of the ladder or stairway. Many of the article's illustrations are of appropriate mediaeval or Renaissance works of art.

265. Wells, Robin Headlam. "A Setting of 'Astrophil and Stella' by Morley." *Early Music* 6 (1978): 230-1.

Suggests that Morley's song *Mistress Mine* was originally a setting of "Only Joy" from Sidney's *Astrophil and Stella*.

266. Wells, Robin Headlam. "Thomas Morley's 'Fair in a Morn'." *Lute Society Journal* 18 (1976): 37-42.

Enquires why Morley chose a tedious poem as the basis of a

most delightful song. The author concludes that the text is a panegyric to Elizabeth I, in the vein of *The Triumphes of Oriana,* which Morley edited.

267. Westrup, Jack. "A Lost English Madrigal Composer." *Listener* 13 (1935): 733-5.

Writes about the Italian madrigals of *Peter Philips,* in the context of the English madrigal school, noting points of similarity and divergence.

268. Wilcox, Helen. "'My mournful style': Poetry and Music in the Madrigals of John Ward." *Music & Letters* 61 (1980): 60-70.

Noticing that nineteen of the poetic sources of Ward's 28 madrigals in his *First Set,* 1613, have been identified, considers the implications of this unusually high proportion: his greater literary awareness, proof that music and poetry were separate forms, and that some poets did not have to rely on composers for musical completion. The author illustrates how Ward set his superior texts, disagreeing with Kerman (*208*) that his settings damage the poetry. Indeed, she seeks to illustrate that Ward's madrigals achieve a uniquely close relationship between poetry and music.

269. Wilson, Christopher R. "Some Musico-Poetic Aspects of Campion's Masques." In *The Well Enchanting Skill* (see *192*), pp.91-105.

Describes the three masques - *Lord Hays, Lords* and *Somerset* - to which Campion contributed. The author demonstrates how he introduced innovations into the structure of the contemporary masque until, in *Somerset,* he lost his sense of direction. Nevertheless the quality of the music itself is high throughout all three, going some way to compensating for the absence of dramatic coherence in *Somerset.*

270. Wilson, Christopher R. "Thomas Campion's 'Ayres Filled with Parts' Reconsidered." *Lute* 23.2 (1983): 3-12.

Debates Campion's motive and method in providing vocal parts for his ayres to turn them into partsongs. The author seeks to establish which form came first, and to what influences, musical and commercial, Campion was subject. All occur in his *Two Bookes of Ayres*, c.1613.

See also 379, 413, 439, 440, 441, 442, 443, 471, 487, 496, 503, 519, 531, 540, 547, 549, 553, 555, 567, 568, 574, 602, WB160, WB174.

V INSTRUMENTAL MUSIC

This section also includes writings about the instruments themselves and their makers, as well as items concerning dance and dance music.

271. Apel, Willi. *The History of Keyboard Music to 1700,* transl. and rev. by Hans Tischler. Bloomington: Indiana University Press, 1972. 025313790X. ML549.A6413.

Outstanding survey with numerous references to Tudor musicians. Deals with nations and with forms of keyboard music, and in so doing places English composers in the context of their continental contemporaries, while exhibiting a firm grasp of the features of the English school. Individual composers and many of their pieces are discussed and analysed, their procedures and idiosyncracies noted along with their generic traits and similarities. There are indices both to names and to works cited.

272. Arneson, Arne J. *and* Williams, Stacie. *The Harpischord Booke: being a Plaine & Simple Index to the Printed Collections of Musick by Different Masters for the Harpischord, Spinnet, Clavichord, & Virginall.* Madison: Index House, 1986. 0936697008. ML128.H35A7.

Lists the contents of over two hundred published collections of harpischord music. Individual works are listed under their composers in the composer index and keyed into a list of bibliographical abbreviations, which in turn directs the reader to the bibliography itself. There are title and editor indices. Several Tudor composers are represented. Works included are only those in the indexed anthologies: complete editions of individual composers are only cited as sources and are not indexed.

273. Arnold, Cecily. "Early Seventeenth-Century Keyboard Parts." *Music & Letters* 33 (1952): 151-3.

Notes origin in the works of *Coprario* of fully worked-out independent keyboard parts to string consorts, and outlines subsequent developments in England.

274. Baines, Frances. "The Consort Music of Orlando Gibbons." *Early Music* 6 (1978): 540-3.

Survey of Gibbons's corpus, with special attention paid to the fantasies for the great double bass, the In nomines and six anonymous fantasies in six parts which, in the opinion of the author, no one but Gibbons could have composed.

275. Baines, Francis. "Fantasias for the Great Dooble Base." *Chelys* 2 (1970): 37-8.

Comes to the conclusion that the instrument in question is a violone with G' as its lowest note, but conjectures an A tuning rather than G. The repertory consists of eleven fantasies, of which two are in four parts and the rest in three, all composed by *Orlando Gibbons*. The identity of this lowest instrument was long a source of controversy.

276. Baker, David. "The Instrumental Consort Music of Robert Parsons (d.1570)." *Chelys* 7 (1977): 4-23.

After a brief discussion of Parsons's life and his church music, refers to each of his authentic consort pieces and provides a complete listing with sources and editions. The author also lists three works which in his opinion are spurious, and explains why. (He does not note that the first In nomine à 7 is ascribed in one source to Byrd). As an editor of some early English consort music he has interesting comments to make concerning Parsons's technique, the structure of his pieces, and the nature of their sources. The article is well illustrated. Subsequent research confirms that Parsons died in 1572: see *133*, page 3.

277. Baker, David *and* Baker, Jennifer. "The Browning (I)." *Chelys* 10 (1981): 4-10.

   Discusses the social background of the form, especially Meyer's promotion of it in *341*, and provides a checklist of all known versions. No second article.

278. Baker, David *and* Baker, Jennifer. "A 17th-Century Dial-Song." *Musical Times* 119 (1978): 590-3.

   Offers a solution to a dial-song composed by W. Syddael in imitation of an In nomine of Robert Parsons. Syddael's effort is printed on pages 42-3 of Charles Butler's *The Principles of Music*, 1636. The authors compare Syddael's work with Osbert Parsley's *The Song Upon the Dial* and suggests Syddael is a pseudonym for Butler himself.

279. Bennett, John *and* Willetts, Pamela. "Richard Mico." *Chelys* 7 (1977): 24-46.

   Comprehensive account of all biographical information known concerning Mico. All his surviving music is for viols, and is of a high standard. For his fruitful relationship with Byrd and the Essex recusants whom both men served see *WB167*.

280. Borren, Charles van den. *The Sources of Keyboard Music in England*, transl. by James E. Matthews. Handbooks for Musicians. London: Novello, 1913; New York: Gray, 1914; repr. eds, Westport: Greenwood, 1970, 08371344437; Dover, NH: Longwood, 1977, 0893411310. ML703.B6712.

   Although the introduction and first three chapters, dealing with history, the sources and biography, have now been superseded by subsequent research, the two remaining chapters are of some value. They deal with the virginalists' new figural material and the musical forms and styles they cultivated. Again, subsequent research on matters such as fingering (see chapter IV) may have shown some advance on the author, but he provides many penetrating insights into this music, and it is his research that has provided the basis for many of those very advances mentioned above.

281. Boston, J.L. "An Early Virginal-Maker in Chester, and his Tools." *Galpin Society Journal* 7 (1954): 3-6.

Refers to *William Goodeman*, active during the reign of Elizabeth I. The author provides evidence of native provincial virginal-making from a period during which it is thought most keyboard instruments were imported or made in London by foreigners. See also *312.*

282. Bream, Julian. "The Morley Consort Lessons." In *Tribute to Benjamin Britten on his Fiftieth Birthday*, ed. by Anthony Gishford. London: Faber, 1963, pp.92-4.

Brief but cogent introduction, though *My Lord of Oxenfords Maske* is not by Byrd (p.93: see *WB129*, p.25).

283. Brookes, Virginia. "The Four-Part In nomines of John Ward." *Chelys* 16 (1987): 30-5.

Provenance and analyses of important corpus of five works. Copiously and attractively illustrated article reprinted from volume four of the *Southern Early Music Forum Journal*.

284. Caldwell, John. *English Keyboard Music Before the Nineteenth Century.* Blackwell's Music Series. Oxford: Blackwell, 1973; repr. ed., New York: Dover, 1985. 0486248518. ML728.C3.

Chapters III-VII are devoted to aspects of Tudor keyboard music, liturgical organ music and secular music of the early sixteenth century; and plainsong settings and fugal forms, secular variations and the dance, and the development of the style from the Elizabethan and Jacobean period. The author describes the instruments on which such music was played, and the circumstances in which it was performed. The analyses of specific pieces are judiciously selected to illustrate the progress and development of the genre. These chapters are valuable not only as a study of Tudor keyboard music, but also for placing it in the continuum from the mediaeval to the Baroque periods, showing what it inherited from one and passed on to the other. Within the period the author elucidates what individual composers learnt from one another. Composers such as Philips usually overlooked in this context are given space proportional to their great abilities, and the pre-eminence of Tudor keyboard music as a whole is confirmed.

285. Caldwell, John. "Keyboard Plainsong Settings in England, 1500-1660." *Musica Disciplina* 19 (1965): 129-53.

Inventory of settings, divided into two tables: pre-Reformation liturgical settings and post-Reformation non-liturgical settings. Alphabetical by title, providing liturgical category and number of verses, composer, sources, modern editions and remarks, in which column any new identifications are announced. The article is well illustrated.

286. Caldwell, John. "Keyboard Plainsong Settings in England, 1500-1600...addenda et corrigenda." *Musica Disciplina* 34 (1980): 215-9.

Provides new information concerning sources and editions, other new information from individuals, and new entries in the two tables, with a note of further points, and misprints and mistakes. There is a particularly important discovery concerning "Tallis's so-called Fantasy."

287. Caldwell, John. "The Organ in the British Isles until 1600." *Organ Yearbook* 2 (1971): 4-12.

Reviews the history of the organ in Britain, with quotations from contemporary sources, from c.700 A.D. The author gives evidence, where it survives, of construction and specifications.

Much of this, notably the iconography, relates to the pre-Tudor period, but he provides a summary of what is known of the background to the development of the British organ up to Tudor times, and the state of that development by 1600.

288. Chaplin, Sylvia A. "English Virginal Music between 1560 and 1660." *Music Teacher* 63 (July 1984): 8-9; (August 1984): 10-11, 29; (September 1984): 14-15, 19.

Comprehensive introduction to all aspects of performance and repertory. This is the best such article on Elizabethan keyboard music, its value lying in its concentration on the music itself, with no lionizing of individual composers.

289. Charteris, Richard. "Another Six-Part Fantasia by Martin Peerson?" *Chelys* 9 (1980): 4-9.

Suggests that the anonymous fantasia no.45 in Archbishop Marsh's Library, a unicum, is by Peerson. The article is well illustrated.

290. Charteris, Richard. "Jacobean Musicians at Hatfield House, 1605-1613." *Research Chronicle* 12 (1974): 115-36.

Generation of *Coprario*, listed from contemporary sources.

291. Charteris, Richard. "John Coprario's Five- and Six-Part Pieces: Instrumental or Vocal?" *Music & Letters* 57 (1976): 370-8.

Offers conclusive evidence that 49 of Coprario's works in five parts and eight in six parts, hitherto described as fantasias, and of which all but four have Italian titles, are vocal in origin: transcriptions, or at least arrangements, of Italian madrigals.

292. Charteris, Richard. "The Origin of Alfonso Ferrabosco the Elder's Six-Part Fantasia C224." *Chelys* 16 (1987): 12-15.

Announces his discovery that this work is a transcription of a chanson *Sur la rousée*, and makes comparisons with other contemporary settings of the same text. Updates *643*.

293. Coates, William. "English Two-Part Viol Music, 1590-1640."
Music & Letters 33 (1952): 141-50.

Discusses 31 pieces for two unaccompanied viols in a
manuscript given to the Rowe Library, King's College,
Cambridge, in 1939.

294. Cole, Elizabeth. "In Seach of Francis Tregian." *Music & Letters*
33 (1952): 28-32.

Provides illustrated evidence to support the identification of
Tregian as the compiler of both "Tregian's Anthology" (*GB-Lbl*
Egerton 3665: see *560*) and the Fitzwilliam Virginal Book (see
295).

295. Cole, Elizabeth, "Seven Problems of the Fitzwilliam Virginal
Book: an Interim Report." *Proceedings of the Royal Musical
Association* 79 (1952-3): 51-64.

Addresses the problems, initially expressed here deftly in
verse, as to what the book was; who compiled it, when and
where; how and why it was compiled; and who shared in its
compilation. The role of the Tregian family is fully discussed, as
is the effect on the book's contents of the family's religious
proclivities, expressed in their patronage of Roman Catholics
and apparent avoidance of some Protestant composers. Several
dedications to leading contemporary Roman Catholics are
explained or clarified for the first time.

296. Cunningham, Walker. *The Keyboard Music of John Bull.* Studies
in Musicology, 71. Ann Arbor: UMI Research Press, 1984.
274pp. 0835714667. ML410.B93C8.

An outstanding monograph which includes a brief but cogent
biography. The sources and each category of Bull's keyboard
music are discussed in detail. Every piece is scrutinized. Three
appendices provide an annotated table of sources, a facsimile
of the 1740 list of pieces by Bull in J.C. Pepusch's manuscript
collection, and a pavan omitted from the modern edition of his

complete keyboard works. Oliver Neighbour's review in *Early Music* 14 (1986): 92-5 contains important and hitherto unpublished information about Peter Philips and Byrd.

297. Dart, Thurston. "John Bull's "Chapel"." *Music & Letters* 40 (1959): 279-82.

Suggests identity of "Chapel" in the titles of four keyboard pieces ascribed to Bull was Jacques Champion, and proposes that he was composer of three and dedicatee of the fourth.

298. Dart, Thurston. "Sweelinck's 'Fantazia on a Theme Used by John Bull'." *Tijdschrift van de Vereniging voor Nederlandse Muziekgeschiedenis* 18 (1959): 167-9.

Attempts to establish a relationship between Bull's *God Save the King* and two fantasias attributed to Sweelinck. An alternative explanation is offered on pages 92-3 of *296.*

299. Dawes, Frank. "Nicholas Carlton and the Earliest Keyboard Duet." *Musical Times* 92 (1951): 542-6.

Useful for a brief analysis of the duet and of Carlton's other known surviving keyboard pieces, with informative comments on provenance. Also attempts to confirm when the duet was composed, and to clarify uncertainty about the identity of the composer.

300. Dodd, Gordon. "Alfonso Ferrabosco II - the Art of the Fantasy." *Chelys* 7 (1977): 47-53.

General discussion of Ferrabosco's standing as a "leading pioneer of the new Jacobean consort music." Uses quotations from contemporary and subsequent critics to justify labelling him a "first-class, first-rate composer." The article is in six sections which deal with Ferrabosco's biography, the contemporary musical situation, sources, his music, its trademarks and the art of the fantasy. Of these the most useful is the penultimate, in which the author discusses Ferrabosco's use of melody, harmony, rhythm, mode, key and fugue, and how through this technique he achieves unity.

301. Dodd, Gordon. "Coperario or Bull?" *Chelys* 1 (1969): 41.

Suggests that a fantasia for four viols attributed to Coprario is by Bull. See also *341*, pp.299-301, for edition.

302. Dodd, Gordon. "Mr. Weelkes his Second Pavin." *Chelys* 9 (1980): 31-2.

Discusses sources and editions of Weelkes's pavan for viol consort, ascribed in one source to both Morley and Danyel. In a well illustrated article the author also summarizes the editions of Weelkes's other consort pavans.

303. Dodd, Gordon, comp. *Thematic Index of Music for Viols.* London: Viola da Gamba Society of Great Britain, 1980-. Not consecutively paginated.

Provides incipits for all music in British sources intended for performance by viols: consorts, songs and solos. It includes anonymous and foreign works. Organized by composer (anonymous works come at the beginning and are organized by genre), it lists all manuscript and printed sources, and modern editions. There is a comprehensive bibliography and each composer with a substantial corpus is given a short but cogent introduction. The *Index* continues to be updated in instalments, the pages issued for insertion or to replace superseded pages. These instalments contain new composers or sources. From instalment 5, 1989, the *Index* was published at York. The *Index* contains entries for a dozen composers not included in *12*.

304. Doe, Paul. "The Emergence of the In nomine: Some Notes and Queries on the Work of Tudor Church Musicians." In *Modern Musical Scholarship*, ed. by Edward Olleson. Stocksfield: Oriel, 1978, pp.79-92.

Asks whether the In nomine was intended for instrumental or vocal performance. The author emphasizes his comments are speculative, but finds it difficult to make a case for the regular use of viols, and suggests that wind instruments were employed.

305. Donington, Robert *and* Dart, Thurston. "The Origin of the In nomine." *Music & Letters* 30 (1949): 101-6.

Covers the same ground as *369* but with closer reference to the mass by Taverner from which the form originated, and with no history of the development of the form. The authors of the two articles were unaware of one another's findings.

306. Edwards, Warwick A. "The Performance of Ensemble Music in Elizabethan England." *Proceedings of the Royal Musical Association* 97 (1970-1): 113-23.

Distinguishes between the various types of ensemble music. The function of the music, rather than the music itself, dictates the instrumentation. Such functions include the nature of the occasion and the social class of the performers. In the light of this, the author summarizes the types of music that survive, but he declines to be dogmatic about instrumentation as nearly all the manuscript sources date from some time after the music was composed. He mentions those instruments which were in use, noting that the viol was the province of the professional and only became popular with amateurs at the very end of Elizabeth's reign.

307. Ferguson, Howard. *Keyboard Interpretation from the 14th to the 19th Century: an Introduction.* London: Oxford University Press, 1975. 0193184192. ML549.F47.

Gathers and expands all the information concerning keyboard instruments, their music and its interpretation that the author first published in the introductions to various anthologies (listed on p.ix) which he had edited during the preceding decade. Usually the various chapters are divided chronologically so that the "Pre-Classical" section accommodates the Tudor period. However he devotes sections to the virginalists in other chapters concerning ornamentation and fingering. This is a good general introduction that places the Tudor in the historical continuum rather than (equally legitimately, if well done) analysing in detail contemporary practices.

308. Forrester, Peter. "A Scottish Consort." *Lute* 27 (1987): 38-42.

Describes the late sixteenth-century ceiling in Crathes Castle, near Banchory, Kincardineshire. It depicts five (originally seven) Virtues and, of musicological interest, nine Muses, seven of whom play musical instruments. The author describes all the instruments, and suggests that the consort implied by the paintings supports the idea that the instrumentation of Morley's *Consort Lessons* was an attempt to standardize a hitherto looser construction. All seven paintings are reproduced.

309. Foster, Donald H. "The Organ Music of Thomas Tomkins." *Diapason* 61 (July 1970): 23-5.

Selects from Tomkins's corpus those pieces of keyboard music that seem most suitable for playing on the organ. The author concentrates on items with titles containing indicative words such as fancy, voluntary, verse or some plainsong, but he also mentions the dances and variations, and comments usefully on figuration and registration.

310. Gill, Donald. "The Elizabethan Lute." *Galpin Society Journal* 12 (1959): 60-3.

Attempts to clarify the questions of the use of extra bass strings, 1590-1612, and hopes to prove the existence of a definitive type of lute neither "classic six-course" nor Baroque.

311. Glyn, Margaret H. *About Elizabethan Virginal Music.* 2nd ed. London: Reeves 1934; enl. photographic repr., *Elizabethan Virginal Music and its Composers,* 1964. 158pp. ML467.G5.

As the author admitted in the opening words of the first edition, 1924, "The time has not yet arrived for an exhaustive study of virginal music." Originally predated only by *351* and *280*, both of which concentrated on the Fitzwilliam Virginal Book (then the only substantial published source), it has now been superseded by a variety of studies such as *WB129, 284* and

296. For all its shortcomings (see *WB153*) it is an important book in the development of the criticism of Tudor music, and contains some provocative opinions on the genre and on the work of individual composers. After five chapters on background, covering the current standing of virginal music, its origins, character, sources and notations, the author devotes separate chapters to Byrd, Bull, Gibbons, Farnaby and the minor composers. As appendices there are a glossary and an excellent index of composers and references to each of their many works mentioned in the text. Significantly the advances of the ten years between the first two editions warranted a full page of description in the preface to the second edition.

312. Goodman, W.L. "Musical Instruments and their Makers in a Bristol Apprentice Register, 1536-1643." *Galpin Society Journal* 27 (1974): 9-14.

Extracts relevant names and fills in social and musical background where possible: an important study of provincial activities. See also *281.*

313. Harper, John. "The Distribution of the Consort Music of Orlando Gibbons in Sixteenth-Century Sources." *Chelys* 12 (1983): 3-18.

Organized in terms of seven tables. First, lists Gibbons's consort output and its modern editions in volume 48 of *Musica Britannica,* plus numbers in *303* for generic pieces. Next the author lists the published and manuscript sources, with abbreviations, and table III is a summary list of manuscript sources with dates, associations and provenances. The remaining tables deal with the distribution of various sections of Gibbons's output through the sources. He also deals with questions of authenticity and textual transmission, confidently ascribing five anonymous fantasias (numbers 31 and 33-6 in *Musica Britannica*) to Gibbons, and in the case of numbers 37-9, whose ascriptions to Gibbons are arguable, pondering whether they may originally have been composed for vocal performance. There is a conspicuously useful bibliography.

314. Harwood, Ian. "Rosseter's *Lessons for Consort* of 1609." *Lute Society Journal* 7 (1965): 15-23.

Begins with a description of what was known in Europe as the English consort, and in England simply as the consort. The author describes the construction of the consort, the roles of the instruments and the instruments themselves. Rosseter's *Lessons* survive fragmentarily, but the author is still able to discourse about the prints, dedication and contents. At the time of delivering this paper to the Lute Society on 12 December 1964, the author had been able to reconstruct seventeen of the 25 *Lessons* using methods he describes in brief but fascinating detail.

315. Hendrie, Gerald. "The Keyboard Music of Orlando Gibbons (1583-1625)." *Proceedings of the Royal Musical Association* 89 (1962-3): 1-15.

Reviews the manuscript sources of Gibbons's keyboard music, pointing out its contemporary popularity. The author discusses spurious attributions, plus one anonymous piece he believes to be by Gibbons, and, rather than analyse individual pieces, he discusses genres, concluding with a look at Gibbons's attitude to tonality.

316. Hill, Simon *and* Inglehearn, Madeleine. "Reconstructing the Masque of Squires." *NEMA Journal* 13 (1990): 1-13.

Describes the preparations made for a workshop performance of *Campion's* masque of 1613. The authors give insights into how much survives intact (the libretto), how much survives in other sources (and the extent to which much of that may only possibly be related to this masque), and how much had to be imported from elsewhere or provided from scratch (such as the choreographies). This is an illuminating account of the staging, costuming, performing and duration of such a masque.

317. Hipkins, A.J. "The Old Clavier or Keyboard Instruments; their Use by Composers, and Technique." *Proceedings of the Musical*

Association 12 (1885-6): 139-48.

Outdated survey but interesting for its programme of illustrations from music by the virginalists, and for the state of knowledge about early music at that time.

318. Holman, Peter. "The English Violin Consort in the Sixteenth Century." *Proceedings of the Royal Musical Association* 109 (1982-3): 39-59.

Traces the early history of the Italian Jewish string players who made up the royal consort. Initially described as violists, it is evident that they also played violins. By Elizabeth's reign they seem almost always to play violins. The author describes the personnel, their working lives, the technique of playing their instruments and the construction of those instruments. Four illustrations provide iconographical evidence, and he tabulates the four original families of the consort and the succession of places between 1540 and 1642. A book is due in 1993.

319. Holman, Peter. "New Sources of Music by Robert Johnson." *Lute Society Journal* 20 (1978): 43-52.

Aims to establish an up-to-date catalogue of Johnson's instrumental music, supplementing the complete editions of his works for solo lute, 1972. The author lists new sources of existing lute music and newly discovered pieces of lute music attributed to Johnson, and provides a catalogue of instrumental music not for the lute and attributed to Johnson.

320. Horsley, Imogene. "The 16th-Century Variation: a New Historical Survey." *Journal of the American Musicological Society* 12 (1959): 118-32.

Tries to prove that the English virginalists were not the first to exploit variation procedures, but were building on procedures long known on the Continent and which originated in Italy.

321. Hubbard, Frank. "Two Early English Harpsichords." *Galpin Society Journal* 3 (1950): 12-18.

Contains description of the earliest known surviving English harpischord of 1579.

322. Hughes, Charles W. "Richard Deering's Fancis for Viols." *Musical Quarterly* 27 (1941): 38-46.

Comments on the distinguishing stylistic features of Dering's "eleven" (*recte* ten: see *303*) surviving fantasies for viols, pondering why, for one who is supposed to have lived in Italy, his style is so conservative and insularly English.

323. Hulse, Lynn. "Francis and Thomas Cutting: Father and Son?" *Lute* 26 (1986): 73-4.

Offers evidence that Francis the composer and Thomas the lutenist were father and son.

324. Irving, John. *The Instrumental Music of Thomas Tomkins, 1572-1656.* Outstanding Dissertations in Music from British Universities. New York: Garland 1989. 2v. in 1. 235pp. 181pp. 0824020111. ML410.T65I8.

Volume 1 is divided into two parts dealing respectively with the keyboard and consort music. Within either section the author begins by discussing the sources. He devotes seven chapters to the various forms of keyboard music in which Tomkins composed, and one to a survey of the less voluminous consort music. He deals in detail with each piece but also covers aspects of style or technique common to several pieces. Where appropriate he notes Tomkins's debt to other composers. There is a valuable appendix devoted to corrections to the second edition of Tomkins's complete keyboard works, volume 5 of *Musica Britannica*. (The contents of the second volume of this monograph have reappeared as volume 59 in that series.) This is a facsimile of the original dissertation presented in 1985, but the author has provided a new introduction which updates the bibliography. See also *WB172*.

325. Irving, John. "Keyboard Plainsong Settings by Thomas Tomkins."

Soundings 13 (1985): 22-40.

Penetrating analyses with sources, illustrations and historical background noting the circumstances of the composition of each piece and its place in the development of English keyboard music.

326. Jeffery, Brian. "Instrumentation in the Music of Antony Holborne." *Galpin Society Journal* 19 (1966): 20-6.

Discusses the suggested variety of instrumentation implied by the title of Holborne's 1599 collection *Pavans, galliards, almains, and other short aeirs...for viols, violins, or other musicall winde instruments,* and looks at the relationship between instrumental versions of the same piece.

327. Jeffery, Brian. "The Lute Music of Antony Holborne: a Lecture Recital." *Proceedings of the Royal Musical Association* 93 (1966-7): 25-31.

After a short biographical introduction, describes the music itself and some of the problems that arise from it, finally putting it into the context of Holborne's total output and of contemporary English lute music.

328. Jeffery, Brian. "The Lute Music of Robert Johnson." *Early Music* 2 (1974): 105-9.

Review article about the complete edition, 1972. Provides additional information about certain pieces in the edition, a note of lute music not included, criteria for authenticity, an attempt at a chronology of Johnson's lute music and a bibliography of editions, biography and studies.

329. Jennings, John M. "The Fantasies of Thomas Lupo." *Chelys* 3 (1971): 3-15.

Begins with a substantial genealogical background to the Lupo family to establish the identity of the relevant Thomas Lupo. From an anaylsis of surviving fantasies, the author concludes that all those attributed to Thomas Lupo were the work of one individual who died in 1628.

330. Jennings, John M. "Thomas Lupo Revisited - is Key the Key to his Later Music?" *Chelys* 12 (1983): 19-22.

Suggests that the stylistic change in Lupo's later music is explained by a greater awareness of the concept of key.

331. Kastner, Santiago. "Parallels and Discrepancies Between English and Spanish Keyboard Music of the Sixteenth and Seventeenth Century." *Anuario musical* 7 (1952): 77-116.

Endeavours to establish that there was mutual influence between Spanish and English keyboard composers in the later Renaissance period. The author considers which pieces Cabezon had composed before he visited England in 1554-5, and compares the technique of the Tudor organists and the Spanish instrumentalists. Having reviewed the various forms of keyboard music in either country, he suggests that knowledge of Cabezon's music forms the bridge between the Tudor organists and the English virginalists, and closed the gap between Tallis and Byrd, a composer not only susceptible to foreign influences but capable of transfiguring such influences into a new musical currency. The rise of the English virginalists, so influential in northern Europe, was too late to influence the declining Italian-influenced Spanish school, though some English influence permeated Portugal. In *WB129* (p.254) Neighbour dismisses Kastner's opinion that Byrd was influenced by Cabezon. (See also *389.*) Nevertheless the present article is the clearest exposition of this oft-cited proposal.

332. Lasocki, David. "The Anglo-Venetian Bassano Family as Instrument Makers and Repairers." *Galpin Society Journal* 38 (1985): 112-32.

Provides a genealogy of musical members of this family, summarizes their careers, and examines in detail their making and repairing of instruments.

333. Lasocki, David. "Professional Recorder Playing in England 1500-1740. I: 1500-1640." *Early Music* 10 (1982): 23-9.

Traces the development in respect of the Court, the waits and the theatres, all of which aspects contain references to the Tudor period. The ubiquitous *Bassano* family looms large as the author ponders where recorders were played, what music was played on them, who the players were, the sort of training they received, the types of recorders they had, and what other instruments they played.

334. Lasocki, David. "The Recorder Consort at the Engish Court 1540-1673." *American Recorder* 25 (1984): 91-100, 131-5.

Establishes the existence of a consort of five recorder players at the English Court from 1540, increased to six in 1550. Initially all were members of the Italian Jewish *Bassano* family, for the appropriate members of which a genealogy is provided. There follow comprehensive accounts of personnel, standards of performance and repertory. The second part deals with the instruments themselves, and here the author deduces from treatises and inventories the sizes in use. He also discusses administrative and domestic arrangements as well as where the consort actually played and why, and he concludes with a consideration of the status, rewards and privileges of service in Court.

335. Lawrence, W.J. "Music in the Elizabethan Theatre." *Musical Quarterly* 6 (1920): 192-205.

Investigates the extent to which music was in use between the acts of Elizabethan plays, and considers the nature of the performing musical ensembles and their instruments.

336. Lumsden, David. "English Lute Music, 1540-1620 - an Introduction." *Proceedings of the Royal Musical Association* 83 (1956-7): 1-13.

Summarizes published and manuscript sources, describes the instruments for which the music was composed and the forms of those compositions with comments on the technique of composing for the lute. This complements the author's more important article *544.*

337. McCoy, Stewart. "Edward Paston and the Textless Lute-Song." *Early Music* 15 (1987): 221-7.

Suggests that in the Paston manuscripts there exist examples of the textless lute song, a hitherto undefined genre, in which fantasies and In nomines for viols by *Byrd* and his contemporaries were rendered as songs, wherein the top line (missing from all surviving sets) was solmized or sung to an accompaniment transcribed for the lute. See also *WB149.*

338. Marlow, Richard. "The Keyboard Music of Giles Farnaby: a Lecture-Recital." *Proceedings of the Royal Musical Association* 92 (1965-6): 107-20.

Only two keyboard pieces by Farnaby survive outside the Fitzwilliam Virginal Book, suggesting a slight contemporary reputation confined to an immediate circle. The author ponders why so many of Farnaby's works were included in Fitzwilliam, and how authoritative are its texts. He notes that Farnaby was an artisan, not a professional musician; that he was Protestant whereas the compiler of Fitzwilliam was Roman Catholic; and that his development as a composer seems to owe something to Bull. Passing briefly through the small surviving corpus of Giles's son Richard, he discusses Farnaby's own output within five principal categories - contrapuntal forms, pavans and galliards, other dances, folktune variations, and descriptive music - noting general trends and interesting points in specific pieces.

339. Meadors, James. "Dowland's 'Walsingham'." *Journal of the Lute Society of America* 14 (1981): 59-68.

The original text of Dowland's *Walsingham* survives in a damaged, almost illegible and inaccurate form. Received wisdom is that the piece is also musically substandard. The author disputes this and aims to restore the piece to a condition that allows its merits fully to be recognized. To do so he makes reference to other sets of variations on the song, differentiating the techniques of the lutenists from those of the virginalists. Dissatisfied with the modern version in the *Collected Lute Music of John Dowland,* 1974, he does not print a full alternative version but provides a corrective commentary on the 1974 edition.

340. Mellers, Wilfrid. "John Bull and English Keyboard Music." *Music Quarterly* 40 (1954): 364-83, 548-71.

Deals separately with music for organ and for virginals, placing Bull within the development of the contemporary English school of keyboard composers. The author analyses several pieces, some in relation to Bull's known biographical circumstances. An epilogue refers to his vocal and consort music. This is a useful complement to *296* and *345.*

341. Meyer, Ernst H. *Early English Chamber Music from the Middle Ages to Purcell.* 2nd ed., ed. by the author and Diana Poulton. London: Lawrence and Wishart, 1982. 363pp. 0853154112. ML1131.M48.

Still the standard work on the English consort school, concentrating on the music for viols. The author makes much of the sociological aspect of his topic, but this is now of merely historical interest as his interpretations of the rise and eclipse of English consort music originate from a narrowly dogmatic (Karl) Marxist perspective. This is not to dismiss some of his more critical utterances about Establishments (especially ecclesiastical) and the bourgeoisie. He describes what he sees as the origins of English consort music from the Middle Ages, via sacred and secular influences, to the age of plenty beginning with Byrd, followed by the crisis and eclipse beginning around 1620. The text is well illustrated, and he maintains an awareness of continental developments in order to place the present subject in a broad historical context. Of particular value is the attention he gives to lesser composers such as Thomas Holmes (see also *WB173).*

342. Miller, Hugh M. "The Earliest Keyboard Duets." *Musical Quarterly* 29 (1943): 438-57.

Describes the duets by *Farnaby, Carlton* and *Tomkins*, the last two reproduced in full. The author differentiates these two works for one keyboard from Farnaby's for two. He discusses their musical content but says little about whether any of the pieces manifest a specific technique for composing duets, beyond suggesting those by Carlton and Tomkins could be arrangements of consort pieces. He does not mention Byrd's *Ut re mi.*

343. Miller, Hugh Milton. "Forty Wayes of 2 Pts in One of Tho[mas] Woodson." *Journal of the American Musicological Society* 8 (1955): 14-21.

Describes the twenty surviving canons for keyboard in *GB-Lbl* Add. 29996. An appendix reproduces six of them.

344. Miller, Hugh M. "*Fulgens praeclara:* a Unique Keyboard Setting of a Plainsong Sequence." *Journal of the American Musicological Society* 2 (1949): 97-101.

Musical analysis of, and discussion of background to, anonymous work in *GB-Lbl* Add. 29996. Suggests it is by *Thomas Preston*. The entire mass of which it forms part is discussed in less detail in *381*, and the present article is developed in *377.*

345. Miller, Hugh M. "John Bull's Organ Works." *Music & Letters* 28 (1947): 25-35.

Brief review of sources, followed by musical analysis of several pieces, selecting the characteristics of Bull's style, and concludes with some comments on the artistic worth of the corpus, complementing *296* and *340.*

346. Miller, Hugh M. "'Pretty Wayes: for Young Beginners to Looke On'." *Musical Quarterly* 33 (1947): 543-56.

Describes structure and function of sixteen apparently instructional keyboard pieces in *GB-Lbl* Add. 29996.

347. Miller, Hugh M. "Sixteenth-Century English Faburden Compositions for Keyboard." *Musical Quarterly* 26 (1940): 50-64.

Concerns 21 pieces in *GB-Lbl* Add. 29996, which use faburdens as canti firmi. The author provides information about the origins of faburden, musical analysis of the pieces, and contemporary circumstances of their performance, plus lists of pieces and plainsongs on which they are based. The article is well illustrated.

348. Morehen, John. "The Instrumental Consort of Music of Osbert Parsley." *Consort* 30 (1974): 67-71.

Copious description with analyses of Parsley's small but distinguished corpus.

349. Morin, Elisabeth. *Essai de stylistique comparée. (Les variations de William Byrd et John Tomkins sur "John Come Kiss Me Now.")* Semiologie et analyse musicales. Montréal: Les Presses de l'Université de Montréal, 1979. 2v. 112pp. 144pp. 0840504160. MT140.M77. French and English texts.

See *WB131.*

350. Munrow, David. *Instruments of the Middle Ages and Renaissance.* London: Oxford University Press, 1976. 0193213214. ML460.M94.

Cogent, enthusiastic and superbly illustrated introduction, including all the instruments in use in Tudor England. Describes the origins, evolution and contemporary use of each instrument, providing photographs of colleagues playing them, reproductions of appropriate contemporary depictions, and details about the early exponents.

351. Naylor, Edward W. *An Elizabethan Virginal Book: being a Critical*

Essay on the Contents of a Manuscript in the Fitzwilliam Museum at Cambridge. London: Dent, 1905; repr. ed., Da Capo Press Music Reprint Series. New York: Da Capo, 1970. 220pp. 03067817921. ML703.N2.

Detailed study of the Fitzwilliam Virginal Book which had recently been published. Predictably more recent research has rendered much of the author's work redundant, but the monograph has two uses: primarily as a reflection of the state of knowledge about Tudor music at the start of the twentieth century, but occasionally for the author's musical analyses, some of which still provide rewarding insights into the music. Use of the index for individual composers is essential as the music is treated generically.

352. Neighbour, Oliver. "Orlando Gibbons (1583-1625): the Consort Music." *Early Music* 11 (1983): 350-7.

Concentrates on the fantasies, and the progressive 1620 trios in particular, pondering the extent to which the rest of Gibbons's more traditional fantasies relate to them. The author mentions the In nomines and the single set of variations in less detail. Throughout, he is willing to comment on any of Gibbons's technical weaknesses, and he also refers to problems of authenticity.

353. Nelson, Graham. "The Lyra-Viol Variation Sets of William Corkine." *Chelys* 17 (1988): 17-23.

Corkine published seven sets of variations for the lyra viol, respectively two and five in his two books of *Ayres*, 1610 and 1612. They are the earliest collections containing pieces for the solo instrument. The author notes that Corkine employed two styles of composition in these pieces: one idiomatic to the lyra way, and the other derived from divisions. He suggests that Corkine was himself a gifted violist. See also *256*.

354. Neumann, Karl. "Captain Hume's 'Invention for two to play upon one viole' ." *Journal of the American Musicological Society* 22 (1969): 101-6.

Explains the technique, physical as well as musical, required to play *The Princes Almayne.* Reprinted in the *Journal of the Viola da Gamba Society of America* 11 (1974): 102-11.

355. Neumann, Karl. "On Captain Hume's 'Wrong' Notes." *Journal of the Viola da Gamba Society of America* 4 (1967): 21-6.

Attacks Thurston Dart, editor of *Jacobean Consort Music,* volume IX of *Musica Britannica,* for tampering with Hume's original tablature, thereby providing an inaccurate edition of his music in that volume.

356. Newton, Richard. "English Duets for Two Lutes." *Lute Society Journal* 1 (1959): 23-30.

Lists printed and manuscript sources that contain such duets, and adds brief commentaries on each piece.

357. Newton, Richard. "Francis Cutting: a Bibliography." *Lute Society Journal* 1 (1959): 38-47.

Lists Cutting's complete works, including his arrangements, with sources. The author provides a biographical introduction and notes on some of the pieces.

358. Newton, Richard. "The Lute Music of Francis Pilkington." *Lute Society Journal* 1 (1959): 31-7.

Lists Pilkington's fifteen surviving lute solos, with sources. The author includes a brief biographical introduction, a discussion of Pilkington's dedicatees in his lute music, and a short commentary on each piece.

359. Nordstrom, Lyle. "The English Lute Duet and the Consort Lesson." *Lute Society Journal* 18 (1976): 5-22.

Elizabethan music was often freely arranged for a number of different instrumental combinations. Music for broken consort was the result of experimentation involving the rearrangement of other compositions, such as lute duets characterized by grounds in the treble. Having been rearranged for broken consort, these pieces in turn give rise to the equal lute duet.

360. Nordstrom, Lyle. "A Lute Duet of John Dowland." *Journal of the Lute Society of America* 12 (1979): 43-7.

Suggests that *Complaint*, hitherto regarded as a lute solo, is a second lute duet by Dowland.

361. Nordstrom, Lyle. "The Lute Duets of John Johnson." *Journal of the Lute Society of America* 9 (1976): 30-42.

Ponders why Johnson composed so many duets if, as seems likely, they are not pedagogical. The author suspects an element of virtuosity. His brief analysis of Johnson's corpus seems to confirm this. A well-illustrated article concludes with an inventory of the duets, differentiating those ascribed to Johnson, anonymous duets probably by him, and those that have some connection with Johnson.

362. Nordstrom, Lyle. "Two New English Lute Duets." *Journal of the Lute Society of America* 6 (1973): 46-7.

One duet is split between two manuscripts. It was originally identified as a solo, and is attributed to (probably John) Marchant. The other is anonymous and was similarly split.

363. Pallis, Marco. "The Instrumentation of English Viol Consort Music." *Chelys* 1 (1970): 27-35.

Establishes that the term "alto" viol is inappropriate and should not be used to the exclusion of (and only as an advisory alternative to) the correct designation, which is "tenor," even when such parts are immediately below the treble and are high by the tenor's standards. Reprinted in the *Journal of the Viola da Gamba Society of America* 9 (1972): 5-13 under the title "Tenor I or Alto? Some Thoughts on the Instrumentation of the Consort of Viols."

364. Palmer, Frances. "Musical Instruments from the *Mary Rose*: a Report on Work in Progress." *Early Music* 11 (1983): 53-9.

   Describes in detail some of the instruments recovered from the ship the *Mary Rose* which sank off the English coast in 1545: a shawm, a three-hole pipe, a fiddle and a bosun's pipe.

365. Payne, Ian. "Instrumental Music at Trinity College, Cambridge, c.1594-c.1615: Archival and Biographical Evidence." *Music & Letters* 68 (1989): 128-40.

   Provides evidence of a brief flowering of interest in music-making, in the purchase, maintenance and importance of a consort of viols. The author gives new biographical information about the three choirmasters concerned - Hilton the elder, Wilkinson and Mason - and offer some conjectural conclusions about musical activity after 1615, when there are no references in college records. A valuable appendix lists musical instruments from probate inventories and wills of Cambridge University musicians, 1557-1667.

366. Poulton, Diana. "Checklist of Some Recently Discovered English Lute Manuscripts." *Early Music* 3 (1975): 124-5.

   Notes whereabouts and accessibility of originals, editions and points of relevant interest. The list includes the Mynshall, Sampson, Board, Turnbull, Hender Robarts and Burwell manuscripts, though only the first four contain Tudor music. See also *561*.

367. Pringle, John. "The Founder of English Viol-Making." *Early Music* 6 (1978): 501-11.

   Well illustrated review of life, career and instruments of *John Rose.*

368. Prior, Roger. "Jewish Musicians at the Tudor Court." *Musical Quarterly* 69 (1983): 253-65.

   Sets out to identify and enumerate these individuals,

especially their roles in the political events during Henry VIII's reign, and in their native Venice. The author concludes that the number of Jews in Tudor England as a whole has hitherto been underestimated, and that for the musicians England was a refuge.

369. Reese, Gustave. "The Origins of the English In nomine." *Journal of the American Musicological Society* 2 (1949): 7-22.

Simultaneously with *305*, but unaware of their findings, reveals why the term In nomine was applied to this staple form of English consort composition from Taverner to Purcell. The contents of this article complement those of *305, q.v.*

370. Remnant, Mary. *English Bowed Instruments from Anglo-Saxon to Tudor Times.* Oxford Monographs on Music. Oxford: Clarendon, 1986. 0198161344. ML760.A2R45.

After having described the sources for her information, including iconography and construction, devotes chapters to specific instruments, tracing evidence of their usage to the Tudor period and beyond. Only isolated parts of the monograph impinge directly on Tudor music, yet it is important in setting Tudor music-making in its historical context. The author's *terminus a quo* is early Tudor, thereby excluding discussions concerning matters such as the use of viols during Divine Service in the new Church of England. Nevertheless, after the considerations of individual instruments, there are interesting conclusions to subsequent chapters on bowed instruments.

371. Rooley, Anthony. "The Lute Solos and Duets of John Danyel." *Lute Society Journal* 13 (1971): 18-27.

Begins by placing Danyel in the context of fellow composers of lute songs who also composed lute solos. Besides Dowland, whom the author excludes, there were few, and none who were prolific. He offers a few reasons for this before going on to consider ascriptions to Danyel of certain lute solos. His final point is a mild bombshell, suggesting John Danyel be identified with Daniel Bacheler, a prolific composer for the lute about whom "nothing" is known: see, however, *614*.

372. Routh, Francis. *Early English Organ Music from the Middle Ages to 1837.* Studies in Church Music. London: Barrie & Jenkins; New York: Barnes & Noble, 1973. 0214668045. 0064960137. ML628.R69.

Devotes two chapters to Tudor organ music, 1400-1558 and 1558-1656. The author outlines its development against the background of contemporary requirements, sacred (for liturgy) and secular (for the home), describing the various genres in which composers wrote and the instruments of the period, and he devotes separate sections to the leading composers. At the end of either chapter there is a list of composers and extant repertoire keyed into a comprehensive checklist of manuscripts and printed editions. He devotes more space to the music itself in the latter chapter, though even here his references to individual pieces tend to be cursory. He restricts his attention to works such as fantasias and In nomines, more idiomatic to the organ than to the virginals, writing knowledgeably and sympathetically within his chosen boundaries.

373. Russell, Lucy Hallman. "A Comparison of the 'Walsingham' variations by Byrd and Bull." In *Bericht über den internationalen Musikwissenschaftlichen Kongress, Berlin, 1974,* ed. by Hellmut Kühn and Peter Nitsche. Kassel: Bärenreiter, 1980, pp.277-9.

See *WB132*.

374. Sandman, Susan G. "Thomas Robinson's Interpretive Left-Hand Fingerings for the Lute and Cittern." *Journal of the Lute Society of America* 11 (1978): 26-35.

Discusses fingerings and their implications from two of Robinson's collections, *The Schoole of Musicke,* 1603, for lute, and *New Citharen Lessons,* 1609. The author mentions other contemporary writers who refer to fingerings for the left hand. Such fingering is a means to achieving a required style of articulation. She concludes that there are two main categories of fingering instructions, indicating a shift in position and the use of the same finger consecutively on two different frets.

375. Selfridge-Field, Eleanor. "Venetian Instrumentalists in England: a Bassano Chronicle (1538-1660)." *Studi musicali* 8 (1979): 173-221.

Full account of Bassano family's contribution to English musical life. Provides an account of the family's origins and genealogy, chronologies of musical and commercial activities, and an account of patronage. All twenty relevant members of the family are discussed. The appendix contains a thematic index of their musical works with sources and modern editions.

376. Stevens, Denis. "The Background of the In nomine." *Monthly Musical Record* 84 (1954): 199-205.

Musical and liturgical background which nourished the In nomine and its predecessors.

377. Stevens, Denis. "Further Light on *Fulgens praeclara*." *Journal of the American Musicological Society* 9 (1956): 1-11.

Develops *344* and attempts to answer the question "Why was this piece written?" The author analyses it verse by verse, and accepts *Thomas Preston* as its composer.

378. Stevens, Denis. "The Keyboard Music of Thomas Tallis." *Musical Times* 93 (1952): 303-7.

Comprehensive and informative summary of the surviving corpus with comments on contemporary music and on the circumstances in which Tallis's music was performed. Includes a list of keyboard compositions and arrangements, excluding organ scores of Services, with keys to printed texts and manuscript sources.

379. Stevens, Denis. "A Musical Admonition for Tudor Schoolboys." *Music & Letters* 38 (1957): 49-52.

Announces discovery of William Lyly's text for *Tallis's O Ye Tender Babes*, known hitherto only as a keyboard reduction in the Mulliner Book. The author includes a reconstruction of the original song.

380. Stevens, Denis. "Pre-Reformation Organ Music in England." *Proceedings of the Royal Musical Association* 78 (1951-2): 1-10.

Cites sources and their provenance, and describes the circumstances in which the music was played.

381. Stevens, Denis. "Thomas Preston's Organ Mass." *Music & Letters* 39 (1958): 29-34.

Announces recognition of Preston's having set the entire mass for organ, rather than only the first movement, analysed in detail in *344* with further comments in *377*.

382. Stevens, Denis. "A Unique Tudor Organ Mass." *Musica Disciplina* 6 (1951): 167-75.

Careful description of the organ mass by *Philip ap Rhys*, the only reasonably complete example from England, in the context of other contemporary continental organ masses.

383. Strahle, Graham. "Fantasy and Music in Sixteenth- and Seventeenth-Century England." *Chelys* 17 (1988): 28-32.

Defines the term fantasy as it was understood by English composers of the late Renaissance and early Baroque. The author gives examples of how this sensibility manifested itself in their music and he indicates how such a sensibility differentiates this age from the succeeding Age of Reason.

384. Traficante, Frank. "Music for the Lyra Viol: the Printed Sources." *Lute Society Journal* 8 (1966): 17-24.

Lists eighteen printed books containing music for solos and accompaniments, 1601-76. The author gives transcripts of title pages, tunings, commentaries on contents and a list of references for each item.

385. Tuttle, Stephen D. "The Keyboard Music of Tallis and Byrd." *Bulletin of the American Musicological Society* 4 (1940): 31-2.

See *WB114*.

386. Ward, John. "The 'Dolfull Dumps'." *Journal of the American Musicological Society* 4 (1951): 111-121.

Endeavours to define the dump, and reviews the corpus of pieces so entitled.

387. Ward, John M. "The English Measure." *Early Music* 14 (1986): 15-21.

Attempts to define the danced "measure" of Tudor and Stuart England. It was mentioned in literary sources more than any dance except the galliard, but so variously described as to defy simple description. After an exhaustive and well illustrated survey of surviving evidence, the author concludes that the term "measure" referred to choregraphy: since the steps of one dance differ from those of another, the term "measure" must refer to the way those steps are put together, and not to a specific sequence of steps. Any dance with its own pattern of steps and music could be and was called a measure.

388. Ward, John M. "The Lancashire Hornpipe." In *Essays in Musicology: a Tribute to Alvin Johnson*, ed. by Lewis Lockwood and Edward Roesner. Philadelphia: American Musicological Society, 1990, pp.140-73.

Traces the origins, documented in the sixteenth century, of the hornpipe. In a small list of hornpipes surviving from before 1650, only four named composers are known to have written such works, including *Byrd*, *Holborne* and *Aston* from the Tudor period. The author traces both the literary and musical origins of the dance, providing substantial quotations and concluding that it was not a dance likely to be found in polite society. He analyses the musical structure of the surviving dances called hornpipes in their sources, and surmises as to which instruments were used to play them. He goes on to discuss the influence of this style of music and, besides a list of surviving hornpipes, he appends a catalogue of 76 four-bar grounds including many by Tudor composers. His comments on Byrd's *Hornpipe* supplement those in *WB129*, especially pages 121-3.

389. Ward, John M. "Spanish Musicians in Sixteenth-Century England." In *Essays in Musicology in Honor of Dragon Plamenac on his 70th Birthday*, ed. by Gustave Reese and Robert J. Snow. Pittsburgh: University of Pittsburgh Press, 1969, pp.353-64.

Reports on the activities in London of musicians in the service of Philip, Prince of Spain, at the time of his wedding to Mary I, 1554-5. The author is entirely sceptical about any Spanish influence on contemporary or subsequent English music, seeing in this sojourn only the possible seeds of a friendship between Monte, the non-Spaniard in Philip's chapel choir, and Byrd, who are known to have exchanged motets nearly thirty years later.

390. Ward, John M. "Sprightly and Cheerful Musick: Notes on the Cittern, Gittern & Guitar in 16th- and 17th-Century England." *Lute Society Journal* 21 (1979-81): 1-234.

Assembles the scattered information found in the work of the author and other scholars, and attempts to interpret it. (This is in fact a monograph of nineteen chapters.) He differentiates the three instruments and then focusses on the cittern, investigating its use and popularity in various social strata and in consorts with other instruments, the technique of playing it, and the composers who wrote specifically for it. Here he devotes considerable space to Thomas Robinson's *New citharen lessons*, not least providing an inventory of the musical contents, as it was not available in a modern edition. (He suggests that some of the Misereres from *Medulla Musicke*, the famous ghost of 1603 attributed to *Byrd* and the older *Ferrabosco,* arranged by *Robinson*, may appear under Byrd's name in *GB-Lbl* Add. 31391.) Remaining topics include the surviving fragments of *An Instruction to the Gitterne*, published in 1569 and an inventory of music for cittern, gittern and guitar in British manuscripts, 1558-1665. (See also *506* for published sources.)

391. Watson, Sara Ruth. "The 'Lordly Viol' in the Literature of the English Renaissance." *Journal of the Viola da Gamba Society of America* 1 (1964): 51-61.

Enumerates, with quotations, references to the viol, and deduces contemporary attitudes to it compared with the lute and violin. She concludes that such references were rare, but is able to construct an interesting article notwithstanding.

392. Weidner, Robert W. "Change and Tradition in the Early *In nomine*." *Journal of the Viola da Gamba Society of America* 15 (1978): 102-12.

Examines the kinds of changes that appeared within the In nomine tradition during the sixteenth century after the inception of the genre around 1530. The author considers four criteria: the position of the cantus firmus in the texture, pitch authenticity, melodic integrity and whether musical allusion to a pre-existent In nomine occurs. In delivering his conclusions he gives due weight to the prolific contribution of *Tye*. He sees in the apparent yet dynamic conservatism of younger exponents the desire to test their mettle against the willingly-embraced inflexibility of the form.

393. Weidner, Robert W. "The Instrumental Music of Christopher Tye." *Journal of the American Musicological Society* 17 (1964): 363-70.

Discusses various aspects of Tye's technique, with frequent references to specific pieces and some illustrations. The author provides a complete list of consort works with title, number of points, manuscript sources and length in measures. Paul Doe in *12* adds one fragmentary item.

394. Weidner, R.W. "New Insights on the Early 'In nomine'." *Revue belge de la musicologie* 15 (1961): 29-46.

Suggests that Oxford was the birthplace of the In nomine, and explains the extravagant titles of *Tye*'s compositions in this form. He also puts forward the possibility that Tye's Protestantism was the catalyst for its development. There are two tables, one with forms of In nomines listed by composer, manuscript source and form; the other a title grouping for Tye's In nomines, the four groups listed as a footnote, and each work annotated with characteristics.

395. Whittaker, W. Gillies. "Byrd's and Bull's "Walsingham" Variations." *Music Review* 3 (1942): 270-9.

See *WB115*.

396. Woodfield, Ian. *The Early History of the Viol.* Cambridge Musical Texts and Monographs. Cambridge: Cambridge University Press, 1984. 0521244924. ML760.V55W66.

Pages 206-27 are devoted to the viol in sixteenth-century England. Deals comprehensively with the development of the manufacture, use and repertory of the viol family.

See also, 102, 109, 114, 260, 402, 403, 407, 408, 409, 410, 411, 412, 430, 451, 457, 470, 489, 493, 498, 499, 500, 501, 502, 505, 506, 507, 508, 509, 510, 511, 512, 513, 514, 515, 516, 518, 522, 524, 526, 528, 529, 532, 533, 534, 535, 536, 537, 539, 542, 544, 545, 548, 554, 556, 557, 561, 562, 563, 564, 566, 569, 570, 571, 572, 574, 597, 601, 608, WB149, WB167, WB169, WB171, WB172, WB173, WB179. Also section A-VII.

VI PERFORMANCE PRACTICE

397. Bowers, Roger. "The Performing Pitch of English 15th-Century Church Polyphony." *Early Music* 8 (1980): 21-8.

Attempts to formulate guidelines in respect of pitch. This article is valuable for plotting the development of the church choir in the period leading up to the Tudors. By then a choir of five parts was the norm. The author names the constituent voices and gives their ranges, noting that high trebles were unknown in the early sixteenth century. See also *398.*

398. Bowers, Roger. "The Vocal Scoring, Choral Balance and Performing Pitch of Latin Church Polyphony in England, c.1500-58." *Journal of the Royal Musical Association* 112 (1987): 38-76.

Intensely argued investigation into performance practices in pre-Elizabethan church music. States that there were three lattices of five voices based on A, F, and D basses. The author gives the ranges of each voice (treble, alto, two tenors and bass), describing how and why they developed from three-part mediaeval music, and he notes that singers looked to the clef only to learn where the semitones fell. He proceeds to the question of pitch and the distribution of personnel within the choirs of the period, including those where boys took the top two parts rather than merely the topmost part. In particular he analyses in detail the Earl of Northumberland's household chapel choir, devoting a substantial appendix to an evaluation of the evidence that he had already presented in the body of the article. This forms part of a running controversy, verging on feud, with Wulstan, whose views, summarized in chapter 8 of *22* and given final expression in *WB187,* he refutes, as he does those of Bray in *400.*

399. Bray, Roger. "The Interpretation of Musica ficta in English Music c.1490-c.1580." *Proceedings of the Royal Musical Association* 97 (1970-1): 29-45.

Contemporary theorists had very little to say about musica ficta. It almost seems that the composers themselves anticipated having little control over the performers' application of it. By carrying out a study of musica ficta in manuscripts of the period, the author discerns a set of rules which dictate its correct application and performance. See also *405.*

400. Bray, Roger. "More Light on Early Tudor Pitch." *Early Music* 8
      (1980): 35-42.

      Considers evidence that the early Tudor organ was a
      transposing instrument, with supporting evidence from the
      constitution of the Earl of Northumberland's household chapel
      choir. This assists the theories advanced by Caldwell in *403* and
      Wulstan in chapter 8 of *22* and ultimately in *WB187*, but they
      are all refuted by Bowers in *398* using the same Northumbrian
      evidence.

401. Bray, Roger. "16th-Century Musica ficta: the Importance of the
      Scribe." *Journal of the Plainsong and Medieval Music Society*
      1 (1978): 57-80.

      Takes various early manuscript sources and their identifiable
      scribes and analyses their practices. The author tries to draw
      conclusions about how this should affect the attitude of the
      modern editor to the application of musica ficta. An appendix
      provides a brief index to the Caius Choirbook which contains
      music by Fayrfax, Ludford, Cornysh, Turges, Prentyce and
      Pashe.

402. Brown, Alan. "Parthenia: Some Aspects of Notation and
      Performance." *Consort* 32 (1976): 176-82.

      See *WB127.*

403. Caldwell, John. "The Pitch of Early Tudor Organ Music." *Music &
      Letters* 51 (1970): 156-63.

      Argues that early Tudor organ pitch sounded a minor third
      above modern pitch, but is not dogmatic that there was one
      invariable pitch standard. The author analyses data concerning
      contemporary organs, and the extent to which plainsong organ
      settings had their melodies transposed to accommodate the
      pitch at which a choir would sing in altermatim.

404. Copeman, Harold. *Singing in Latin, or Pronunciation Explor'd.*

Oxford: Copeman, 1990. 0951579800. MT883.C65.

Presents the modern evidence as to how Latin was pronounced in England during the Tudor period. The book concerns Latin pronunciation in all European countries throughout the ages but there is a substantial section devoted to the sound of English Latin to 1650, followed by a much shorter section on Scotland, Wales and Ireland. Amongst the book's appendices, the fourth consists of notes on Tudor matters. Of additional interest is an account of how Latin was pronounced in England during the revival of interest in Tudor music in the nineteenth century.

405. Doe, Paul. "Another View of Musica ficta in Tudor Music." *Proceedings of the Royal Musical Association* 98 (1971-2): 113-22.

Urges caution in the application of musica ficta, arguing for fewer accidentals. The author bases his remarks on the evidence offered by the Eton Choirbook and the three *Western Wind* masses, though he concedes that a later composer such as, particularly, Sheppard poses problems. This paper is a response to *399*.

406. Fallows, David. "Early English." *Musical Times* 118 (1977): 949-52.

Mainly a review of several new editions of Tudor music, but on the final page asks urgently for a broadening of the discussion concerning the editorial insertion or omission of accidentals in such music. The latter opinion had, in the author's view, had too reticent an airing: both sides of the argument needed to be clearly stated to assist the scholarly and performing communities. See also *460*.

407. Ferguson, Howard. "Repeats and Final Bars in the Fitzwilliam Virginal Book." *Music & Letters* 43 (1962): 345-50.

Attempts to resolve the problems posed by the apparently redundant concluding breve chords in many Fitzwilliam pieces.

By referring to concordances and analysing the musical structure, the author is able to provide nine suggestions as a rough guide to when the concluding chords should or should not be played, and the extent to which repeats should be observed.

408. Harwood, Ian. "A Case of Double Standards? Instrumental Pitch in England c.1600." *Early Music* 9 (1981): 470-81.

Copiously illustrated and wide ranging exploration of the possibility that around 1600 there existed for instruments two pitch standards a fourth or a fifth apart. Suggests also that one of the two surviving original orpharians may be a bandora, of which no example was thought to survive.

409. Hunter, Desmond. "The Function of Strokes in Sixteenth-Century Sources of English Keyboard Music." *Irish Musical Studies* 1 (1990): 131-49.

Analyses the changing function of strokes in twelve English keyboard sources, c.1530-70. The author discusses all aspects from single to quadruple strokes, and notes that the stroke was used not only as a correction sign but also to indicate embellishment. Where possible he suggests what forms of embellishment the various shakes mean, and endeavours to discern a pattern of development. The paper is well illustrated. See also *WB171*.

410. Koopman, Ton. "'My Ladye Nevell's Booke' and Old Fingering." *English Harpsichord Magazine* 2 (1977): 5-10.

See *WB128*.

411. le Huray, Peter. "English Keyboard Fingering in the 16th and Early 17th Centuries." In *Source Materials and the Interpretation of Music: a Memorial Volume to Thurston Dart,* ed. by Ian Bent. London: Stainer & Bell, 1981, pp.227-57.

Takes as the starting-point Dart's view that many problems of phrasing and musica ficta may be solved by a study of contemporary fingering techniques. The author proceeds to list the sources: 29 contain fingerings of which ten are important, one further is printed, and the remainder contain isolated fingerings. He provides an index by composer and source to fingered pieces, and includes sections on techniques, interpretation and ornaments. The whole is comprehensively illustrated. At the same time the author has compiled *The Fingering of Virginal Music* (London: Stainer & Bell, 1981), which is intended as a practical anthology of instructively fingered pieces, published as a companion to *411*. See also *412*.

412. Lindley, Mark. "Early Fingering: Some Editing Problems and Some New Readings for J.S. Bach and John Bull." *Early Music* 17 (1989): 60-9.

Provides corrigenda, with explanation, to the fingering given for Bull's *Miserere* in the companion to *411*.

413. Monson, Craig. "Consort Song and Verse Anthem: a Few Performance Problems." *Journal of the Viola da Gamba Society of America* 13 (1976): 4-11.

Discusses the problems of performance practice revealed by an inspection of original sources of music in these two genres. In particular the author investigates the doubling of voices with viols, the employment of two trebles, whether instrumentalists sang as well, the role of other instruments than viols, and the occurrence of vocal improvization.

414. Phillips, Peter. "Performance Practice in 16th-Century English Choral Music." *Early Music* 6 (1978): 195-9.

Some thoughts both for and against the upward transposition of Tudor church music. Suggests that countertenors were trained to alternate head and chest registers contrary to modern practice.

415. Pike, Lionel. "The First English 'Basso continuo' Publication." *Music & Letters* 54 (1973): 326-34.

It is the author's opinion that *Peter Philips's Gemmulae*

sacrae of 1613 was the first publication of music by an English composer to include a basso continuo, not Philips's *Cantiones sacrae* of 1612, whose basso continuo part is dated 1617, though this is thought by some to be a misprint for 1612 (see for instance *14,* p.780). The author discusses the historical and literary background of the *Gemmulae,* and compares their style with that of other pieces by Philips and of music by his contemporaries. Of particular interest are the author's views on the realization of the basso continuo, the aspect of the collection which gives it its historical significance.

416. Pike, Lionel. "Triple Rhythms in Peter Philips' Vocal Music." *Consort* 28 (1972): 88-105.

Uses evidence from Philips himself as to how he required the relevant notational signs to be interpreted. Copiously illustrated.

417. Routley, Nicholas. "A Practical Guide to Musica ficta." *Early Music* 13 (1985): 59-71.

Comprehensively surveys problems associated with conventional provision or non-provision of accidentals in early music.

418. Spencer, Robert. "Performance Style of the English Lute Ayre c.1600." *Lute* 24 (1984): 55-68.

Is of the opinion that modern singers are too restrained in their performances of ayres. The author quotes writers on singing from the sixteenth and seventeenth centuries to further his case, and he follows this section with an account of the circumstances in which ayres were composed and performed around 1600, with suggestions about performing ayres today. Spencer added a postscript in 25 (1985): 40. Confusingly, immediately before this on pages 31-9, comes "The Art of Singing," Anthony Rooley's painstaking but breezy "personal reply" to Spencer's original article. Confusion worse confounded, on page 81 occurs "Singing Lute Songs: a Final Word," Spencer's slightly tetchy response to Rooley's reply.

See also 22, 38, 109, 307, 316, 599, WB144, WB171, WB187.

VII THEORY AND CRITICISM

419. Barnett, Howard B. "John Case - an Elizabethan Music Scholar."
     Music & Letters 50 (1969): 252-66.

Case was a respected philosopher at Oxford who in 1588
published *Apologia musices*. Two years previously *The Praise of
Musicke* was published anonymously. It has never been
established except circumstantially that Case was responsible
for both works. The author weighs up the arguments and
provides a brief biography of Case, an articulate spokesman for
music in a society bent increasingly on restricting music in
worship. It is the author's opinion that Case wrote both works.
See also *420* and *425*.

420. Binns, J.W. "John Case and 'The Praise of Musicke'." *Music &
     Letters* 55 (1974): 444-53.

Disputes Barnett's conclusions in *419* and argues that Case
did not write *The Praise of Musicke* for two reasons: that Case
himself implied as much in his own writings and that, *pace*
Barnett, Case's *Apologia musices* is not a translation of the
earlier English work. See also *425*.

421. Boyd, Morrison Comegys. *Elizabethan Music and Musical
     Criticism*. 2nd ed. Philadelphia: University of Pennsylvania
     Press, 1962. 363pp. ML286.2.B59E48.

Assembles comments made 1558-1625 on English music,
summarizes works on musical theory published in England
between those dates, illustrating the Elizabethan attitude to
music. The author provides copious background material, such
as on the rise of metrical psalters, and deals specifically with
various aspects of music, vocal, instrumental, ecclesiastical or
dramatic, as well as with England's relations with the continent.
His opinions and conclusions are entrenched around 1940, when
the first edition was published, and tend to be beholden to the

authors, especially Morley, from whom he quotes. The structure of the book is cumbersome, impeding narrative flow which in turn removes any sense of perspective and interaction among the musicians cited. It retains its usefulness as a reference tool in the absence of anything exactly comparable.

422. Carpenter, Nan Cooke. "The Study of Music at the University of Oxford in the Renaissance (1450-1600)." *Musical Quarterly* 41 (1955): 191-214.

Gives copious account of the teaching of music and names the better known musicians who held the Oxonian baccalaureate. The author also describes subsequent developments into the seventeenth century and notes some important performances.

423. Hallmark, Rufus. "An Unknown English Treatise of the 16th Century." *Journal of the American Musicological Society* 22 (1969): 273-4.

Summary of the findings concerning a musical treatise in Latin by *John Dygon,* in fact a paraphrased adaptation of part of a work by Gaffurius.

424. Irving, John. "Thomas Tomkins's Copy of Morley's 'A Plain and Easy Introduction to Practical Music'." *Music & Letters* 71 (1990): 483-93.

Studies the manuscript annotations by Tomkins and those subsequent owners whom he is able to identify. This copy of the first edition is not in *RISM*. The author uses the evidence of Tomkins's own annotations (the two composers were both pupils of Byrd) and of *GB-Bl* Add. 29996 which Tomkins owned, to suggest when he had obtained his copy of Morley's book. This leads the author to consider the scribal hands in Add. 29996, and to suggest the presence of the same hand in this and two other significant contemporary manuscripts of instrumental music. In the first of two important appendices he transcribes all the prefatory material from the front flyleaves written by the two owners before the presentation of the book to the library of

Magdalen College, Oxford in 1952. The second appendix reproduces for the first time in print Tomkins's canonic workings of Morley's "playnesong" added in manuscript by Tomkins to his copy of Morley's book.

425. Knight, Ellen E. "The Praise of Musicke: John Case, Thomas Watson, and William Byrd." *Current Musicology* 30 (1981): 37-51.

See *WB101*. See also *419* and *420*.

426. Maynard, Judson Dana. "'Heir beginnis countering'." *Journal of the American Musicological Society* 20 (1967): 182-96.

Discusses that section of *GB-Bl* Add. 4911, an anonymous Scottish treatise on music of about 1580, that deals with a form of discant called countering. The author edited the entire treatise for his doctoral thesis (Indiana, 1961), and gives the scribe's fourteen rules in the original Scots with parallel modern English paraphrases. To this he adds a commentary on the historical background to the treatise, its musical examples and provenance.

427. Morley, Thomas. *A Plain and Easy Introduction to Practical Music,* ed. by Alec R. Harman. 2nd ed. London: Dent, 1962. 325pp. MT6.M86.

By Byrd's most famous pupil, and no doubt expressing some of Byrd's teachings. It covers all aspects of singing and composing music for the aspiring contemporary musician, and has remained indispensable for an understanding of the musical life of the Tudor period. Arguments continue as to how much of the book is original and how much Morley incorporated from others. The present edition sheds light on the latter, though the extent to which Morley incorporated the theories of Byrd, also the book's dedicatee, remains open to further research. A facsimile of the original edition of 1597 was published in London by the Shakespeare Association in 1937, with an introduction by E.H. Fellowes. See also *424* and *433*.

428. Morris, R.O. *Contrapuntal Technique of the Sixteenth Century.*
Oxford: Clarendon, 1922. 74pp. + 49pp. of examples
separately paginated. ML446.M67.

Although superseded in some areas by subsequent research,
and perhaps too cavalier in tone for the roundhead musicologist,
this remains a fine introduction to polyphonic technique at the
time of the Tudors. For its time it was seminal: disrespectful of
established "authorities" on strict counterpoint, whose opinion
the author was able to overthrow with a combination of
familiarity with, and sympathy for, Renaissance polyphony. He
cites many examples from Tudor composers, but his use of
illustrations also from continental musicians helps to place the
Tudors in contemporary perspective. His chapters deal with
modes, rhythm, melody, harmony, specific contrapuntal
techniques, form and some technical features of the English
school.

429. Nixon, Paul J. "William Bathe and his Times." *Musical Times* 124
(1983): 101-2.

Biography of important Elizabethan musical educator.

430. Payne, Ian. "The Provision of Teaching on the Viols at Some
English Cathedral Churches, c.1594-c.1645: Archival
Evidence." *Chelys* 19 (1990): 3-15.

Deals with York, Ely, Lincoln and Peterborough. Information
is sketchy before c.1600. The provision of viols was not usually
undertaken earlier than the mid 1590s. Before this, apt boys, not
necessarily choristers, were taught to play keyboard instruments
mainly. With the reduction in the number of daily services, after
the Reformation, from ten to three, learning an instrument was a
constructive way of occupying the time available to musical
boys.

431. Price, David C. "The Elizabethan Household and its Musical
Education." *Consort* 32 (1976): 193-9.

Looks at the social and religious background of the age to

provide evidence for the significant advance in the appreciation by amateurs of the advantages of being musically literate. The author gives examples of the provision of teaching as well as playing by resident musicians. The households in question come from within a narrow stratum of contemporary society.

432. Rainbow, Bernarr. "Bathe and his Introduction to Musicke." *Musical Times* 123 (1982): 243-7.

Account of the contents of William Bathe's *A Brief Introduction to the Skill of Song* (c.1587-90), a new version of the first musical textbook to appear in the English language, which Bathe published in 1584 but of which no copies survive. The author describes the background to Bathe's thinking and attempts to date the new version. Subsequently a letter from Cecil Hill on pages 530-1 of the same volume states that a mid-seventeenth-century copy of the 1584 treatise survives (in manuscript in Aberdeen University Library) and has been edited for publication, 1979, and that the new version was entered at Stationers' Hall in 1596.

433. Stevenson, Robert. "Thomas Morley's 'Plaine and Easie' Introduction to the Modes." *Musica Disciplina* 6 (1951): 177-84.

Compares what Morley wrote in 427, concerning church modes, with what contemporary continental theorists had written about the topic. The author sees this as interesting on three counts: first, Morley was well educated and connected, and his opinion may be taken to represent the most enlightened opinion of Elizabethan England. Secondly, as a capable linguist, he would have been able to read the theorists' works, with their finer nuances, in the original languages. Thirdly, there must have been some reason behind those passages where Morley departed from the unanimous opinion of his continental contemporaries concerning church modes. He concludes that Morley regarded the topic as being of limited importance and that the subject had never become an indigenous part of musical education in England.

See also 171, 346, 626, 628, WB147, WB156.

VIII PATRONAGE AND DEDICATIONS

434. Ashbee, Andrew, *ed. Records of English Court Music.* Vol.IV (1603-1625). Snodland: Ashbee, 1991. 258pp. 0950720755. ML286.A8.

Aims to present a new calendar of the musical material from the Lord Chamberlain's papers and to incorporate related records of English Court music and musicians. As administrative head of the royal household away from domestic matters, the Lord Chamberlain controlled all musical activities at Court and all payments had to be approved first by him. This is an indispensable biographical and historical tool that corrects and updates a variety of details and assumptions in preceding and even contemporary monographs. This is part of a series of seven projected volumes. See section A-VII below, for details of those forthcoming that have most relevance to Tudor music. As an indication of the quality of the series, volume II won the first C.B. Oldman Prize awarded annually by the United Kingdom Branch of the International Association of Music Libraries for the year's best book of music bibliography, librarianship or reference by an author domiciled in the British Isles. In particular, volume IV updates *632* and confirms on p.197 that Hume was Scottish.

435. Baillie, Hugh. "A London Gild of Musicians, 1460-1530." *Proceedings of the Royal Musical Association* 83 (1956-7): 15-28.

Account of The Company of Parish Clerks or Fraternity of St Nicholas, with details of activities, duties and members, and description of the contemporary musical background.

436. Baldwin, David. *The Chapel Royal, Ancient & Modern.* London: Duckworth, 1990. 0715623494.

The Chapel Royal dates from the Middle Ages and is the

monarch's personal and mobile chapel, consisting not of buildings but of a body of musicians as well as of clergy. During the Tudor period of the Reformation, the Chapel Royal was nearly alone in sustaining the cathedral style of Divine Service in England, having beforehand recruited the best musicians in the country. This primarily historical study provides the background for the often political activities of the Chapel's personnel throughout the centuries. Several of the 26 chapters (especially 3, 5, 7, 9, 17, 19, 20 and 24) refer to Tudor music, mentioning junior and adult singers as well as instrumentalists. There is a complete list (Appendix II) of Chapel Royal personnel so far as it is known. Of the greatest musicological value is the discussion in chapter 17 about the emergence around 1600 of the post of organist.

437. Bennett, John. "A Tallis Patron?" *Research Chronicle* 21 (1988): 41-4.

Biographical account of Anthony Roper, named in the will of Joan, Thomas Tallis's widow and heir.

438. Brett, Philip. "Edward Paston (1580-1630): a Norfolk Gentleman and his Musical Collection." *Transactions of the Cambridge Bibliographical Society* 4 (1964): 51-69.

See *WB63*, where the date of publication is given wrongly as 1984.

439. Brett, Philip. "English Music for the Scottish Progress of 1617." In *Source Materials and the Interpretation of Music (see 411),* pp. 209-26.

Against the background of the Scottish Progress of James VI of Scotland and I of England, which the author describes in detail, he comments on the two works composed for it by *Orlando Gibbons:* the anthem *Great King of Gods* and the song *Do Not Repine.* The former is well known, though unfortunately better so as a modern contrafactum "Great Lord of Lords," but the music of the latter was only rediscovered and published in 1961, edited by Brett himself. He now subjects the piece for the first time to musical analysis, with comments on its style and on its place in the history and development of English music. He concludes with some suggestions about the circumstances of its first performance.

440. Chibbett, Michael. "Dedications in Morley's Printed Music." *Research Chronicle* 13 (1976): 84-94.

Investigates motives for all of Morley's dedications, and gives biographical backgrounds of dedicatees.

441. Cutts, John P. "Robert Johnson: King's Musician in His Majesty's Public Entertainment." *Music & Letters* 36 (1955): 110-25.

Account of his work for the theatre.

442. Dart, Thurston. "A Suppressed Dedication for Morley's Four-Part Madrigals of 1594." *Transactions of the Cambridge Bibliographical Society* (1963): 401-5.

Although Morley's *Madrigalls to Foure Voyces* was published apparently without a dedication, rendering it unique among English books of madrigals, as well as the first such book ever published, the author produces evidence that it was to have been dedicated to Sir John Puckering, Lord Keeper of the Great Seal of England, who for reasons unknown refused to accept the dedication.

443. Godt, Irving. "Prince Henry as Absalom in David's Lamentations." *Music & Letters* 62 (1981): 318-30.

The son and heir of James VI of Scotland and I of England, Prince Henry, died in 1612. His death provoked a torrent of lamentation. The author suggests that as many as thirteen contemporary settings of the non-liturgical text from II Samuel xviii 33, in which David laments the death of his son Absalom, are elegies for Henry symbolized as Absalom. He also notes that there are nine settings of David's lament for his friend Jonathan, II Samuel i 17-27, which could symbolize Henry as Jonathan. Four appendices provide manuscript sources, lists of settings of the Absalom and Jonathan texts, and memory of Henry himself: fifteen settings or cycles that are not Biblical but are more overt in their reference to him.

444. Hogwood, Christopher. *Music at Court.* London: Gollancz, 1980. 0575028777.

Chapter II, "Britannia triumphans," provides a succinct account of music in the Tudor Court, referring to Queen Elizabeth's use of music for prestige and entertainment.

445. Hoppe, Harry R. "John Bull in the Archduke Albert's Service." *Music & Letters* 35 (1954): 114-15.

Archival references to Bull's service in the Spanish Netherlands 1613-14 and irregularly until 1618, by which time Bull had already been organist of Antwerp Cathedral for a year. See also *625*.

446. Hulse, Lynn. "The Musical Patronage of Robert Cecil, fourth earl of Salisbury (1563-1612)." *Journal of the Royal Musical Association* 116 (1991): 24-40.

Gives account of Cecil's musicians and apprentices, including a table giving identities, dates of service, and known service to Cecil. Another table lists pieces dedicated to him. The author endeavours to reconstruct from available evidence Cecil's musical resources (instruments), his musicians' duties, his exploitation of patronage and his understanding of music.

447. Hulse, Lynn. "Sir Michael Hickes (1543-1612): a Study in Musical Patronage." *Music & Letters* 66 (1985): 220-7.

Provides an account of Hickes's musical activities and of his acquaintance with Anthony Holborne and Ferdinando Heybourne (or Richardson).

448. Mackerness, E.D. *A Social History of English Music.* Studies in Social History. London: Routledge and Kegan Paul, 1964. ML286.M25.

Bracing and rather sceptical account that, when dealing with musical aspects of the Tudor period, does not always go along with the received wisdom as to the musicality of that epoch: see chapter II, "Renaissance, Reformation and the Musical Public."

449. Philipps, G.A. "John Wilbye's Other Patrons: the Cavendishes and their Place in English Musical Life During the Renaissance." *Music Review* 38 (1977): 81-93.

Although Wilbye spent his professional life in the employment of the Kytsons, he dedicated his two collections of madrigals to members of the Cavendish family. The author provides a comprehensive account of this family and their many contacts with, and influences upon, English music of the time.

450. Philipps, G.A. "Patronage in the Career of Thomas Weelkes." *Musical Quarterly* 62 (1976): 46-57.

Ponders why such a talented musician apparently achieved so little in terms of career advancement. The author discusses the dedicatees of Weelkes's published collections, and suggests that Weelkes's unseemly behaviour was the result of professional disappointments, not the cause.

451. Poulton, Diana. "Captain Digory Piper of the 'Sweepstake'." *Lute Society Journal* 4 (1962): 17-22.

Biography of dedicatee of Dowland's famous galliard (and its preceding pavan), including evidence that Piper was a pirate.

452. Price, David C. *Patrons and Musicians of the English Renaissance.* Cambridge Studies in Music. Cambridge: Cambridge University Press, 1981. 250pp. 0521228069. ML286.2.

Patronage by private families of musicians in Elizabethan England was brought about by the Reformation and increased musical literacy. The Reformation ejected many musicians out of the church into the houses of families who could afford to employ them for entertainment and status or, if Catholics, as Kappellmeisteren. These families had in recent years become wealthier and better educated, and were both materially and intellectually equipped to patronize displaced musicians. The author gives details of patronage by specific families in various parts of England, and discusses the attitudes of Roman Catholics and Protestants. He also deals with the related matter of publication, in which many dedicatees are effusively and informatively acknowledged, and ponders whether much can be deduced about trends in musical literacy or taste from reviewing the ownership of manuscripts in private hands during this period. Three appendices list music publications 1563-1632, recipients of dedications 1570-1632, and dedications implying a special relationship between patron and composer 1588-1632. Substantial and significant though it is, this monograph contains many errors in respect of Byrd alone. The publisher has undertaken to incorporate the corrections into any future edition. Meanwhile factual statements concerning individual composers should be checked against reliable biographies, though it is to be hoped that all the inaccuracies herein have been visited upon the one composer.

453. Shire, Helena Mennie. "Musical Servitors to Queen Mary Stuart." *Music & Letters* 40 (1959): 15-18.

References to *James Lauder* and *William Kinloch* in contemporary documents which shed light on their activities and movements.

454. Stevens, Denis. "Music in Honour of Queen Elizabeth I." *Musical Times* 101 (1960): 698-9.

Brief account of anthems and madrigals that directly or indirectly mention the queen.

455. Vining, Paul. "Gibbons and his Patrons." *Musical Times* 124 (1983): 707-9.

Biographical accounts of the dedicatees of Gibbons's two published collections: Sir Christopher Hatton (*The First Set of*

Madrigals and Mottets, 1612) and Edward Wray (*Fantazies of III. parts,* c.1620).

456. Warren, Charles W. "Music at Nonesuch." *Musical Quarterly* 54 (1968): 47-57.

Describes the place of Nonesuch Palace in the history of England. The author provides an account of musical activities in the chapel, and as part of entertainments. He also notes the collections of musical instruments and manuscripts (containing the earliest reference to Tallis's *Spem in alium* in forty parts), and the musical contacts of the Earl of Arundel and Lord Lumley, successive owners of Nonesuch during the latter half of the sixteenth century. Unfortunately *The Lumley Library: the Catalogue of 1609,* edited by Sears Jayne & Francis R. Johnson (British Museum Bicentenary Publications. London: British Museum, 1956) is inadequate as a bibliographical tool for music (see pp.284-6) but Warren conveys adequately the musical proclivities of the palace's Elizabethan owners. The true extent of the library's musical holdings are investigated by John Milsom in "The Nonsuch Music Library," from *Sundry Sorts of Music Books,* ed. by Chris Banks *et al* (London: British Library, 1993). See also *255* and *491.*

457. Westfall, Suzanne R. *Patrons and Performance: Early Tudor Household Revels.* Oxford: Clarendon, 1990. 01981218800. PN2590.C66W48.

Chapter **4,** about minstrels, contains several references to music in these revels, and Appendix B consists of a list of solo instrumentalists under the headings of individual instruments, with some examples of payments to soloists.

458. Woodfill, Walter L. *Musicians in English Society, from Elizabeth to Charles I.* Princeton: Princeton University Press, 1953; repr. ed. Da Capo Press Music Reprint Series. New York: Da Capo, 1969. ML286.2.W6.

Provides copious information about the practicalities of being a musician during the late sixteenth and early seventeenth centuries. The author devotes separate sections to professional musicians in the City of London, the provinces, the Church and the Court, with a fifth part on amateurs. From this he conveys a picture of the social and practical circumstances of practising musicians, their wages, professional bodies, terms of employment and employers, and how all these varied over the years. He also draws attention to contemporary attitudes to music itself and to musicians who, from Gentlemen of the Chapel Royal to vagabond minstrels, impinged on all the strata of contemporary society. No specific successor has revised this monograph but *434* updates many of its biographical and historical premises.

See also *70, 234, 337, 669, WB165.*

IX BIBLIOGRAPHY

This section, besides bibliographical items, includes authentication, computers, discography, editing, palaeography, printing and video. For recent recordings in all formats see *Opus* (Nashville: Schwann), published quarterly, for American releases, and *The Classical Catalogue* (Harrow: General Gramophone Publications), published biannually, for British releases.

459. Aplin, John. "The Origins of John Day's 'Certaine Notes'." *Music & Letters* 62 (1981): 295-9.

   Produces evidence that *Certaine Notes*, published in 1565 but known to have been intended for publication as early as 1560, was in fact an Edwardian compilation which originated before 1552, date of the second Edwardine Prayer Book.

460. Blezzard, Judith. "Editing Early English: Some Further Evidence." *Musical Times* 119 (1978): 265-8.

   Continues the discussion begun in *406* concerning chromaticism in Tudor music. Basing her comments on the Lumley books (see *491*), which date from 1549, the middle of the period in question, and which were copied soon after the music was composed, the author is able to make deductions, aided by the relative repetitiveness of the music, as to which precepts were being followed by the scribes. She concludes that the evidence favours neither those editors who wish to purge the music of accidentals, nor those who wish to insert them.

461. Blezzard, Judith. "Reconstructing Early English Vocal Music: History, Principle and Practice." *Music Review* 45 (1984): 85-95.

Draws attention to the problems of reconstruction when sections of a piece are missing. Editors disagree among themselves, and can be shown to have been unadventurous when a long-lost part reappears. The attitude of eighteenth and nineteenth century scholars to early music was condescending, and editors were prepared to "correct" or recompose existing passages. The author charts the course from complacency to consideration, marking Arkwright as a pioneer of the newer attitude in his *Old English Edition* of 1893, and on to the desire for authenticity in the late twentieth century.

462. Bray, Roger. "John Baldwin." *Music & Letters* 56 (1975): 55-9.

Examines Baldwin's career as a copyist. The author lists the four manuscripts for which Baldwin is known to have been responsible, and discusses Baldwin's reliability, where his sources are known, and the extent to which he modernized older music and why. With the aid of a chronology of Baldwin's life, the author attempts to provide datings for each of the manuscripts.

463. Byard, Herbert. "A Sternhold and Hopkins Puzzle." *Musical Quarterly* 56 (1970): 221-9.

Primarily a summary of the publishing history of Sternold and Hopkins's psalter and of rival psalters, but the author also attempts to set out what evidence there is to support the claim of the parish of Awre, in the diocese of Gloucester, that it was there that the *Psalmes of David in English metre* by Sternhold were first uttered.

464. Caldwell, John. *Editing Early Music.* Early Music Series, 5. Oxford: Clarendon, 1985. 125pp. 0198161433. ML63.C29.

Essential textbook for anyone working on Tudor music. Even if one is not involved oneself in editing, it is important to understand the principles involved. These are spelt out in general terms in the first chapter, while in the third they are applied to the music of the period 1450-1600. The author deals with every possible problem including barring, note values, naming of vocal parts, time signatures, transposition, ligature, presentation of verbal text and many other related issues, all provided with sensible but undogmatic conclusions and advice. There is a practical concluding chapter on the presentation of edited copy. Four appendices cover special signs and conventions, suggested standardized part-names and abbreviations, sample score layouts and the editorial treatment of accidentals. There is a good bibliography.

465. Clark, J. Bunker. "Some Problems of Transcribing Music with Many Sources: The Verse Anthem *O Praise God in His Holiness* by Edward Smith." In *Notations and Editions: a Book in Honor of Louise Cuyler*, ed. by Edith Borroff. Dubuque: Brown, 1974, pp.69-105.

Deals with techniques of transcription in the form of advice to potential editors. There are three clear reproductions of different sources and a complete text of the anthem, its only modern edition. See *12* for confirmation that Smith is an earlier composer than the author assumes.

466. Coover, James and Colvig, Richard. *Medieval and Renaissance Music on Long-Playing Records.* Detroit Studies in Music Bibliography, 6. Detroit: Information Service, 1964. ML156.2.C67.

Organized in three parts. First, anthologies of mediaeval and Renaissance music subdivided chronologically as chant, mediaeval, Renaissance and addenda, listed alphabetically by title and given a running number. Part two is an index to anthologies and individual discographies by composer. The final part is a performer index classified by instrument or medium. The main catalogue runs only to 1960 and is followed by a first supplement 1960-1. It is essential to read the introduction to part II as it is intricately organized. See *467* for supplement.

467. Coover, James *and* Colvig, Richard. *Medieval and Renaissance Music on Long-Playing Records: Supplement, 1962-71.* Detroit Studies in Music Bibliography, 26. Detroit: Information Co-ordinators, 1973. 0911771448. ML156.2.C67.

Supplements *466*, and also contains addenda and corrigenda to original edition and first supplement.

468. Croucher, Trevor. *Early Music Discography, from Plainsong to the Sons of Bach.* London: Library Association; Phoenix: Oryx, 1981. 2v. 0853656134. ML156.2.

Lists all such records commercially available in Europe and North America at the end of June, 1980. Volume 1 is a record index organized chronologically - Early Renaissance, Late Renaissance and Early Baroque relate to Tudor Music - with running numbers. Volume 2 consists of composer, plainsong, anonymous work and performer indexes keyed to the running numbers in volume 1.

469. Day, Timothy, *comp. A Discography of Tudor Church Music.* London in British Library, 1989. 317pp. 0712305033. ML156.4.R4D4.

Lists all known commercial recordings and also tapes of BBC broadcasts in the National Sound Archive. The compiler provides a magisterial introduction which not only reflects the growing interest from the late nineteenth century, but also the changing attitudes to performance practice and authenticity. The 190 footnotes are a valuable resource in themselves, as are the discographical sources in the preface. The main list of recordings is chronological, followed by an index of composers and their works, an index of performers, and an annotated chronological list of recordings of broadcast talks held on tape at the Archive in London.

470. Deutsch, Otto Erich. "Cecilia and Parthenia." *Musical Times* 100 (1959): 591-2.

Traces the model for the title-page of *Parthenia* to a Dutch engraving of St Cecilia.

471. Dowling, Margaret. "The Printing of Dowland's Second Booke of Ayres." *Library*, 4th ser., 12 (1932): 365-80.

Account of the progress of Dowland's 1600 publication through the printing house, and of the court cases it provoked.

472. Fenlon, Iain *and* Milsom, John. "'Ruled Paper Imprinted': Music, Paper and Patents in Sixteenth-Century England." *Journal of the American Musicological Society* 37 (1984): 139-63.

See *WB31*.

473. Humphries, Charles *and* Smith, William C. *Music Publishing in the British Isles, from the Beginning until the Middle of the Nineteenth Century: a Dictionary of Engravers, Printers, Publishers and Music Sellers, with a Historical Introduction.* 2nd ed. Oxford: Blackwell, 1970. 063112330X. ML112.H8.

Arranged as alphabetical sequence with supplement to the first edition. Entries include the subjects' extramusical activities, dates active, and locations of businesses with, where appropriate, a commentary enlarging upon their musical activities and their relationships with others in the music trade. Informative about those active in Tudor times, and those who continued to deal in Tudor music subsequently. See also John A. Parkinson's *Victorian Music Publishers: an Annotated List* (Warren: Harmonie Park Press, 1991) which, although not an essential tool for the study of Tudor music, is of interest in that it continues the work begun by Humphries and Smith into the twentieth century.

474. Illing, Robert. "The English Metrical Psalter of the Reformation."

Musical Times 128 (1987): 517-21.

Defines "the English metrical psalter" as a group of anthologies c.1548-64, of which ten distinct editions seem to have survived. These the author describes individually, to unravel confusions, and then goes on to discuss sources of the verses and melodies, rhythm and tonality, the various editions of East's psalter (1592-1633; see *475-6*), Hart's psalter (Edinburgh, 1635) and the musical companions to the English metrical psalter.

475. Illing, Robert. *Est - Barley - Ravenscroft and the English Metrical Psalter.* Adelaide: Libraries Board of South Australia, 1969. ML3166.I43.

Bibliographical study that attempts to relate all the editions of the psalter associated with East, Barley and Ravenscroft. It is well illustrated, though the illustrations could be clearer, and the author tabulates surviving copies. The first psalter of this group appeared in 1592 with a reissue in 1594 and two more in 1604 and 1611, all prints of East's original. Barley's revision is undated (see the author's "Barley's Pocket Edition of Est's Metrical Psalter," *Music & Letters* 49 (1968): 219-23), conjecturally 1599, but two concluding issues by Ravenscroft are dated 1621 and 1633. Psalters assumed considerable importance after the Reformation and this one was the only harmonized version of the psalm melodies at this time in England. See also *481*.

476. Illing, Robert. "A Metrical Trinity: Est, Barley, Ravenscroft." *Musical Times* 110 (1969): 977-8.

Account of relationship between three related metrical psalters (see *475*) and *The Whole Booke of Psalmes*, 1562, with their immediate publishing histories, and modern editions from 1844.

477. Johnson, Gerald D. "William Barley, 'Publisher & Seller of Bookes', 1591-1614." *Library*, 6th ser., 11 (1989): 10-46.

First comprehensive study of the whole career of Barley, holder of the music patent in succession to Tallis, Byrd and Morley during the early seventeenth century. The four sections deal with his life, Barley and the book trade, the early music books and the music patent. These are followed by nine tables illustrating Barley's career as a publisher, identifying each publication.

478. King, Alec Hyatt. "The Significance of John Rastell in Early Music Printing." *Library*, 5th ser., 26 (1971): 197-214; repr. in *Musical Pursuits: Selected Essays.* London: British Library, 1987, pp.7-31.

Establishes Rastell as printer of the earliest mensural music printed in England, of the earliest broadside in Europe with music printed from type, of the earliest song printed in an English dramatic work and of the first attempt anywhere at printing a score. Conveniently the succeeding essay in *Musical Pursuits*, pages 32-7, "Rastell Reunited," complements and supplements the main article. (See p.xii for original source.)

479. King, A. Hyatt. *Some British Collectors of Music c.1600-1960.* Sandars Lectures, 1961. Cambridge: Cambridge University Press, 1963. ML406.K55.

Provides important information about the preservation of Tudor manuscripts and prints, indicating the varying degrees of esteem in which Tudor music has been held. Many collectors were involved in the great revival of practical interest in such music, which began before 1900. For Tudor matters, access to the text is best achieved by referring to the names of individual composers or collectors in the index. Particularly useful is Appendix B, "Classified List of Past Collectors," Group 2, "Collectors Whose Music has been Conserved Intact, in Whole or Part," which provides location and name of recipient, usually a library.

480. Kratzenstein, Marilou *and* Hamilton, Jerald. *Four Centuries of Organ Music, from the Robertsbridge Codex through the Baroque Era: an Annotated Discography.* Detroit Studies in

Music Bibliography, 51. Detroit: Information Co-ordinators, 1984. 0899900208. ML156.4.06K7.

Chapter 2 is devoted to Renaissance England, and is divided into "Anthologies" and "Individual Composers." Entries are given running numbers, and there is an index of composers. Lists of works are given under the main entries, which contain brief annotations, naming the organ in use and summarizing any further contents that are not played on an organ. Otherwise the entries give artiste, title of disc, label and number, with date of release if known.

481. Krummel, D.W. *English Music Printing, 1553-1700.* Bibliographical Society Publications, 1971. London: Bibliographical Society, 1975. 0197217885. ML112.K75.

From a Tudor standpoint, valuable for chapter II, "The Politics of the Music Patents," and chapter IV, "Part Books," in which form was published nearly all Tudor vocal music that was published. Chapter III, "Psalm Books," reflects a then significant but now neglected area of Tudor activity aimed at a domestic, devotional and musically undemanding market, hence of ephemeral or at best peripheral importance in the development of English music during the Tudor period.

482. Lavin, J.A. "William Barley, Draper and Stationer." *Studies in Bibliography* 22 (1969): 214-23.

Queries all previous research and articles on Barley as a printer, offering evidence that although he was a publisher and bookseller, he was never a printer. Until 1606 he called himself a bookseller and draper, after which he became a freeman of the Stationers' Company and called himself a stationer.

483. Nixon, Howard M. "Day's *Service Book,* 1560-1565." *British Library Journal* 10 (1984): 1-31.

Using close bibliographical analysis, argues that, contrary to long held belief, John Day's *Certaine Notes* was not published in 1560 with a second edition five years later (entitled *Mornyng* and *Evenyng Prayer and Communion),* but was published in four partbooks for the only time in 1565. The author lists and comments upon the surviving parts. Confusion about the number of editions arose because, although it was proposed to publish the service book under the former title in 1560, publication was delayed until 1565, when the title was changed. However, in some copies the former title page, carrying the earlier date, was not cancelled. He detects a break in printing, and confirms this by a close analysis of the state of the woodcut initials that begin each new piece of music, in all four parts.

484. Payne, Ian. "The Handwriting of John Ward." *Music & Letters* 65 (1984): 176-88.

In the light of the discovery of a third specimen of Ward's non-musical handwriting, the author tests those claims made for Ward's having been involved in the copying of a variety of music manuscripts. He supports these investigations with the suggestion that the hitherto anonymous song *Mount Up My Soul* was composed by Ward and survives in his hand. He concludes that, despite the opportunities offered by proximity to the musical circle of Thomas Myriell, Ward's musical hand survives with any degree of probability only in one item.

485. Rapson, Penelope. *A Technique for Identifying Textual Errors and Its Application to the Sources of Music by Thomas Tallis.* Outstanding Dissertations in Music from British Universities. New York: Garland, 1989. 3v. in 2. 368pp. 0824020235 ML3797.R36.

Seeks to advance beyond the favoured eclectic method of textual criticism in establishing a musical text that is as near as possible to the composer's original wishes. To this end the author enunciates a theory which, exploiting computer technology, will enable an editor to arrive at an objectively achieved final text. The method involves identifying where there is a choice of sources, and those occasions when incontrovertibly wrong readings emerge. The direction of the flow of these errors through subsequent sources may be ascertained, and the least erroneous source can be recognized and reconstructed. The author provides full operational apparatus including programs and musical texts. She admits that the system has inconveniences but asserts that it holds good, citing examples of when it corroborates the proven conclusions of other scholars, and she suggests some subsidiary uses for the technique. This study is highly relevant to specialists concerned with textual editing but is only incidentally about Tallis. The thesis dates from 1981 and was not updated for publication.

486. Steele, Robert. *The Earliest English Music Printing: a Description and Bibliography of English Printed Music to the Close of the Sixteenth Century.* Illustrated Monographs, 11. London: Bibliographical Society, 1903; repr. ed. with corrs, Meisenheim: Hain, 1965. 108pp. ML112.S8.

Though largely superseded by *481*, this is an important document in being the first monograph to be devoted to the designs and typefaces of early English printed music. The corrected reprint provides two pages of addenda and corrigenda which embody the more important alterations made by the author in an annotated copy which he presented to the British Museum in 1941. The body of the book is a chronological list of music printed in England up to 1600, with full bibliographical description. Besides introductory matter there are synopses of known and doubtful editions and of ghosts, and many illustrations. The whole is conspicuously well laid out and pleasant to use. Although it reflects a discipline in an embryonic state, and is written from a bibliographical rather than a musicological standpoint, it is a seminal work of great significance in the revival of interest in music of the Tudor period. It still conveys some useful information, and its felicitous structure makes it gratifying to observe where knowledge has moved on.

487. Ward, John M. "Barley's Song Without Words." *Lute Society Journal* 12 (1970): 5-22.

Seeks to explain why William Barley included four songs without words in *A New Booke of Tabliture,* 1596. Although vocal parts are provided, only incipits of text are given, and those are as headings. The author suggests that Barley adopted this procedure because printing from woodblocks did not allow him to do otherwise. He conjectures that Barley's readers may have known the intended texts or may have sung different texts to the same music, as this was not an uncommon practice.

See also *57, 102, 155, 188, 229, 530, 604, 605, 606, 629, WB149, WB151, WB153, WB157, WB161, WB162, WB169, WB170, WB177, WB184.*

X SOURCE MATERIALS

This chapter includes studies of individual manuscripts and publications which have a bibliographical bias and are not limited to the work of one composer. As to the question of where to locate these or other sources, Tudor music is well served by bibliographical tools. English church music, both printed and in manuscript, may be located through *59*, though locations discovered for printed sources will then have to be found in *8* or *13*. Similarly, Latin church music can be located through *82*, thence to *8 or 13* again for printed sources. These two tools provide locations for all printed secular items whether vocal or instrumental. Music for viols, including songs or any ensemble employing the viol, may be located, whether printed or in manuscript, through *303*, and lute music through *544*. Keyboard music may be located through a book published too late for inclusion in the main sequence of this guide, John Harley's *British Harpsichord Music*. Volume 1: *Sources* (Aldershot: Scolar, 1992). Again this covers printed and manuscript sources, though access is only by composer, not by individual pieces: for these, use *372*. Otherwise only small recesses of the secular manuscript repertory remain untouched, and for these the best starting-point remains Augustus Hughes-Hughes's *Catalogue of Manuscript Music in the British Museum*. Volume 2: *Secular Vocal Music*. Volume 3: *Instrumental Music, Treatises, etc.* (London: British Museum, 1906-9).

488. Aplin, John. "Sir Henry Fanshawe and Two Sets of Early Seventeenth-Century Part-Books at Christ Church, Oxford." *Music & Letters* 57 (1976): 11-24.

Description of *GB-Och* Mus. 56-60 and 61-66. The author is particularly interested in why John Ward figures so prominently, the key being his relationship with Fanshawe, Remembrancer of the Exchequer at the time of the death of James I's son and heir Prince Henry in 1612. These partbooks contain several laments on his death, including two by Ward. The author provides lists of the contents of both sets and of Mus. 67, from which it may be seen that the partbooks contain a wealth of instrumental consort music plus sacred and secular vocal music of composers (including a few Italians) from Tye onwards.

489. Ashbee, Andrew. "Instrumental Music from the Library of John Browne (1608-91), Clerk of the Parliaments." *Music & Letters* 58 (1977): 43-59.

Complementary article to *524*. Lists the manuscripts, now in various locations, that once belonged to, and were partially copied by, Browne. As well as providing palaeographical information about each manuscript, the author lists their contents and tabulates the number of contributions to each manuscript by individual composers. This is one of the largest and most important surviving collections, albeit now dispersed, of English consort music from the sixteenth and seventeenth centuries.

490. Bergsagel, John D. "The Date and Provenance of the Forrest-Heyther Collection of Tudor Masses." *Music & Letters* 44 (1963): 240-8.

Describes *GB-Ob* Mus. Sch. e. 376-81. Predominantly a bibliographical study. The author suggests that the manuscript originated as a Festschrift for the new Cardinal College around 1530. He details its additions (in which *John Baldwin* had a hand) and changes of ownership before its return to Oxford in 1627. See also *WB169*.

491. Blezzard, Judith. "The Lumley Books: a Collection of Tudor Church Music." *Musical Times* 112 (1971): 128-30.

Introductory account of *GB-Lbl* Royal App. 74-6, originally a set of four but of which the bass partbook is lost. It formed part of the library of Henry Fitzalan, 12th earl of Arundel, which was merged with that of his son-in-law Lord Lumley in 1580. This set is second only in importance to the Wanley Books (see *575*) as a source of Edwardine liturgical music. See also *456.*

492. Blezzard, Judith. "A New Source of Tudor Secular Music." *Musical Times* 122 (1981): 532-5.

Description of *GB-Lbl* Add. 60577, a fifteenth-century manuscript with substantial sixteenth-century additions consisting of vocal canons, lute dances and keyboard pieces. These seem to have been copied c.1560-80 and are all anonymous except for a keyboard piece ascribed to John White (d.1560).

493. Boston, John L. "Priscilla Bunbury's Virginal Book." *Music & Letters* 36 (1955): 365-73.

Supplement to *510*, describing and analysing contents.

494. Bowers, Roger *and* Wathey, Andrew. "New Sources of English Fifteenth- and Sixteenth-Century Polyphony." *Early Music History* 4 (1984): 297-346.

Pages 298-304 describe a hitherto unknown and otherwise undocumented work by *Ludford.*

495. Bray, Roger W. "British Museum Add. MS. 17802-5 (the Gyffard Part-Books): an Index and Commentary." *Research Chronicle* 7 (1969): 31-50.

Contains shorter pieces of Latin church music for the Sarum rite mainly by the generation from Taverner to Tallis, especially Tye, Sheppard and John Blitheman, but with pieces by younger composers such as John Mundy and "Byrd" (though William is not specified).

496. Bray, Roger. "British Museum, R.M. 24 d 2 (John Baldwin's

Commonplace Book): an Index and Commentary." *Research Chronicle* 12 (1974): 137-51.

Consists of 209 varied items in score, from Bedyngham to Bull, including both sacred and secular music from England and the continent. It is rich in Byrd, Taverner, Sheppard, Parsons and the Mundys, and contains madrigals by Marenzio. See also *497* and *WB169*.

497. Bray, Roger. "The Part-Books Oxford, Christ Church, Mss 979-983: an Index and Commentary." *Musica Disciplina* 25 (1971): 179-97.

In the hand of *John Baldwin*. Contains 172 predominantly sacred vocal items by Byrd and his contemporaries. See also *496* and *WB169*.

498. Brett, Philip. "*Musicae modernae laus*: Geoffrey Whitney's Tribute to the Lute and its Players." *Lute Society Journal* 7 (1965): 40-4.

In 1586 Plantin of Leiden published Whitney's *A Choice of Emblemes*, the first English emblem book. Of 248 items it contains only two that are musical, showing a lute and a lyre. The author describes both devices, and quotes the undistinguished poem accompanying the lute device. However, he believes he has discovered the original presentation copy which contains 49 fewer emblems. One of the musical ones is dropped, but the manuscript contains a musical emblem excluded from the print. He describes and reproduces the emblem and quotes the accompanying poem in full, that mentions "Johnsonne" approvingly, whom he identifies as John Johnson. Finally he ponders why this emblem was dropped from the print.

499. Charteris, Richard. "Consort Music Manuscripts in Archbishop Marsh's Library, Dublin." *Research Chronicle* 13 (1976): 27-63.

Comprehensive introduction, with appendix containing

thematic catalogue. The composers are of the generation of Coprario and his successors beyond Gibbons. See also *500* and *537*.

500. Charteris, Richard. "New Information About Some of the Consort Music in Archbishop Marsh's Library, Dublin." *Consort* 43 (1987): 38-9.

Half of the article takes vigorous issue with *537*, but the rest identifies other sources copied by one of the scribes whose hand may be seen in the Marsh manuscripts. See also *499*.

501. Charteris, Richard. "A Rediscovered Source of English Consort Music." *Chelys* 5 (1973-4): 3-6.

Brings to scholarly attention *US-LAuc* F1995 M4, which contains 26 fantasias in three parts by Coprario, Gibbons, Jenkins, the younger Robert Johnson and Lupo of which two, one each by Johnson and Lupo, are otherwise unknown.

502. Clark, J. Bunker. "Adrian Batten and John Barnard: Colleagues and Collaborators." *Musica Disciplina* 22 (1968): 207-29.

Disputes le Huray's claim in *93* (pp.172-6) that Batten was not the compiler of the Batten organ book. The author outlines le Huray's arguments and follows up with his own, based on new evidence. Some of this is palaeographical, but the most important evidence is that which links it with Barnard's *The First Book of Selected Church Musick*, 1641. He also provides a list of the contents of *GB-Lrc* 1045-51, the set of partbooks that Barnard used to prepare *The First Book* for publication.

503. Cutts, John P. "A Bodleian Song-Book: Don C.57." *Music & Letters* 34 (1953): 192-211.

Introduction, list and commentary devoted to a manuscript that contains songs by John Wilson, Robert Ramsay, the younger Robert Johnson and John Hilton, and later composers.

504. Cyr, Mary. "A Seventeenth-Century Source of Ornamentation for

Voice and Viol: British Museum MS. Egerton 2971."
Research Chronicle 9 (1971): 53-72.

Consists of Italian and English songs and pieces for lyra viol.
Compiled before 1622, it is important for evidence about
performance practice.

505. Danner, Peter. "Dd.4.23 or English Cittern Music Revisited."
Journal of the Lute Society of America 3 (1970): 1-12.

Commentary on, and inventory of, largest known collection of
music for solo cittern (prefix *GB-Cu*). Notes the idiosyncracies of
the cittern, such as its range, tuning and use of chord patterns,
and how this affects music composed or arranged for it,
compared with other instruments.

506. Dart, Thurston. "The Cittern and its English Music." *Galpin
Society Journal* 1 (1948): 46-63.

Account of development of cittern during Tudor period,
including references to printed and manuscript sources from
Britain and abroad. Updated in 6 (1953): 112-13. See *390* for
updated list of English manuscript sources.

507. Dart, Thurston. "An Early Seventeenth-Century Book of English
Organ Music for the Roman Rite." *Music & Letters* 52 (1971):
27-38.

Suggests that *GB-Och* Mus. 89 was the organ book of
Richard Dering, none of whose music for organ survives
anywhere else. The author begins with an extract from a paper
he read in 1964 on "The Classification and Dating of the
Sources of English Keyboard Music, 1560-1630," in which he
proposed a division of the material into eight categories. He
discerns Mus. 89 as part of the seventh, "Books for Day-to-Day
Use by Professional Keyboardists." Many of the pieces are
anonymous, but deductions from the Roman ritualistic content,
and the identities of the few named composers, lead him to a
Brussels provenance, where Dering was organist of the convent
of English Benedictine nuns. Subsequently, though a recusant,

he returned to England as organist of the chapel of Charles I's French Catholic queen, an explanation of the manuscript's preservation in England.

508. Dart, Thurston. "Henry Loosemore's Organ Book." *Transactions of the Cambridge Bibliographical Society* 3 (1960): 143-51.

Provides provenance and inventory for an important organ book compiled c.1625-c.1645 by Loosemore for use in accompanying the chapel choir of King's College, Cambridge. Twenty of the 83 works are unica. Two are accompaniments for instrumental pieces. Composers represented span the period from Tallis to Loosemore himself who died in 1670. The anthem, *This is the Day,* without a composer's name is now known to be by Parsley (see *12*). See also *106*.

509. Dart, Thurston. "Lord Herbert of Cherbury's Lute-Book." *Music & Letters* 38 (1957): 136-48.

Description, with summary of contents. The music is by continental composers and contemporary English lutenists such as Bacheler, Robert Johnson, Holborne, Ferrabosco the younger and, uniquely for the lute, Coprario. See also *557*.

510. Dart, R. Thurston. "Morley's Consort Lessons of 1599." *Proceedings of the Royal Musical Association* 74 (1947-8): 1-9.

Account of contents and the circumstances of compilation and publication, with a note on the instrumentation and Morley's reason for choosing it.

511. Dart, Thurston. "New Sources of Virginal Music". *Music & Letters* 35 (1954): 93-106.

Describes contents of the following manuscripts: Dublin Virginal Book, Lord Middleton's (or the Willoughby) Lute-Book, *GB-Ob* Mus. d. 143, *GB-Cu* Dd. 4. 22 (another lutebook), Lady Jean Campbell's Book (mainly lute music), Clement Matchett's Virginal Book, Duncan Burnett's Virginal Book, and the Bull

Virginal Book (also known as the Bull Manuscript). The author gives locations for the named manuscripts. The lutebooks are present because they contain one or more pieces for keyboard.

512. Dart, Thurston. "The Printed Fantasies of Orlando Gibbons." *Music & Letters* 37 (1956): 342-9.

Primarily important for authoritatively proposing a publication date of c.1620 for the undated *Fantazies of III. parts*, previously thought to predate *Parthenia*, 1612/3. Argues that some of Gibbons's fantasies for three stringed instruments are in effect early trio sonatas, and that in others he imitated the style of Coprario and Lupo. See also *274, 313 and 352* which update some of Dart's conclusions, though not the date of the *Fantazies*.

513. Dickinson, A.E.F. "A Forgotten Collection: a Survey of the Weckmann Books." *Music Review* 18 (1956): 97-109.

Account of *D-Bsb* Ly. A1 and A2 compiled by Matthias Weckmann around 1630, and which contain keyboard pieces by several English composers such as Byrd, Bull, Philips and Farnaby. The author's commentary places their music in a continental perspective. The contents of either book are listed, the pieces identified and the circumstances of the compilations elucidated. The books provide an indication of the influence of the English virginalists on continental composers.

514. Dodd, Gordon. "The Coprario-Lupo Five-Part Books at Washington." *Chelys* 1 (1970): 36-40.

Account of provenance and contents of *US-Lc* M.990.C66F4 which consists of two volumes. The former contains consort works by Coprario, with two apparent insertions by Michael East, while the latter was known as the Dolmetsch Manuscripts and mainly contains works by Lupo but with a few by Coprario.

515. Edwards, Warwick. "The Instrumental Music of Henry VIII's Manuscript." *Consort* 34 (1978): 274-82.

In his introduction the author describes the manuscript, and deplores the absence of any articles which are more than mere introductions to Henrician instrumental music, with its problems of definition and form. He in turn is quite clear in his own definition of "instrumental" at least for the purposes of the present study. He then discusses the contents of this manuscript in the contexts of wordless compositions by continental, English and unnamed composers.

516. Edwards, Warwick. "The Walsingham Consort Books." *Music & Letters* 55 (1974): 209-14.

Announces discovery of *GB-HUu* DDHO/20/1-3, companions to a cittern partbook at Mills College, Oakland, California, containing 34 pieces in various forms of incompleteness, from only a title to those that survive in Morley's *Consort Lessons*. The author describes the remaining partbooks in detail and, deducing evidence from the music itself, endeavours to establish their provenance. He concludes that the scribe was probably Daniel Bacheler.

517. Elliott, Kenneth. "The Carver Choir-Book." *Music & Letters* 41 (1960): 349-57.

Account of *GB-En* Adv. 5.1.15 which contains, amongst many British and continental pieces, the entire surviving corpus of Robert Carver, placing him in the context of his contemporaries as well as indicating the repertory of the Scottish Chapel Royal. In a strongly bibliographical study the author lists the contents, and suggests a reordering that would reflect the probable original order before the book achieved its present form.

518. Ellis, Osian. "Ap Huw: Untying the Knot." *Soundings* 6 (1977): 67-80.

Detailed consideration of Welsh manuscript of harp music consisting of accompaniments in tablature for pre-existing tunes. The accompaniments were composed, and the manuscript was compiled, by Robert ap Huw (c.1580-1665) around 1613, *GB-Lbl* Add. 14905. The article is copiously illustrated.

519. Fallows, David. "The Fayrfax Manuscript." *Musical Times* 117 (1976): 127-30.

Attempts to place the manuscript in the context of the history of English music at a time when, because of the Wars of the Roses, it was cut off from European developments. The manuscript itself contains music by several contemporary composers in addition to that of Fayrfax, and consists of secular songs. The author concludes with comments on the nature and collation of the manuscript.

520. Fenlon, Iain, ed. *Cambridge Music Manuscripts*. Cambridge: Cambridge University Press, 1982. 05211244528. ML141.C3.

Includes comprehensive state-of-the-art descriptions, with bibliographies, of several Tudor sources including the Fitzwilliam Virginal Book and the Caius Choirbook. It was published to coincide with an exhibition held at the Fitzwilliam Museum, Cambridge, in 1982.

521. Fenlon, Iain. "Instrumental Music, Songs and Verse from Sixteenth-Century Winchester: British Library Additional MS 60577." In *Music in Medieval and Early Modern Europe: Patronage, Sources and Texts*, ed. by Iain Fenlon. Cambridge: Cambridge University Press, 1981, pp.93-116.

The manuscript was begun during the second half of the fifteenth century and continues until the 1560s. It contains many non-musical items, but its musical content bears witness to the growth of musical literacy over this period. It is particularly valuable for its keyboard pieces, including several unica and a version of *Hugh Aston's Ground.*

522. Fitzgibbon, H. Macauley. "The Lute Books of Ballet and Dallis." *Music & Letters* 11 (1930): 71-7.

Of some use for the list of references to the tunes in either collection which occur in contemporary English literature.

523. Ford, Wyn K. "An English Liturgical Partbook of the 17th Century." *Journal of the American Musicological Society* 12 (1959): 144-60.

Account of the Dunnington-Jefferson manuscript in York Minster Library, a bass partbook containing liturgical compositions of the period of Byrd and Gibbons. The author concludes that it originated at Durham Cathedral. There is a complete list of contents, with concordances excluding, for sheer volume, the partbooks at Durham. These are now listed in Brian Crosby's *A Catalogue of Durham Cathedral Music Manuscripts* (Oxford: Oxford University Press, 1986).

524. Fortune, Nigel *and* Fenlon, Iain. "Music Manuscripts of John Browne (1608-91) and from Stanford Hall, Leicestershire." In *Source Materials and the Interpretation of Music* (see *411*), pp.155-68.

Identifies a number of manuscripts that were owned and in part copied by Browne, Clerk of the Parliaments. The essay deals with the source materials and the music itself is discussed in *489*.

525. Fugler, Paul. "The Lambeth and Caius Choirbooks." *Journal of the Plainsong & Mediaeval Music Society* 6 (1983): 15-25.

Reassesses the likelihood of a common origin for these two early sixteenth-century choirbooks, both containing much music by Fayrfax and Ludford, amongst others. The author lists the contents of both books, and provides full bibliographical, palaeographical and historical analyses and comparison. Postdates *520*.

526. Fuller Maitland, J.A. "The Notation of the Fitzwilliam Virginal Book." *Proceedings of the Musical Association* 21 (1894-5): 103-14.

Describes provenance and physical appearance of the book itself, and gives a detailed account of the problems facing its editor in respect of time signatures, positioning of notes, accidentals, slurs and ornaments. This paper is important for its reflection of the problems faced by the book's first editor. See also *520*.

527. Gaskin, Hilary. "Baldwin's Commonplace Book: Problems of Space in a Sixteenth-Century Score-Book." *Soundings* 10 (1983): 18-22.

Comprehensive account of John Baldwin's copying practice, based on *GB-Lbl* Royal 24.d.2. See also *WB169* and *496*.

528. Gervers, Hilda F. "A Manuscript of Dance Music from Seventeenth-Century England: Drexel Collection MS 5612." *Bulletin of the New York Public Library* 80 (1976-7): 503-52.

Large collection (191 items) of keyboard music by Byrd, Gibbons and their contemporaries. Discusses the manuscript (physical properties, scribes, notation, repertory), instruments (including ornamentation and fingering), composers (nineteen names; many pieces remain unattributed) the history of the manuscript and the titles (dance tunes, ballad verses, descriptive titles, themes borrowed from contemporary composers and miscellaneous titles). There is a complete list of contents.

529. Gill, Donald. "The Sources of English Solo Bandora Music." *Lute Society Journal* 4 (1962): 23-7.

Summary of, and commentary upon, manuscripts and printed sources.

530. Greer, David. "Manuscript Additions in Early Printed Music." *Music & Letters* 72 (1991): 523-35.

Records results of a survey of nearly all the music printed in London 1571-1632 now in the Library of Congress and the Folger Shakespeare Library. As a result the author is able to list nine newly discovered identifiable pieces: one by Simon Ives, two by Michael East, one by Robert Parsons, three by John Hilton and two by Corkine (see *195*). He explains the problems of identifying the composers (Parsons is a much later one than the famous one who drowned in the Trent in 1572) and notes that even among the known pieces discovered amongst these manuscript addenda, some variants are of interest. He identifies over half the additions as being in the hand of Conyers D'arcy (1570-1653). The appendix lists the 22 items of printed music containing manuscript additions, which include thirteen hitherto unknown pieces amongst which are the nine attributed items mentioned above. This is work in progress and the author writes that he hopes to produce more articles on this and related topics.

531. Harper, John. "Orlando Gibbons: the Domestic Context of his Music and Christ Church MS21." *Musical Times* 124 (1983): 767-70.

   Several works by Gibbons published in *The First Set of Madrigals*, 1612, survive without underlay in slightly different versions in this manuscript, which also contains fantasies and fully texted verse anthems. From this it seems that Gibbons's ostensibly vocal works were conceived instrumentally, inspired by the genres of English song and fantasy. The author summarizes the contents of the manuscript, some of which are not by Gibbons, and suggests a provenance.

532. Harwood, Ian. "The Origins of the Cambridge Lute Manuscripts." *Lute Society Journal* 5 (1963): 32-48.

   Investigates the origins of the nine manuscripts in Cambridge University Library which relate to the lute: four partbooks for broken consort, one for solo cittern, the remaining four mainly for solo lute. The author describes the group as the most important single source of English music from the period around 1600. Previously it had been thought that the manuscripts were of an East Anglian provenance, but by identifying Matthew Holmes as the scribe of the manuscripts, the author is able to place their origins in Westminster and Oxford.

533. Irving, John. "Consort Playing in Mid-17th-Century Worcester: Thomas Tomkins and the Bodleian Partbooks Mus.Sch.E.415-18." *Early Music* 12 (1984): 337-44.

Investigates the claim that these partbooks were used by Tomkins and his friends for music-making in Worcester. After an initial brief description of the manuscripts the author discusses Tomkins's social milieu and concludes that there is circumstantial evidence to support the claim. He mentions concordances, describes the rehearsal marks on the parts, and the characteristics of some of the pieces, suggesting that some were composed for two violins on the uppermost parts rather than the customary viols, and that Tomkins himself played a keyboard continuo. There is a list of contents and a wealth of illustrations.

534. Irving, John A. "Matthew Hutton and York Minster MSS. M.3/1-4(S)." *Music Review* 44 (1983): 163-77.

Copious account of manuscript of 1667 important as a source of viol music by *Tomkins* and *Ward*.

535. Irving, John. "A Note on British Library Add. MSS 30826-8." *Consort* 43 (1987): 17-23.

Describes manuscript containing consort music by many composers not famous in that medium. Included is a transcription and reconstruction of a pavan by *Tomkins* unique to this source and hitherto unpublished, with a note of its first modern performance.

536. Irving, John A. "Oxford, Christ Church MSS 1018-1020: a Valuable Source of Tomkins's Consort Music." *Consort* 40 (1984): 1-12.

Detailed description of manuscript with incipits of twelve items by Tomkins. As all are anonymous, other texts are compared except in the case of no.6, a unicum. There are some remarks on the dating of certain pieces, and both the quality of the text and the importance of the manuscript are assessed.

537. Irving, John. "Two Consort Manuscripts from Oxford and Dublin: their Copying and a Possible Dating." *Consort* 42 (1986): 41-9.

Suggests that, *pace 499,* manuscripts *EIRE-Dm* Z 3.4.1 and 7 were copied by the same scribe who also copied part of *GB-Ob* Mus. Sch. C.64. up to thirty years earlier than Charteris proposes. Important from the Tudor perspective for palaeographical and bibliographical evidence employed by the author, with many references to the consort music of *Tomkins.* See also *500.*

538. Joiner, Mary. "British Museum Add MS. 15117: a Commentary, Index and Bibliography." *Research Chronicle* 7 (1969): 51-109.

A musical commonplace book, the latest work dateable 1616, the collection probably compiled during the last few years leading up to that date, but containing music as early as c.1560. Errata in 8 (1970): 102.

539. Kelly, Thomas F. "Notes on the Jane Pickering Lute Book, with Special Emphasis on the Music for Two Lutes." *Journal of the Lute Society of America* 1 (1968): 19-23.

Lists and provides commentary on the fifteen duets in this book followed by a more cursory glance at the rest of the contents. Though the manuscript is dated 1616, all the pieces in Jane Pickering's hand predate 1600. See also *356.*

540. Kerman, Joseph. "An Elizabethan Edition of Lassus." *Acta Musicologica* 27 (1955): 71-6.

Lists contents of *Recueil du mellange d'Orlande de Lassus* (London: Vautrouller [*sic*], 1570) and from them draws some conclusions about contemporary Elizabethan taste, textual and musical.

541. King, Alec Hyatt. "Fragments of Early Printed Music in the Bagford Collection." *Music & Letters* 40 (1959): 269-73; repr. in *Musical Pursuits* (see *478*), pp.38-42.

Reproduces trancription of what survives of the text of *Bull's* oration as Professor of Music, Gresham College, 1597. This is the one source that indicates he was a pupil of *Byrd*.

542. Kinkeldy, Otto. "Thomas Robinson's "Schoole of Musicke": a Lute Book of Shakespeare's Time." *Bulletin of the American Musicological Society* 1 (1936): 7.

Account of what little was then known of Robinson's life, followed by informative and detailed summary of the contents of his *Schoole*, 1603.

543. le Huray, Peter. "The Chirk Castle Partbooks." *Early Music History* 2 (1982): 17-42.

Introduction to, and description of, contents of important Welsh manuscript of Anglican church music. Includes annotated inventory and a note on evidence concerning the transposition of organ accompaniments. See *WB158* for a minor correction.

544. Lumsden, David. "The Sources of English Lute Music (1540-1620)." *Galpin Society Journal* 6 (1953): 14-22.

Describes all the known English sources of music for the solo lute, with some brief remarks on the types of music they contain. The author excludes English music in continental sources, all pieces not for solo lute and all sources devoted to transcriptions of vocal music. Notes on other sources include ghosts and items lost, untraced, ineligible or involved in a change of ownership. See also *366*.

545. Mark, Jeffrey. "The Orlando Gibbons Tercentenary: Some Virginal Manuscripts in the Music Division." *Bulletin of the New York Public Library* 29 (1925): 847-60.

Interesting for contemporary view of resurrection of

Gibbons's reputation, from a slightly sceptical perspective. Useful for its account of recent publishing activities, and for comprehensive descriptions of appearances and contents of Drexel manuscripts 5611 and 5612. One particularly considerate illustration juxtaposes the first twelve bars of *Peascod Time* in the original source and in a modern edition.

546. Mateer, David G. "John Sadler and Oxford, Bodleian MSS Mus. e. 1-5." *Music & Letters* 60 (1979): 281-95.

Provides a brief biography of Sadler (1513-91) about whom little is known, and describes his manuscript in detail: first bibliographical and then in respect of its contents. The author suggests the manuscript was compiled c.1565-85. He notes its Roman Catholic bias - nearly all the 43 compositions are in Latin, by musicians from Fayrfax to Morley with known or suspected Catholic sympathies - and he draws attention to Sadler's illustrations, which lend themselves to political interpretations favourable to Catholicism though of scrupulous loyalty to the queen. This is one of the most important of Tudor manuscripts.

547. Mateer, David. "Oxford, Christ Church Music Mss 984-8: an Index and Commentary." *Research Chronicle* 20 (1986-7): 1-18.

Includes biography of Robert Dow, the original owner. The manuscript, compiled 1581-8 by Dow himself but with contributions by *Baldwin* (see *WB169*, p.160), is an important source of the sacred and secular vocal music for the generation up to and including Byrd. Some foreign composers are also present.

548. Meer, John Henry. "The Keyboard Works in the Vienna Bull Manuscript." *Tijdschrift voor Muziekwetenschap* 18 (1957): 72-105.

Comprehensive study of *A-Wn* 17.771. The author suggests a provenance and devotes several pages to a description of the notation. Having observed that all the eleven pieces for keyboard are ascribed to Bull (wrongly in the case of a fantasia by Sweelinck) he lists and then discusses all the ten authentic items, referring to concordances, published editions, provenances of individual pieces and historical perspective. He proceeds to comment on the figuration, modality, tonality and harmony of the Vienna pieces and considers the instrument for which they were composed, concluding with a few observations about continental influence on English composers and the reverse.

549. Monson, Craig. *Voices and Viols in England, 1600-1650: the Sources and the Music.* Studies in Musicology, 55. Ann Arbor: UMI Research Press, 1982. 360pp. 0835713024. ML286.2.M65.

Traces the history of what the author calls the verse idiom, the English musical style combining voices and viols in those forms that have come to be known as the consort anthem and the consort song. He adheres to secular manuscript sources, even though these contain sacred as well as consort pieces, nevertheless revealing much about musical tastes and the processes of compilation within a certain social stratum during this period. He surveys the sources geographically - London, Eastern Counties, West Country and Oxford - but also devotes separate chapters to *GB-Lbl* Add. 37402-6 and *GB-Ob* Tenbury 1162-7. There are inventories of the sources scrutinized, and indexes for titles of vocal works and for manuscripts cited.

550. Morehen, John. "A Fragmentary Bass Manuscript in St. John's College Library, Oxford." *Music & Letters* 53 (1972): 56-8.

Classified as Box 235, this manuscript of c.1600 contains fragments of four works. One is Byrd's *Prevent Us O Lord* but despite a scrutiny of concordances of this piece, and of known sources containing the texts of other fragmentary works, none of the other three can be identified. Since the fragment was discovered too late for inclusion in *59* the author provides incipits for the unidentified fragments.

551. Morehen, John. "The Gloucester Cathedral Bassus Part-Book MS

93." *Music & Letters* 62 (1981): 189-96.

Important manuscript containing music by composers from Tallis to Batten, including several otherwise obscure local composers. The author establishes that Tomkins was in Gloucester around the time the manuscript was being compiled, 1640-1, and may have provided texts of two works omitted subsequently from *Musica Deo sacra*, 1668. The compiler of the partbook was almost certainly the Gloucester Cathedral organist, John Okeover, and the repertory suggests that his choir was of above average standard. The author tabulates the contents, and provides incipits for the two anonymous unica.

552. Morehen, John. "The Southwell Minster Tenor Partbook in the Library of St. Michael's College, Tenbury (MS. 1382)." *Music & Letters* 50 (1969): 352-64.

Provides complete list of the contents of this manuscript of 1617 containing 86 items. It is claimed to be the earliest datable source of English liturgical music. The author analyses it bibliographically and goes to great lengths to try to establish the identity of its scribe and its provenance beyond the wording of the dedication. He also ponders the whereabouts of the other seven partbooks in the set. The article closes with incipits of the anonymous works. According to the author this is a source of liturgical music rather than a liturgical source of music. It is now cited as *GB-Ob* Tenbury 1382.

553. Noden-Skinner, Cheryl. "A Tudor Chansonnier: British Library Royal Appendix MSS 41-44." *Current Musicology* 36 (1984): 101-12.

Palaeographical study, with list of contents, of a modest volume which nevertheless sheds a little further light on the presence of continental (in this instance French) songs in Tudor England.

554. Nordstrom, Lyle. "The Cambridge Consort Books." *Journal of the Lute Society of America* 5 (1972): 70-103.

Introduction to, and inventory of, *GB-Cu* Dd. 3.18, 5.20, 5.21 and 14.24, four remaining partbooks of a set of six containing music for broken consort. The author's purpose is to clarify the confusion that existed concerning the contents of the books, their relationship to one another, and their relationship to other manuscripts and printed sources.

555. Oboussier, Philippe. "Turpyn's Book of Lute-Songs." *Music & Letters* 34 (1953): 145-9.

Commentary on contents of manuscript, four of whose songs are unica, and two more of which are known only in other versions.

556. Payne, Ian. "British Library Add. MSS 30826-28: a Set of Part-Books from Trinity College, Cambridge?" *Chelys* 17 (1988): 3-15.

Gives reasons for his suggestion that Trinity College may feature in the provenance of this set. Only three of the original five partbooks survive, and they contain dances for viols. The author is able to provide East Anglian backgrounds for most of the composers, two of whom were organists at the college. Two others may have had connexions with the college, the name of which appears in an anonymous piece. Finally he suggests the identity of the copyist, a college layclerk. The article is excellently illustrated. The author has reconstructed the music for publication.

557. Price, Curtis A. "An Organizational Peculiarity of Lord Herbert of Cherbury's Lute-Book." *Lute Society Journal* 11 (1969): 5-27.

Demonstrates that Herbert's book is organized in seven large sections by key not, *pace 509*, in the order in which Herbert collected the pieces. A list of contents is appended, giving folio, key, hand (I or II) and title in manuscript.

558. Rubsamen, Walter H. "Scottish and English Music in a Newly-Discovered Manuscript." In *Festschrift Heinrich Besseler zum Sechzigsten Gerburtstag,* ed. by Institut für

Musikwissenschaft der Karl-Marx-Universität. Leipzig: VEB, 1961, pp.259-84.

Discusses provenance and contents of Raitt MS, with special emphasis on where it supplements the first edition of *Music of Scotland 1500-1700*, volume XV of *Musica Britannica*.

559. Sandon, Nick. "The Henrician Partbooks at Peterhouse, Cambridge." *Proceedings of the Royal Musical Association* 103 (1976-7): 106-40.

Account of incomplete set of sacred partbooks belonging to Peterhouse now housed in Cambridge University Library as Peterhouse manuscripts 471-4. The tenor of the set is missing. The author provides a description of the books and an analysis of their contents, concentrating on individual items and their significance. There are four appendices: on watermarks, evidence for layers in the manuscripts, an inventory, and biographical information about the composers.

560. Schofield, Bertram *and* Dart, Thurston. "Tregian's Anthology." *Music & Letters* 32 (1951): 205-16.

Summary of contents of *GB-Lbl* Egerton 3665, over a thousand villanelle, madrigals and instrumental pieces in three, four or five parts mainly by English and Italian composers of the sixteenth and early seventeenth centuries. The authors provide incipits of "new instrumental pieces" but the promised "fuller investigation" was never published.

561. Spencer, Robert. "Three English Lute Manuscripts." *Early Music* 3 (1975): 119-24.

Illustrated and copious notes on the Mynshall, Sampson and Board manuscripts, all of which contain Elizabethan music. See also *366*.

562. Spencer, Robert. "The Tollemache Lute Manuscript." *Lute Society Journal* 7 (1965): 38-9.

List of contents, including brief comments, with short introduction describing provenance.

563. Spencer, Robert. "The Weld Lute Manuscript." *Lute Society Journal* 1 (1959): 48-57.

Lists contents of manuscript probably from the last years of Elizabeth I's reign. The author describes the search for the manuscript itself, of which he provides a full physical description, and discusses its provenance.

564. Spring, Matthew. "The Lady Margaret Wemyss Manuscript." *Lute* 27 (1987): 5-29.

Comprehensive account of minor but substantial Scottish lute manuscript of mid-1640s, which includes seventeen songs by Morley and Campion in a version for solo voice and bass instrument (probably viol). The author provides a physical description of the manuscript and discusses in detail its provenance, contents and lute music. The article is well illustrated and closes with an inventory which includes concordances of the music for lute. See also *179.*

565. Stevens, Denis. "The Manuscript Edinburgh, National Library of Scotland, Adv. Ms. 5.1.15." *Musica Disciplina* 13 (1959): 155-67.

Survey, with inventory, of contents of the *Carver* Choirbook, also known as the Scone Antiphonary. The author writes from a doggedly English perspective, seemingly forgetting he was dealing with a Scottish manuscript.

566. Stevens, Denis. *The Mulliner Book: a Commentary.* London: Stainer & Bell, 1952. 77pp. ML93.M9.

After a copious introduction, suggesting the sort of keyboard instrument for which the contents of the book were composed and summarizing the contents of five contemporary manuscripts, the author comments on the pieces themselves in chapters devoted to music based on liturgical cantus firmi, and to arrangements of sacred and secular vocal music. He sets pieces in their domestic and continental context, mindful of contemporary developments in musical taste, preference and expediency. The two appendices list plainsongs on which Mulliner pieces are based and provide eleven transcriptions of pieces for cittern and gittern which are in tablature in the manuscript.

567. Stevens, John E. "Rounds and Canons from an Early Tudor Songbook." *Music & Letters* 32 (1951): 29-37.

Refers to what is now cited as *GB-Lbl* Add. 31922, which contains twelve rounds, six puzzle-canons and three canons from the reign of Henry VIII. All nine canons are discussed in turn, and a list of rounds is appended.

568. Vlasto, Jill. "An Elizabethan Anthology of Rounds." *Musical Quarterly* 40 (1954): 222-34.

Description of *GB-CKc* KC 1 of 1580. The contents are fully listed with commentary, including concordances from the subsequent publications of Ravenscroft.

569. Ward, John M. "The Fourth Dublin Lute Book." *Lute Society Journal* 11 (1969): 28-46.

This is what the author calls the Marsh Lute Book, one of the largest and best sources for early Elizabethan lute music. After a comprehensive bibliographical introduction, he provides an inventory giving paginations and numberings of each item, titles and comments which include not only information about composers, but also an indication of whether the piece in question is a unicum and whether there are concordances and/or cognates. There is an index to the inventory. This is the third article by the author on Trinity College's lutebooks: see *570.*

570. Ward, John. "The Lute Books of Trinity College, Dublin." *Lute Society Journal* (1967): 17-40; 10 (1968): 15-32.

Inventories of three manuscripts, the Dallis and the two Ballet lutebooks, the latter listed consecutively, make up these two articles. The first article begins with a general introduction, and there are further introductions in both articles specific to the respective lutebooks. The inventories contain pagination and numeration, hand (first Ballet only), titles and comments on such matters as authorship, concordances and presence in other catalogues. "Additions to the Inventory of TCD MS. D.3.30/I" in the same journal, 12 (1970): 43-4, refers to the Dallis lutebook. See also *569*.

571. Ward, John. "The Lute Music of MS Royal Appendix 58". *Journal of the American Musicological Society* 13 (1960): 117-25.

Transcribes the contents of this (now) British Library (*GB-Lbl*) manuscript into staff notation. The author provides an informative commentary on the eight lute pieces and fragment of instruction which form part of the manuscript, probably copied 1551. He summarizes, and gives published sources for, the remaining contents. Much emphasis in the commentary is given to concordances. The article is well illustrated.

572. Ward, John M. "The So-Called 'Dowland Lute Book' in the Folger Shakespeare Library." *Journal of the Lute Society of America* 9 (1976): 5-29.

Suggests that although manuscript V.b.280 is probably in Dowland's handwriting it was never, contrary to recent tradition, owned by him. The author concludes that it was the notebook either of a teacher or of a student of the lute. There are several illustrations and an inventory.

573. Warren, Charles W. "The Music of Royal Appendix 12-16." *Music & Letters* 51 (1970): 357-72.

Description of a British Library manuscript originally from the Nonsuch Library, wherein the music consists of a complete cycle of Lamentations and Benedictus antiphons for the Office of Tenebrae. With copious illustrations the author analyses the anonymous polyphonic music, and concludes with some suggestions about authorship: *Byrd* (for whom he offers some resemblances), *Philips* or *Dering,* whose Christian name appears on one partbook.

574. Willetts, Pamela J. "Silvanus Stirrop's Book." *Research Chronicle* 10 (1972): 101-7.

Pieces for lyra viol and songs, compiled during 1620s containing music by Giles, Ford, Robert Johnson and Hume. Inventory, with addendum in 12 (1974): 156.

575. Wrightson, James. *The "Wanley" Manuscripts: a Critical Commentary.* Outstanding Dissertations in Music from British Universities. New York: Garland, 1989. 323pp. 0824023374. ML3166.W74

Concerns *GB-Ob* Mus. Sch. e. 420-2, three partbooks of an original set of four from the reign of Edward VI. The Wanley manuscripts are the largest surviving collection of Anglican music from this period, and of ninety pieces, nearly 75% are unica. The tenor partbook is missing but the author reconstructs relevant passages, when required, for illustration. (The original thesis was in two volumes. The second was a transcription of the Wanley music with the missing tenor part editorially reconstructed. The material from this volume has been published separately by A-R Editions of Madison.) In an exhaustive study, he examines the circumstances of the compilation of the manuscripts and discusses their content both musical and verbal. Where there is firm information he imparts it, but does not try to force conclusions onto contentious matters such as the attributions of the many anonymous pieces. The manuscripts are a major source of music composed for the newly created Church of England, and he provides a penetrating insight into this aspect of musical life in the middle of the Tudor period. The original thesis dates from 1984 and he provides a new introduction which also updates the bibliography.

See also 23, 32, 59, 80, 81, 82, 93, 94, 151, 162, 178, 201, 219, 229, 231, 240, 242, 243, 244, 245, 246, 250, 256, 261, 270, 280, 303, 308, 313, 314, 319, 356, 366, 384, 390, 415,

442, 462, 465, 590, 610, 612, 669, WB145, WB146, WB169, WB171. Also section A-VII.

XI TUDOR MUSIC SINCE THE SEVENTEENTH CENTURY

This chapter contains items that deal with the survival of Tudor music, in performance (both live and recorded) and study, since the death of Tomkins, its longest lived practitioner, and with the opinion in which it has been held down the years. Purcell copied out much Renaissance music, including anthems by Tallis, Byrd, Giles, Gibbons and Batten. Signs of Renaissance influence in his music have been investigated in some articles by F.B. Zimmerman, and these are listed with abstracts in his Composer Resource Manual (volume 18) *Henry Purcell: a Guide to Research* (New York: Garland, 1989) on pages 309 (item three), 312 (item three) and 315 (item one). Included in the present volume are biographies of those active in the revival of interest in Tudor music. One little known source of information about the revival of Tudor music in the twentieth century is the Carnegie United Kingdom Trust's papers, deposited in the Scottish Record Office, Edinburgh. They contain references to the famous series Tudor Church Music (London: Oxford University Press, 1922-9, 10v.; see *670*) which the Trust sponsored.

576. Anderton, H. Orsmond. "Thomas Tallys." *Musical Opinion* 37 (1914): 282-3.

Virtually worthless except for its account of the six performances of *Spem in alium* known to have taken place during the nineteenth century.

577. Andrews, Hilda. *Westminster Retrospect: a Memoir of Sir Richard Terry.* London: Oxford University Press, 1948. 186pp. ML423.T27A5.

Biography of one of the most important figures in the Tudor revival. As a Roman Catholic convert he enthusiastically introduced Latin music by English Renaissance composers while he was organist at Downside Abbey (1896-1901) and

Westminster Cathedral (1901-24), while the book's appendix reveals the prodigious extent of his editing activities, not all of them devoted to the choral repertory. See also *607*.

578. Blezzard, Judith. "Tallis Fantasia: a Renaissance Tune Reborn." *Overture* (Deutsche-Englishe Musikgesellschaft) 1 (1987): [4-9].

Analysis of Vaughan Williams's *Fantasia on a Theme by Thomas Tallis*. Gives weight to the significance of Tallis's tune not only in its own time but also in the broader ramifications of Vaughan Williams's response to it in respect of his own musical development and awareness, and that of English music as a whole. See also *123*.

579. Boorman, Peter. *A Souvenir Brochure Issued to Mark the Tercentenary of the Death of Thomas Tomkins with Details of the Commemorative Festival Held in the Cathedral from August 13th to 17th.* St Davids: St Davids Cathedral, 1956. [55pp.]

Contains three main articles: "The Thomas Tomkins Tercentenary Festival," essentially a biographical summary by Boorman, "An Assessment of the Work of Thomas Tomkins," by David Harries; and "The English Viols," by Harry Danks. Also of interest are "The Festival Programme" and "The Tomkins Memorial Organ Case," the latter illustrated.

580. Bumpus, John S. *A History of English Cathedral Music 1549-1889.* 2v. London: Laurie, 1908; repr. ed. in 1v., Farnborough: Gregg, 1972. 580pp. O576282448. ML3131.B86.

As Watkins Shaw states in his introduction to the reprint, these volumes were pioneer work when they first appeared. Only the first three chapters impinge directly on the Tudors, but there are subsequent references to the survival of Tudor music in the Anglican Church, such as in the activities of Ouseley. Indeed this is a uniquely Victorian view of its survival during previous centuries. As a source of information about Tudor music it has been superseded by *71, 91, 95, 117, 141* and parts of *22*, but it remains an important document in the Tudor revival for what it tells us of contemporary attitudes to Tudor music and to its survival.

581. Campbell, Margaret. *Dolmetsch: the Man and his Work.* London: Hamilton; Seattle: University of Washington Press, 1975. 02418911760. 02954167. ML424.B65C3.

Comprehensive though eulogistic biography of a leading light in the revival of early, including Tudor, music in Britain. A chapter is devoted to "Discovering the Elizabethans."

582. Crosby, Brian. "A Service Sheet from June 1680." *Musical Times* 121 (1980): 399-401.

Transcribes, and explains provenance of, a manuscript sheet listing the music sung at Mattins and Evensong daily during June 1680 in Durham Cathedral, giving both setting and anthem. Many Tudor works are included. The author lists those works still in the Durham repertory three hundred years on, noting that Mattins had been sung only on Sundays since 1970, and states that the current choir planned to sing music from the repertory of its ancestor during a week in June, 1980.

583. Cummings, W.H. "Organ Accompaniments in England in the Sixteenth and Seventeenth Centuries." *Proceedings of the Musical Association* 26 (1899-1900): 193-211.

Taken up with a violent argument between the author and Henry Davey (who was capable of being wrong about musical history: see *WB153*, p.141). Davey maintained that the Puritans destroyed cathedral organs because of the floridity of contemporary organ accompaniments to Divine Service. Cummings maintained that the examples of such floridity chosen by Davey were arrangements of the pieces in question never intended as accompaniments to be played with voices. Davey was present at the lecture and the account of the "discussion" afterwards is most lively. More prosaically it reflects contemporary knowledge and preoccupations about Tudor music. Much critical water has since flowed under the bridge: see, *inter alia, 91.*

584. Day, Thomas. "A Renaissance Revival in Eighteenth-Century England." *Musical Quarterly* 57 (1971): 575-92.

Describes, and attempts to account for, an apparent revival of interest in Renaissance music in England during the eighteenth century. The author quotes from several contemporary writers and refers to publications, the founding of societies for enthusiasts, and the contents of contemporary manuscripts. Although Tallis and Byrd benefitted most from this revival, interest was not confined to English music. The movement preceded, but did not seem to influence, revivals of early music on the continent during the following century.

585. Fellowes, Edmund H. *Memoirs of an Amateur Musician.* London: Menthuen, 1946. 220pp.

From the standpoint of Tudor music, this autobiography of its most voracious editor is disappointing. Only chapter XI, on musicology and research and, to a lesser extent, the following one on lecturing, give insights into any of the author's many and prodigious activities. Understatement rather than modesty is to blame: for instance, despite a reasonably informative if breezy description of the rediscovery of Byrd's *Great Service*, he omits the date, even the year, when this occurred. (It is to be found in *WB41.* Ironically the date was misprinted in *WB163* but was corrected in a subsequent letter and appears accurately in *WB183.*) Nevertheless in the context of the Tudor revival it provides a brisk insight into the motivation of one of its prime movers.

586. Foster, Myles Birket. *Anthems and Anthem Composers: an Essay upon the Development of the Anthem, from the Time of the Reformation to the End of the Nineteenth Century.* London: Novello, 1901; repr. ed. Da Capo Press Music Reprint Series. New York: Da Capo, 1970. 0306700123. ML3260.F75.

Primarily of interest in respect of indicating the state of the Tudor revival by 1900. The author lists chronologically all composers he knows to have composed anthems and under these separate personal headings lists their surviving anthems with sources. Chapters III-VII (of 25) relate to the Tudors. The lists are often inaccurate, the sources more so. Nevertheless they throw up some titles otherwise unknown. Most if not all are likely to be errors but the matter is discussed in *WB161*.

587.   Giles, Peter. *The Counter Tenor*. London: Muller, 1982. 058410474X. ML1400.

Chapter 8,"The Post-War Renaissance," contains interesting background to the revival of early, and specifically Tudor, music from the standpoint of the rediscovery of the countertenor as a solo voice.

588.   Hardwick, Michael *and* Hardwick, Mollie. *Alfred Deller: a Singularity of Voice*. London: Proteus, 1980. 197pp. 09060701631. ML420.D44H4.

Biography of a crucial figure in the revival of early, including much Tudor, music who singlehandedly re-established the countertenor voice.

589.   Haskell, Harry. *The Early Music Revival: a History*. London: Thames & Hudson, 1988. 232pp. 0500014493. ML457.H35.

General introduction to the revival, encompassing the rehabilitation of original instruments and the rise of the authenticity movement. Chapters 2 and 6-8 have specific British content, but Tudor composers crop up throughout the book, the value of which is that it provides an international context for the revival of interest in Tudor music.

590.   Hogwood, Christopher. "Thomas Tudway's History of Music." In *Music in Eighteenth-Century England: Essays in Memory of Charles Cudworth*, ed. by Christopher Hogwood and Richard Luckett. Cambridge: Cambridge University Press, 1983, pp.19-47.

Consisting mainly of prolonged quotation from *GB-Lbl* Harl. 7337-42, provides an early example of a reverential attitude, mid-eighteenth century, to Tallis and Byrd in particular. See also *612*.

591. Holst, Gustav. "My Favorite Tudor Composer." *Midland Musician* 1 (1926): 4-5.

> *Weelkes.* Enthusiastic, but of only mild interest, because of Holst's own planetary stature. Much cited but probably little read; worth the effort, once.

592. Howes, Frank. *The English Musical Renaissance.* London: Secker & Warburg; New York: Stein and Day, 1966. ML289.H69.

> Contains a significant chapter on the Tudor revival, indicating the part played by English Renaissance music during the English Musical Renaissance of the late nineteenth and early twentieth centuries. It is rewarding to read the previous chapter on the folk music revival which refers to the impact of folk tunes recycled through Tudor music, in such pieces as keyboard variations. The author's only serious misjudgment is to dismiss the possibility of a revival of the viol.

593. Hughes, Anselm. *Septuagesima: Reminiscences of the Plainsong & Mediaeval Music Society, and of Other Things, Personal and Musical.* London: Plainsong & Mediaeval Music Society, 1959. 77pp.

> Interesting account of an aspect of the Tudor revival, of whose ethos the Society formed part. Founded in 1888, it began publishing in 1890 and the author joined in 1910. Only the earliest Tudor music, notably the then anonymous mass *O quam suavis* of c.1500 (now attributed to *John Lloyd*) comes into the Society's orbit, but the author is a good narrator and mentions many luminaries of the Tudor revival, along with their activities.

594. Johnstone, H. Diack. "The Genesis of Boyce's 'Cathedral Music'."
     Music & Letters 56 (1975): 26-40.

   Details the events leading up to the publication of *Cathedral Music* (1760-73). The original idea was Maurice Greene's, Boyce's teacher, who bequeathed all his manuscripts to his pupil. The author quotes from contemporary advertisements, and he lists the contents of both surviving manuscripts likely to have been prepared by Greene for this project before his death in 1755. Of interest is the paucity of Tudor material in what should be an hospitable environment.

595. King, Alec Hyatt. "William Barclay Squire, 1855-1927: Music Librarian." *Library*, 5th ser., 12 (1957): 1-10; repr. in *Musical Pursuits* (see *478*), pp.187-99.

   Full account of life and work of one of the pillars of the Tudor revival, especially as an editor.

596. Lovell, Percy. "'Ancient' Music in Eighteenth-Century England." *Music & Letters* 60 (1979): 401-15.

   Summary of the various manifestations of interest in Renaissance music in England c.1714-60, including criticism, preservation, transmission and performance. The roles of various historians and antiquarians are discussed, including Tudway, Travers, Pepusch, Hawkins, Boyce and Immyns. Continental composers were much admired, and among the English, most attention is paid to Tallis and Byrd.

597. Marshall, Arthur W. "Viols in the Late 18th and 19th Centuries." *Viola da Gamba Society of Great Britain Newsletter* 73 (1991): 9-13.

   Proceedings of a conference, 2 March 1991, in London. There were four papers: "Viols in Victorian England," by John Catch; "Dolmetsch and the Arts and Crafts Movement," by Elizabeth Liddle; "Reminiscences of Arnold Dolmetsch," by Cecile Dolmetsch; and "Makers of Viols," by Michael Fleming. Marshall reports a wealth of material on an unpromising topic.

Though playing the viol was supposed to have ceased in England with the death of Abel, its "last" virtuoso, in 1787, Catch and Fleming were able to prove that there continued to be not only players but manufacturers. The two speakers on the Dolmetsch phenomenon placed it in different but complementary contexts, Miss Liddle in relation to contemporary culture, and Miss Dolmetsch in relation to his individual achievement, specifying when he gave his first recital using a consort of viols in 1891.

598. Marshall, John. "When Music was Musyck." *Scotsman Magazine* 6 (1985): 22-3.

Brief but informative introduction to *Carver's* music, with an account of the revival in performances of his music in the years leading up to his quincentenary.

599. Mee, J.H. "Points of Interest Connected with the English School of the Sixteenth Century." *Proceedings of the Musical Association* 14 (1887-8): 145-72.

Completely superseded factually, but interesting for an early airing of the problem of performing pitch, in this instance concerning *Tallis's* Te Deum.

600. Miller, H.W. *Notes on Old English Music: Being the Substance of a Lecture Delivered Before Members of the Richmond Parochial Library, November 17, 1874.* London: Cramer, 1874. 58pp. ML285.2.M45.

Apparently unknown introduction, interesting nowadays for its place in the literature of the Tudor revival and for its provenance.

601. Northcott, Bayan. "The Forms of Fantasy." *Independent* (10 February 1990): 33.

Good summary of the development and influence of the English consort school via Purcell to the twentieth century, concentrating on the fantasy and the In nomine.

602. Ochs, Michael. "E.H. Fellowes in Pursuit of Morley's 'Aires'."
     Notes 45 (1989): 878-86.

     Transcriptions, some complete, others partial, of 33 letters
     from Fellowes to the New York music critic Richard Aldrich
     documenting, with commentary, Fellowes's efforts to gain
     access to the unique print of Morley's *The First Booke of Ayres*,
     1600, in a private American collection. The letters date from
     1916-32 and are now in the Eda Kuhn Loeb Music Library,
     Harvard University. The print, found to be defective when it
     finally materialized, formed the basis of Fellowes's edition of
     1932.

603. Powell, Michael. *Alfred Deller: a Recorded Legacy 1949-1979*.
     York: Alfred Deller Memorial Trust, 1981. 50pp.

     Discography of important figure in the Tudor revival (see
     588). Lists only by recording, chronologically. There are no
     indexes, but the author provides full analyses of contents.
     Recordings by the Deller Consort are included as are reissues.

604. Roche, Elizabeth. "Early Music and the BBC." *Musical Times* 120
     (1979): 821-3, 912-4.

     Charts the amount of time devoted by the British
     Broadcasting Corporation's radio networks to music composed
     before 1640. The former article is subtitled "World War II to
     1957," the latter "1957 to Date." Although this item deals with all
     early music, there are plenty of references to Tudor composers,
     and it is instructive to compare their coverage with that of their
     continental contemporaries. Unlike the composers and music
     mentioned in *605,* those in the present survey are prominent
     less for commercial reasons than for what the BBC perceived to
     be educational purposes.

605. Roche, Elizabeth. "Early Music on Records in the Last 25 Years."
     Musical Times 120 (1979): 34-36, 215-17.

     Discographical study of early music, copiously tabulated, and with many references to Tudor composers. The study includes composers up to and including those born before 1590 and/or who died before 1650. The opportunity to compare coverage of Tudor composers with that of their continental contemporaries is interesting, not least in revealing the perceived commercial popularity of certain composers and works.

606. Roche, Elizabeth. "The Elizabethan Competitive Festival 1923-6." *Early Music* 11 (1983): 519-22.

Celebrates the sixtieth anniversary of an attempt to establish an annual competitive festival based entirely on Elizabethan music. Called the Elizabethan Music Festival, it ran for four years at the Kingsway Hall, London. Insufficient finance and, latterly, support, along with contemporary social factors, saw to its demise, but the author commends it as an heroic failure.

607. Roche, Elizabeth. "'Great Learning, Fine Scholarship, Impeccable Taste': a Fiftieth Anniversary Tribute to Sir Richard Terry (1865-1938)." *Early Music* 16 (1988): 231-6.

Detailed account of Terry's place in the resurrection of Tudor church music through his work as choirmaster at Downside Abbey and Westminster Cathedral. Contains copious quotations from Downside magazines and other contemporary journals and newspapers. It is particularly valuable for details of recitals and service lists. The author provides a judicious summary of his career, personality, achievements, influence and legacy. For a longer and more subjective contemporary memoir, see *577*.

608. Sandford, Gordon. "Percy Grainger and the Viol Consort." *Consort* 43 (1987): 35-7.

A sidelight on the Tudor revival, interesting for reference to some apparently unpublished editions by Grainger of English consort pieces.

609. Shaw, H. Watkins. "Extracts from Anthony Wood's 'Notes on the Lives of Musicians,' Hitherto Unpublished." *Music & Letters* 15 (1934): 157-62.

Transcribes extracts from Wood's famous notes of c.1695. Of a dozen selected composers, all are from the early Baroque period except *Taverner*. Shaw adds a commentary to make good Wood's errors and omissions. For Wood's notes on Byrd and for further information about Wood's manuscript as a whole, see *WB154*.

610. Terry, Charles Sanford. "John Forbes's "Songs and Fancies"." *Musical Quarterly* 22 (1936): 402-19.

Comprehensive account of the first secular music to be published in Scotland (Aberdeen, 1662), of interest for the amount of material from the works of the Elizabethan madrigalists. Includes bibliographical description of all three seventeenth-century editions, list of contents, concordances and commentary. Only the cantus part was published, or has survived.

611. Van der Merwe, Peter. *Origins of the Popular Style: the Antecedents of Twentieth-Century Popular Music.* Oxford: Clarendon, 1989. 0193161214. ML6120.

Finds some antecedents in Tudor music, using two keyboard pieces by *Byrd* as particular examples: *John Come Kiss Me Now* for "the blue seventh" and *The Woods So Wild* for its double tonic which he relates to the chants of football supporters centuries later.

612. Weber, William. "Thomas Tudway and the Harleian Collection of 'Ancient' Church Music." *British Library Journal* 15 (1989): 187-205.

Describes the origins of *GB-Lbl* Harl. 7337-42. As well as imparting new information and a political insight unusual in musicological writings, the author explains the reasons for the survival of Tudor church music during the early Hanoverian period, the musical climate of which is regarded as inimical to the preservation of such music. See also *590*.

*See also 95, 123, 132, 142, 230, 364, 428, 526, 545, WB144,
WB152, WB154, WB162, WB164, WB182, WB184, WB186. Also
section A-VII.*

XII INDIVIDUAL COMPOSERS

This chapter contains biographical studies of composers and surveys
of their work too broad to be accommodated in preceding chapters.
For Byrd, see Appendix.

613. Greening, Anthony J. "Amner Reconsidered." *Musical Times* 110
(1969): 1131-3.

Introduction to life and work of John Amner, putting the case
for his ability as a composer and advocating wider performance
of his music. The author lists the contents of his *Sacred
Hymns,* 1615, and goes on to discuss the more distinguished
items from it and from among his unpublished works. He
concludes with a source-list of Amner's music not in *Sacred
Hymns.*

614. Batchelor Anne. "Daniel Batcheler: the Right Perfect Musician."
Lute 28 (1988): 3-12.

The best biographical account of an elusive individual, one of
the most important lutenist-composers of his day. The author is
a descendant.

615. Brennecke, Ernest. "A Singing Man of Windsor." *Music & Letters*
33 (1952): 33-40.

Account of life, works (listed) and surviving manuscripts of
John Baldwin. Confirms him as composer of *Coridon and
Phyllida*, sung for the queen at Elvetham in 1591. See also *165*.

616. Bridge, Joseph C. "The Organists of Chester Cathedral. Part I.
1541 to 1644. *Journal of the Chester and North Wales
Architectural Society* 19 (1913): 63-90.

Thomas Bateson... pages 73-7. Still the most substantial biography, with details concerning payments while Organist of Chester Cathedral and his marriage in Dublin, plus substantial excerpts from his will.

617. Clark, J. Bunker *and* Bevan, Maurice. "New Biographical Facts about Adrian Batten." *Journal of the American Musicological Society* 23 (1970): 331-3.

Announces discovery of details of date and place of birth, and of Batten's musical career as chorister, layclerk and organist.

618. Ford, Robert. "Bevins, Father and Son." *Music Review* 43 (1982): 104-8.

Brief biographies of Elway and his son Edward with whom he was hitherto confused. Provides lists differentiating the compositions of the two and disposing of some false ascriptions. This article updates information in *619*.

619. Hooper, Joseph Graham. *The Life and Works of Elway Bevin.* Bristol: Hooper, 1971.

Indispensable as the only monographic introduction to Bevin and his music, though the biographical information is updated in *618*. All of Bevin's works are listed and are discussed individually. These discussions are sound in dealing with provenances and sources, but weak - descriptive and superficial - in what passes for analysis. Similarly the treatment of Bevin's surviving prose work, *A Briefe and Short Instruction of the Art of Musicke,* 1631, is satisfactory as introduction but unsuccessful in trying to summarize the contents, resorting to a succession of quotations. So prolific are the illustrations that they obscure the basic layout of the book, but they are of great interest, and are well reproduced.

620. Stevens, Denis. "William Blitheman: a Note." *Musical Times* 104 (1963): 37.

Brief introduction to the life and work of Blitheman, whose Christian name is now known to have been John.

621. Cameron, Francis. "John Bull: A Retrospect: Homage to Thurston Dart." *Studies in Music* 5 (1971): 43-53.

Biographical, primarily important for account of Bull family preceding John and for hitherto unpublished English translations of Hereford Chapter Acts relating to Bull.

622. Chappell, Paul. *A Portrait of John Bull, c.1563-1628.* Hereford: Hereford Cathedral, 1970. 25pp. ML410.B93C5.

Good short introduction to Bull's life, with cogent references to the music where appropriate.

623. Dart, Thurston. "John Bull, 1563-1628." *Musical Times* 104 (1963): 252-3.

Anecdotal and mainly biographical introduction to Bull, some of which has been superseded by more recent research. Mentions the site of Bull's grave.

624. Dart, Thurston. "A Letter of Recommendation Written for John Bull in 1617." *Revue belge de musicologie* 17 (1963): 121-4.

Letter (in Dutch, without translation) from the Wardens of the Guild of Our Lady to the Treasurer of Antwerp Cathedral in support of Bull's appointment as Organist. Dart provides much relevant biographical and historical detail, including a commentary on the letter. See also *445* and *625*.

625. Dart, Thurston. "An Unknown Letter from Dr John Bull." *Acta musicologica* 32 (1960): 175-7.

Text of letter in original Flemish, with English translation, from Bull to the mayor and aldermen of Antwerp, giving his version of why he fled England for Flanders. This is in support of his application for employment in Antwerp, and is a response to accusations quoted in *445*. See also *624*.

626. Lindley, David. *Thomas Campion.* Medieval and Renaissance Authors, 7. Leiden: Brill, 1986. 242pp. 9004076018. ML410.C3.

Consists of four chapters, on the poetry, the music, poetry and music, and the masques. The investigation of Campion's ostensibly light poetry is a necessary precursor to the next two chapters. The author is mainly preoccupied with subject matter and "right handling" in this first chapter as he discusses the lyrics in Campion's published collections. Moving on to the music, the author first considers the circumstances in which it was composed and its manner of performance, referring to such matters as ornamentation, declamation and rhythm. This chapter is copiously illustrated. The third chapter relates Campion's theoretical writings, and others of the time, to his often experimental technique is setting words to music. Several songs are closely analysed. In the final chapter the author takes in turn the masques in which Campion collaborated and, in describing the action and quoting generously from the texts, shows how Campion commented on, and realized, the symbolic actions.

627. London, S.J. "Thomas Campion, M.D. (1567-1620), Scamp of Fleet Street." *New York State Journal of Medicine* 67 (1967): 3269-74.

Racy account of Campion's life and work, with particularly detailed emphasis on his role in the Overbury case, in which a noblewoman poisoned Sir Thomas Overbury to prevent his blackmailing her.

628. Wilson, Christopher. *Words and Notes Coupled Lovingly Together: Thomas Campion, a Critical Study.* Outstanding Dissertations in Music from British Universities. New York: Garland, 1989. 397pp. 0824020480. ML410.C3W54.

Considers in seven chapters both the music and the poetry of Campion. The author provides a review of Campion criticism from the nineteenth century. He places Campion's corpus in the context of contemporary musicians, poets and patrons. In a section on doubtful works in chapter 1 he queries the hitherto accepted ascription to Campion of five cantos, apparently his earliest published poems, appended to a pirated edition of Sidney's *Astrophil and Stella* from 1591. This thesis dates from 1982. For the published edition the author provides a new preface, reviewing new publications relating to Campion and noting continuing lacunae. He also provides a substantial addendum to an already comprehensive bibliography. He is of the opinion that some of the inadequacies in Campion scholarship can be attributed to the fact that many Campion scholars are literary critics, not musicologists.

629. Turbet, Richard. "Scotland's Greatest Composer: an Introduction to Robert Carver (1487-1566)." In *Bryght Lanternis: Essays on the Language and Literature of Medieval and Renaissance Scotland*, ed. by J. Derrick McClure and Michael R.G. Spiller. Aberdeen: Aberdeen University Press, 1989, pp.48-54.

Provides brief biography and survey of Carver's surviving music, an annotated bibliography of criticism (all items included within the present *Guide*), a critical discography, and a short summary of his position in the musical history of Europe. Since the end of 1988, when this paper was completed, the complete surviving works of Carver have been recorded on three compact discs by Cappella Nova conducted by Alan Tavener on the ASV label, numbers CD GAU 124, 126 and 127, released to critical acclaim during 1991. Despite its date *630* (*q.v.*) was published substantially later than the present paper.

630. Woods, Isobel. "Towards a Biography of Robert Carver." *Music Review* 49 (1988): 83-101.

Marshals every known scrap of evidence concerning Carver's life. The author brings together disparate historical sources and establishes his probable dates of birth and death, and the crucial dates of his monastic career. She also notes connections he had with Scone Abbey, Stirling and the Chapel Royal, then also at Stirling. According to Kenneth Elliott, the author of the booklets accompanying the compact discs of Carver's complete surviving works (see *629*), further biographical information is to appear in an issue of *The Innes Review.* It is known that Carver, through his uncle, had a sojourn in Aberdeen. See also *127.*

631. Charteris, Richard. "Autographs of John Coprario." *Music & Letters* 56 (1975): 41-6.

Attempts to establish which of the surviving manuscripts of Coprario's works are autograph. Several that are claimed to be so are disputed. The author carefully analyses each source and uses bibliographical, biographical and palaeographical evidence to support his opinions.

632. Charteris, Richard. *John Coprario: a Thematic Catalogue of his Music, with a Biographical Introduction.* Thematic Catalogue series, 3. New York: Pendragon, 1977. 113pp. 0918728053. ML134.C65A15.

Indispensable to anyone interested in Coprario (né Cooper). Contains the fullest published biography about him. In the catalogue the music is divided into instrumental and vocal, then subdivided by form or other suitable category. The author first gives incipits running numbered within subdivisions, followed by tables giving each item's source(s) and, where appropriate, scoring, Meyer (or other such) number and any published editions. He includes anonymous works probably by Coprario and spurious attributions, under separate headings. Appendices provide references to host sources and a list of sources from which each incipit is taken and parts cited. Manuscript and printed sources are described in detail (with references for the former) and where appropriate in the catalogue proper he provides a commentary. See also *633* and *434.*

633. Charteris, Richard. "A Postscript to `John Coprario: a Thematic Catalogue of his Music, with a Biographical Introduction' (New York, 1977)." *Chelys* 11 (1982): 13-19.

Supplement and addendum to *632.*

634. Dart, Thurston. "Two English Musicians at Heidelberg in 1613."

Musical Times 111 (1970): 29-32.

Seeks to establish that *Coprario* and *Orlando Gibbons* were present at the wedding of King James's daughter Princess Elizabeth and Duke Frederick V. The author does his best to confirm that Orlando is the "Gibbons" mentioned in a contemporary book about the wedding, and he ponders the circumstances of his selection for the ceremony and of his journey.

635. Platt, Peter. "Dering's Life and Training." *Music & Letters* 33 (1952): 41-9.

Attempts to confirm the details of Dering's biography in order to throw light on the style and chronology of his compositions. In particular the author seeks to establish where Dering received his training, and at what stage he converted to Roman Catholicism.

636. Frank, Priska. "A New Dowland Document." *Musical Times* 124 (1983): 15-6.

Announces the discovery of a hitherto unknown receipt signed, and possibly written, by Dowland. A transcription is provided, as well as comments on the document's provenance and contents, and the circumstances of its being drawn up.

637. Poulton, Diana. *John Dowland.* 2nd ed. London: Faber, 1982. 528pp. 0571180221. ML410.D808.

The standard work on Dowland's life and music. The eight chapters cover his life, music for solo lute, songbooks, songs with sacred texts, consort music, translations, patrons and friends, and posthumous reputation. Two appendices, the latter by David Mitchell, deal with manuscripts containing lute music by him which were not described in the main narrative, and with fretting and tuning the lute. The author shows great awareness of other people's researches. She considers all documents relevant to Dowland's life, and describes from his standpoint all contemporary sources, both manuscript and printed, of his music. The unwieldy "Bibliography and Finding Lists" contains a bibliography to 1970; manuscript sources listed by location; abbreviations; finding lists of all pieces including arrangements and pieces based on, or quoting, those of Dowland; spurious attributions; a list of relevant facsimile editions; and a post-1970 bibliography. There is a general index and an index of Dowland's works.

638. Richardson, Brian. "New Light on Dowland's Continental Movements." *Monthly Musical Record* 90 (1960): 3-9.

Versions of Dowland's *My Lady Hunsdon's Puffe* occur in two continental sources, Italian and German, neither ascribing it to Dowland. Basing his arguement on what was then known of Dowland's movements on the continent, the author attempts to establish a relationship between this work of Dowland and Donino Garsi, who in the Italian source claims the work as his own.

639. Sparr, Kenneth. "Some Unobserved Information About John Dowland, Thomas Campion, and Philip Rosseter." *Lute* 27 (1987): 35-7.

Reveals that all three composers signed the Stammbuch or *liber amicorum* of Hans von Bodeck. A native of East Prussia, now Poland, he was in London while touring England. Dowland provided a piece of lute music, and Campion a song. The book itself did not survive the Second World War and is known only through an article of 1929 by Hanns Baner, who does not describe Rosseter's entry.

640. Ward, John M. "A Dowland Miscellany." *Journal of the Lute Society of America* 10 (1977): 5-153.

Intended as a supplement to the first edition of *637* itself. The five sections are about the biography, the music, the index of works, background material and addenda. The first deals substantially with contemporary sources. The second is subdivided into seven subsections, on Dowland and his contemporaries, choosing the text to edit, mistakes and variants, playing directions, lute lessons, the revising of *The First Booke,* and the use of voice(s) and/or instrument(s). The third section is keyed into *637* and provides illuminating comments on, and additions to, its index; few of the former are incorporated into *637.* The fourth section contains 26 items, some of which provide texts of unpublished contemporary documents, while others are short essays on matters or people, such as Holborne and Robinson, peripherally relevant to Dowland. The final section consists of half a dozen late random thoughts. By way of an appendix, see Ward's ""Excuse me": a Dance to a Tune of John Dowland's Making," in *Libraries, History, Diplomacy, and the Performing Arts: Essays in Honor of Carleton Sprague Smith,* ed, by Israel J. Katz. Festschrift Series, 9. Stuyvesant: Pendragon, 1991, pp.379-88.

641. Owen, A.E.B. "Giles and Richard Farnaby in Lincolnshire." *Music & Letters* 42 (1961): 151-4.

   Establishes that at one time Giles Farnaby lived at Aisthorpe and was in the service of the Saunderson family as tutor in music. The author is also able to deduce the date of birth of Giles's son Richard and to draw some conclusions about Richard's movements after 1608.

642. Warren, Edwin B. *Life and Works of Robert Fayrfax, 1464-1521.* Musicological Studies and Documents, 22. Dallas: American Institute of Musicology, 1969. 213pp. ML410.F28W3.

   Deals comprehensively with the composer's biography, the sources of his surviving music, and the music itself, both sacred and secular. A concluding chapter considers his style, and there is an impressive bibliography. The monograph is conspicuously well illustrated, and it updates all the preceding articles on Fayrfax by the author.

643. Charteris, Richard. *Alfonso Ferrabosco the Elder (1543-1588): a Thematic Catalogue of his Music with a Biographical Calendar.* Thematic Catalogue Series, 11. New York: Pendragon, 1984. 237pp. 0918728444. ML134.F34A13.

The biographical calendar forms an introduction to a catalogue in which items are arranged by form, such as motets. The entries include incipit, voices, manuscript sources, modern edition, text and commentary. Dubia appear at the end of the main catalogue, while spuria appear as one of seven appendices, which also include English versions of Ferrabosco's French and Italian works. See also *292*.

644. Charteris, Richard. "Autographs of Alfonso Ferrabosco I-III." *Early Music* 10 (1982): 208-10.

Differentiating the signatures of the three men (succesive generations), aided by recent discoveries, has helped to identify a hitherto unattributed letter, and confirms that none of the surviving music of I or II is autograph.

645. Charteris, Richard. "A Memorial for Alfonso Ferrabosco the Elder." *Musical Times* 129 (1988): 393-6.

Summarizes Ferrabosco's biography and output, and emphasizes his considerable influence on contemporary English composers. The author concludes with a review of the revival of interest in Ferrabosco's music, from 1894 to his own most recent researches.

646. Duffy, John. *The Songs and Motets of Alfonso Ferrabosco, the Younger* (1575-1628). Studies in Musicology, 20. Ann Arbor: UMI Research Press, 1980. 479pp. 0835711102. ML410.F2978.

After a biographical introduction and chapters on poetry and music and on Ferrabosco's harmonic practice, by far the largest part of the book (nine of fourteen chapters) is devoted to the songs, especially those in the masques (four chapters). Amongst the appendices are concordances to the ayres, manuscript songs, and motets and anthems, plus transcriptions of the fifteen motets with a table of variants, and texts and translations. The author's particular claim for the songs is their important role in the development of a specifically English declamatory sensibility, a claim pursued throughout the many close analyses in the narrative.

647. Emsden, C.S. "Lives of Elizabethan Song Composers: Some New Facts." *Review of English Studies* 2 (1926): 417-22.

Useful for the section on *Thomas Ford* (pp. 419-20) in which the bequests in his will, many to various fellow musicians, are detailed.

648. Fellowes, Edmund H. *Orlando Gibbons and his Family: the Last of the Tudor School of Musicians*. 2nd ed. London: Oxford University Press, 1951; repr. ed., Hamden: Archon, 1970. 109pp. 020800489. ML410.G295F4.

The only general monograph devoted to Gibbons. While the biographical matter has withstood the test of time, musicological research and attitudes have moved on. Fellowes's comments on genres and pieces are inadequate. Furthermore many anthems have been reconstructed, and some reascribed to others, so knowledge of the repertory has expanded. Performance practice, especially of verse anthems and the *Second Service* (see the notes by Sally Dunkley accompanying compact disc GAU 123 performed by the Choir of King's College, Cambridge on the ASV label; also *WB158*), has improved, so that Fellowes's lack of enthusiasm is shown to be a shortcoming in his critical faculties or in contemporary performances rather than in Gibbons's music. There is no attempt by Fellowes to place Gibbons in the continuum of English musical development. In the absence of other such monographs it must be read with discrimination, scepticism and tolerance.

649. Moroney, Davitt. "Orlando Gibbons." *Music and Musicians* 23 (June 1975): 20-2.

Good general introduction to the life and work of Gibbons, with a particularly illuminating paragraph on his best-known verse anthem *This is the Record of John*.

650. Thewlis, George A. "Oxford and the Gibbons Family." *Music & Letters* 21 (1940): 31-3.

Mainly concerned to try to unravel the activities of William, father of Orlando.

651. Vining, Paul. "Orlondo Gibbons: the Portraits." *Music & Letters* 58 (1977): 415-29.

The surviving representations of Gibbons, none contemporary, amount to a bust in Canterbury Cathedral (source of two subsequent engravings) and a painting. It is the latter which mainly concerns the author, who goes into great detail to establish its provenance, and postulates that it is a copy of an original contemporary portrait.

652. Fraser, Russell A. "A Minor Elizabethan Composer." *Music & Letters* 33 (1952): 329-32.

Brief account of the life and works of *John Hall*, c.1529-66.

653. Marlow, Richard. "Sir Ferdinando Heyborne alias Richardson." *Musical Times* 115 (1974): 736-9.

Copious account of Elizabethan courtier, amateur composer and pupil of Tallis, mainly devoted to his biography, but with a summary of his works and their sources, with some judicious comments.

654. Jeffery, Brian. "Anthony Holborne." *Musica disciplina* 22 (1968): 129-205.

Brings together all available biographical information, describes and lists his instrumental music, and places him in the context of the musical life of his time. The author also notes Holborne's literary connexions, and suggests that some of the titles of his instrumental pieces are related to emblem literature. He includes a thematic index of Holborne's works.

655. Harris, Colette. "Tobias Hume - a Short Biography." *Chelys* 3 (1971): 16-18.

Concentrates on biographical aspects of Hume, not his music. The author cites the few existing biographical sources and their contents, and adds judicious interpretations of the information where appropriate. It has been established in *434* that Hume was Scottish

656. Baillie, Hugh. "Nicholas Ludford (c.1485-c.1557)." *Musical Quarterly* 44 (1958): 196-208.

Within the limitations of current knowledge, attempts to provide an authoritative biography, with a list of works and substantial commentary.

657. Bergsagel, John D. " An Introduction to Ludford (c.1485-c.1557)." *Musica disciplina* 14 (1960): 105-30.

Comprehensive introduction to life and works, with analyses and illustrations.

658. Rose, Bernard. "John Mason: a Clarification." *Musical Times* 113 (1972): 1231.

Establishes the identity of the composer, giving full surviving details of his career, and removing from consideration a contemporary of the same name.

659. Hunt, J. Eric. "Merbecke: his Life and Times." *Gregorian* (October 1990): 4-15.

Concentrates on details of Merbecke's religious proclivities (especially his prosecution for Lutheranism) and work on his *Booke of Common Praier Noted*, 1550. This had currency for only two years until the second Edwardine *BCP*, but was taken up by the Oxford Movement during the Anglo-Catholic revival in the Church of England during the nineteenth century. In the course of a bibliographical consideration of the fourteen surviving copies of Merbecke's publication, the author puts a vigorous case against the existence of a second edition, arguing that differences among the copies can be explained by the primitive nature of English music printing technology.

660. Marbeck, John. *The Work of John Marbeck*, ed. by R.A. Leaver. The Courtenay Library of Reformation Classics, 9. Appleford: Sutton Courtenay Press, 1978. BX5130.M33.

Useful background about Merbecke from a theological perspective. In chapter 3 on music and liturgy, the editor discusses both Merbecke's Latin music and his noting of the new Book of Common Prayer which ironically, in view of its popularity in the twentieth century, became redundant only two years after its initial publication. He places Merbecke's music and theological development within the context of the religious ferment of the time.

661. Brennecke, Ernest. *Milton the Elder and his Music.* Columbia University Studies in Musicology, 2. New York: Columbia University Press, 1938; repr. ed., Octagon, 1973. 224pp. ML410.M679B7.

Unavoidably known as the father of a famous son, Milton was a cathedral chorister who went on to contribute to *The Triumphes of Oriana* as well as to collections of sober religious music. This study of his life and works is anecdotal in tone but sustains interest in a minor but decent talent. Of particular value are a chronological list of his extant music, a cogent and relevant bibliography, and fifty pages of musical examples.

662. Brown, David. "Thomas Morley and the Catholics: Some Speculations." *Monthly Musical Record* 89 (1959): 53-61.

Suggests that Morley's Roman Catholicism is a more complicated matter than is usually thought. The author bases his argument on two known sources: first Morley's own Latin church music, which forms a small corpus of outstanding quality (though see *118* and *119*); secondly a letter in which the duplicitous Catholic intriguer Charles Paget, writing from the Low Countries, exposed Morley's faith and to which the government agent Thomas Phelippes suggested a reply, both letter and reply confirming that Morley was on an assignment there to obtain information about Roman Catholics in England.

Brown possibly resolves the problem of Morley's being a Catholic yet spying on other Catholics, in identifying Morley as the author of a letter objecting to two gentlemen in election for the office of Sherriff of Worcestershire as being known Roman Catholics. Brown argues that Morley was a Catholic who preferred rule by the Church of England to that by Spain, the only realistic Catholic alternative, as the lesser of two evils.

663. Dart, Thurston. "Morley and the Catholics: Some Further Speculations." *Monthly Musical Record* 89 (1959): 89-92.

Supports the arguments in *662*, and emphasizes the nature of the Latin texts Morley chose to set, either Marian or deeply penitential. See also *118* and *119*.

664. Gordon, Philip. "The Morley-Shakespeare Myth." *Music & Letters* 28 (1947): 121-5.

Seeks to disprove the "myth" that Morley and Shakespeare were artistically associated in any way.

665. Nutting, Geoffrey. "Thomas Morley: Friend or Foe of the Absurd?" *Parergon* 14 (April 1976): 32-42.

Discusses Morley's attitude to absurdity in music, based on selective analysis of his madrigals and on his comments in *427*. The author notes how Morley reflects absurdity in wordsetting and in changes of metre and pace, but examples are few and far between. He concludes that Morley is aware, in his writings, of absurdity as a human condition, but treats it lightly in his music.

666. Shaw, Watkins. "Thomas Morley of Norwich." *Musical Times* 106 (1965): 669-73.

Relates all that is known about Morley's connection with Norwich, from his birth until he resigned as Organist in 1587.

667. Zimmerman, Franck. "Italian and English Traits in the Music of Thomas Morley." *Anuario musical* 14 (1959): 29-37.

Draws attention to Morley's heavy reliance on Italian theorists and composers in his own theoretical writing, in his choice and treatment of poetic texts, and in the forms and style in which he chose to compose: this last a most important section.

668. Willetts, Pamela J. "The Identity of Thomas Myriell." *Music & Letters* 53 (1972): 431-3.

Establishes Myriell's identity, despite the claims made for him in other earlier articles cited here, which seem to refer to other men of the same name.

669. Willetts, Pamela J. "Musical connections of Thomas Myriell." *Music & Letters* 49 (1968): 36-42.

Comparison of manuscripts in Oxford and London has brought to light a group of connections between musicians at whose centre is Myriell, compiler of "Tristitiae remedium," an important manuscript source of English music dated 1616. See also *549* and *668*.

670. Buck, P.C. *et al. Short Biographical Notes and Description of Manuscript Sources for the Tudor English Church Music Series, Kalmus Volumes 6649-6728.* New York: Kalmus, 1973, pp.5-14.

Originally published as introduction to *Tudor Church Music* (1922-9). Of the nine notices on the life and works of the composers herein, only the sections on *Osbert Parsley* and *Robert Whyte* are now worth perusing. Indeed the item on Parsley is the most substantial biographical writing about him, while the section on Whyte's music is sympathetic to the point of being combative. These two essays can also be found in *TCM* volumes X and V (1929 and 1926) respectively.

671. Ford, Wyn K. "Concerning William Parsons." *Music & Letters* 37 (1956): 333-5.

Biographical introduction. Bases his report on the researches of W.H. Grattan Flood, whom he proves to be unreliable (as Flood is on most biographies of composers he claimed to have investigated). The author conjectures that the Parsons in question was not as important as Flood says he was. It should be added that this composer is best known for being the likely composer of an anthem also attributed, probably erroneously, to Tallis: see *681*.

672. Jones, Audrey. "Martin Peerson: Some New Facts." *Monthly Musical Record* 85 (1955): 172-7.

Summarizes the known biographical information concerning Peerson, corrects some perceived errors and adds a few more details. It is a shame that in attempting to raise Peerson's status the author succumbed to denigrating such a fine composer as Michael East. Such an approach calls into question her assessment of Peerson who, it could be argued, does not require such misbegotten comparisons in any case.

673. Wailes, Marilyn. "Martin Peerson." *Proceedings of the Royal Musical Association* 80 (1953-4): 59-71.

Biographical introduction with some comments on his music.

674. Petti, A.G. "Peter Philips, Composer and Organist, 1561-1628." *Recusant History* 4 (1957-8): 48-60.

Attempts a biography of Philips in the light of newly discovered information. This remains the standard source, to which little of substance has been added except the fact of his having been a pupil of Byrd (see *WB153*, p.278).

675. Mateer, David. "Further Light on Preston and Whyte." *Musical Times* 115 (1974): 1074-7.

Announces the discovery of documentary evidence revealing the presence at Trinity College, Cambridge of Thomas Preston, 1548-59, and Robert Whyte, 1554-61. The author quotes copiously from his sources, especially concerning Preston, and suggests Whyte's still unknown date of birth must be around

1540 in the light of his being listed as a chorister as late as 1554-5.

676. Thompson, Edward. "Robert Ramsay." *Musical Quarterly* 49 (1963): 210-24.

Comprehensive introduction to Ramsay's music and to what little is known of his life.

677. Mark, J. "Thomas Ravenscroft, B.Mus. (c.1583-1633)." *Musical Times* 65 (1924): 881-4.

More useful as a broad introduction of his music than as biography. It is conspicuously well illustrated. See *678* concerning Ravenscroft's date of birth.

678. Payne, Ian. "Thomas Ravenscroft: a Biographical Note." *Musical Times* 127 (1986): 707-9.

Disputes the usually accepted date of Ravenscroft's birth, 1592 (though see *677*), and suggests c.1587.

679. Jeffreys, John. *The Life and Works of Philip Rosseter.* Wendover: Roberton, 1990. 97pp. 0951372017.

The "life" begins only in 1597, when Rosseter was 28, as nothing before this is known, and even his age is a point of contention. The author completed this book in 1952 and delayed publication in the hope that more biographical material would emerge. He deals with Rosseter as composer and lutenist, as well as describing his theatrical activities, and devotes the final chapter to Rosseter's family. There is neither bibliography nor index, but of three addenda, one provides biographical notes on individuals mentioned in the text; another, notes on the plays performed by the child actors under Rosseter when he was Master of the Children of the Queen's Revels; and the third refers briefly to the legal case concerning Dowland's *Second Booke of Ayres* described in *471*. An insert forming a late addendum provides Robert Spencer's list of titles and sources of the solo lute music, preceded by Jeffreys's introduction, and this compensates for the inadequacies of content and detail in what is nevertheless the only monograph devoted to Rosseter.

680. Vlam, Christiaan *and* Dart, Thurston. "Rosseters in Holland." *Galpin Society Journal* 11 (1958): 63-9.

Traces three musicians from this family, beginning with Philip, the most famous, also Dudley and Thomas.

681. Doe, Paul. *Tallis*. 2nd ed. Oxford Studies of Composers, 4. London: Oxford University Press, 1976. 71pp. 0193141221. ML410.T147D6.

Good introduction in five chapters, covering the old musical tradition before the Reformation, Tallis's ritual music of the mid-sixteenth century, his Elizabethan motets, music for the Anglican church and instrumental music. Nearly all of Tallis's pieces receive at least a passing mention, and the book is well illustrated. The list of works in the main provides only published sources: see the same author's entry on Tallis in *12* for a more informative listing.

682. Turbet, Richard. "Tallis and Byrd." *Musical Opinion* 106 (1983): 301.

See *WB30.*

683. Turbet, Richard. "Thomas Tallis and Osbert Parsley (died 1585)." *Brio* 22 (1985): 50-5.

Updates and supplements bibliographies in *12*, including some items not chosen for the present *Guide*, and provides selective critical discographies for both composers.

684. Hand, Colin. *John Taverner: his Life and Music.* Eulenburg Books. London: Eulenburg, 1978. 128pp. 090387524. ML410.T186H3.

Good introduction that judiciously sifts the sketchy biographical evidence, and discusses all the surviving music. Its three chapters deal respectively with Taverner's life, music and musical style, and the appendix contains an annotated list of manuscript sources. The author is open-minded about the problematical *Quemadmodum,* the only source of which is textless, though its title suggests a setting of Psalm XLII. See page 7 of the booklet accompanying compact disc CDC 7496612, *Masterworks from Late-Medieval England and Scotland* sung by the Taverner Choir on the EMI Reflexe label, 1989, in which Sally Dunkley relates how Hugh Keyte discovered the correct text for this piece (not the one given in *53*) and edited it for choral performance.

685. Josephson, David S. *John Taverner: Tudor Composer.* Studies in Musicology, 5. Ann Arbor: UMI Research Press, 1979. 283pp. 0835709906. ML410.T186J7.

Comprehensive study of Taverner's life and works. Begins with the outstanding biography of the composer. The author offers evidence that Taverner was resident in London during the second decade of the sixteenth century. After the relatively straightforward accounts of Taverner's spells in Tattershall and Oxford, he is able to use contemporary documents to provide an account more detailed than hitherto of the composer's last years in Boston, disposing of the myth that he was a cruel suppressor of local monasteries, and that far from giving up music when he moved there, Taverner continued his musical activities. The author then discusses the sources of Taverner's church music, each piece of music within liturgical categories, and the songs. His discussion of the church music includes acute insights into Taverner's technique and development. Significantly he is even barking up the right tree in respect of the problematical *Quemadmodum*: see *684* for the reference to the subsequent solution.

686. Stevens, Denis. "John Taverner." In *Essays in Musicology, in Honor of Dragon Plamenac on his 70th Birthday,* ed. by Gustave Reese and Robert J. Snow. Pittsburgh: University of Pittsburgh Press, 1969, pp. 331-9.

Divided into separate sections on life and works. The

biographical information is superseded by *685*. Works are listed with references to numbers in *Tudor Church Music* (see *52 and 53)* whose editions are now superseded by those of *Early English Church Music* (London: Stainer and Bell, 1978-90). The bibliographical information is superseded by *12*. Nevertheless, the introduction to the works is thorough, and refers to specific sections of individual pieces to make a point or to characterize Taverner's procedures. Such insights from a critic of Stevens's calibre render this essay worthwhile.

687. Evans, David R.A. "The Life and Works of John Tomkins." *Welsh Music* 6 (Spring 1980): 56-62.

Informative and comprehensive account of the small but estimable output of the brother of the famous Thomas, with detailed biographical introduction.

688. Rose, Bernard. "Thomas Tomkins 1575?-1656." *Proceedings of the Royal Musical Association* 82 (1955-6): 89-105.

Introduction to Tomkins's keyboard, vocal and consort output with illuminating comments on his compositional technique. See *689* for his correct date of birth.

689. Stevens, Denis. *Thomas Tomkins, 1572-1656.* London: Methuen, 1957; corr. repr. ed., New York: Dover, 1967. ML410.T6558.

Outstanding introduction to Tomkins's life and music. In view of the size of Tomkins's corpus, a substantial number of works are mentioned and discussed in the text. In six chapters the author deals in appropriate detail with the Tomkins family, Tomkins's life, *Musica Deo sacra*, the *Songs* of 1622, and the keyboard and consort music. There are lists of the music by category, giving printed and manuscript sources, and a discography. See also *22, 91* and *117*.

690. Turbet, Richard. "Thomas Tomkins: Discography and Bibliography." *Welsh Music* 7 (Summer 1984): 44-9.

Critical discography of major recordings of Tomkins's music.

Several more recordings of his church music have since appeared but hardly any keyboard music. The bibliography updates the list in *12*, and a supplement was published in *7* (Autumn/Winter 1984-5): 122; these include some writings not selected for the present *Guide.*

691. Ford, Robert. "John Ward of Canterbury." *Journal of the Viola da Gamba Society of America* 23 (1986): 51-63.

Seeks to demonstrate that there were two composers of this name, the one in the title (1571-1617) who wrote the church music and madrigals, and his son (1592-1638) who wrote the music for viols. The author uses copious genealogical and palaeographical evidence to prove his point, though he is forced to admit that there is no evidence for the birth of the proposed son. He summarizes the musical analyses used to differentiate the technique of the vocal composer from that of the consort composer. He also mentions other John Wards in order to clear the ground for his two main contenders.

692. Brett, Philip. "The Two Musical Personalities of Thomas Weelkes." *Music & Letters* 53 (1972): 369-76.

Attempts to confirm the pre-eminence of Weelkes as a madrigalist rather than as a composer of church music. This article was written as part of an elongated preparation for 199?Bs and suggests that even in Weelkes's ostensibly most revolutionary Italianiate manner, his structural tendencies firmly linked him to *Byrd* and the native tradition. The author is keen to reverse the perspective of *694*, which advocates the church music at the expense of the madrigals, and he proposes that although Weelkes grasped the Italianate manner in his madrigals, he remained mindful of the advantages, when composing madrigals, of the formal approach to poetry observed by Byrd and others in the native tradition.

693. Brown, David. "Thomas Weelkes." *Recorder and Music Magazine* 2 (1967): 137-8.

Ideal as a brief summary of Weelkes's career and works.

694. Brown, David. *Thomas Weelkes: a Biographical and Critical Study.* London: Faber, 1969. 223pp. 057108933X. ML410.W36B8.

   The only monograph devoted to Weelkes and fortunately of resoundingly high quality. There are twelve chapters. The first is biographical, while two others discuss his madrigal style and the final one is a general assessment. The rest deal with specific parts of his output: the madrigalian collections of 1597, 1598, 1600 and 1608; the miscellaneous works, mainly instrumental; the full and verse anthems; and the Services. The author places Weelkes's life and music in their contemporary context. Nearly all the surviving works are discussed, and some are analysed at some length. In *692* Brett endeavours to redress what he sees as a bias in the present monograph in favour of Weelkes's sacred music against his madrigals. Notwithstanding, Brown argues a cogent case for the various sources of Weelkes's influence, though his book predates Alan Brown's suggestion that Weelkes was a pupil of Byrd: see *William Byrd: Keyboard Music: II,* 2nd ed., Musica Britannica, 28 (London: Stainer & Bell, 1976, rev. repr. 1985), p.198. As well as pointing out, particularly in respect of the madrigals, who influenced Weelkes and whom in turn he influenced, he also notes Weelkes's many self-quotations in his church music. Of particular value is his numbering of Weelkes's ten surviving Services. Only the first two bear contemporary numberings, and as they survive in a variety of sources and in various states of fragmentation, this has imposed order on a chaos of cumbersome or non-existent titles.

695. Collins, Walter S. "Recent Discoveries Concerning the Biography of Thomas Weelkes." *Music & Letters* 44 (1963): 123-31.

   Contains some domestic information and details about the conduct of choristers and services. See also *699*.

696. Dickinson, A.E.F. "Thomas Weelkes (c.1575-1623)." In *The Music Masters, including "Lives of the Great Composers."* Vol 1: *From the Sixteenth Century to the Time of Beethoven,* ed.

by A.L. Bacharach. Dublin: Fridberg, 1948, pp.361-6.

Summary introduction to life and works. Most of the author's remarks on the former have been superseded, notably in *694*, but his observations about the vivid illustrations in the madrigals are provocative for all their brevity.

697. Fellowes, Edmund H. "Thomas Weelkes." *Proceedings of the Musical Association* 42 (1915-16): 117-43.

More biographical detail is now available, but this paper contains a wide-ranging and informative introduction to the madrigals.

698. Fincham, Kenneth. "Contemporary Opinions of Thomas Weelkes." *Music & Letters* 62 (1981): 352-3.

Hitherto unpublished attestations of 1615 as to the skill of Weelkes as Cathedral Organist at Chichester: a change from the usual litany of drunkenness, blasphemy, dismissal and debt.

699. McCann, Timothy J. "The Death of Thomas Weelkes in 1623." *Music & Letters* 55 (1974): 45-7.

Announces discovery of the original copy of Weelkes's inventory at the time of his death. The author draws various inferences concerning Weelkes's personal circumstances during the last year of his life. He includes a transcription of the original, as the later copy which had to be used in *695*, which substantially predates the present article, is "careless."

700. Shepherd, John. "Thomas Weelkes: a Biographical Caution." *Musical Quarterly* 66 (1980): 505-21.

Examines the nine documents that provide evidence about the progressive degradation of Weelkes's life. As a result the author argues forcefully that Weelkes was not the habitual and unruly drunkard many critics have presumed him to be, and urges caution in interpreting contemporary documents about him.

701. Spector, Irving. "Robert White's Music." *Consort* 23 (1966): 100-8.

Provides useful biographical introduction, and reviews Whyte's musical output, with analyses of several pieces.

702. Whytehorne, Thomas. *The Autobiography of Thomas Whythorne,* ed. by James M. Osborn. Oxford: Clarendon, 1961. 328pp. ML410.W647A3.

The only surviving first-hand monographic account of the life of a professional musician in Elizabethan England. The editor provides a useful introduction to the autobiography itself, though subsequent research has long overtaken many of his comments on musical matters, such as Whytehorne's supposed role in the development of the English madrigal (see for instance *208*, though see also *254* for a more supportive view). The text reproduces Whytehorne's "new orthography" based on phonetic spelling, and on page 1 Whytehorne's own title for his work is reproduced.

703. Brown, David. *Wilbye*. Oxford Studies of Composers, 11. London: Oxford University Press, 1974. 55pp. 0193152207. ML410.W6986B8.

This exemplary study of the music is effectively in three chapters, with a short introduction and conclusion. The two outside chapters deal with the madrigals of 1598 and 1609 respectively. Between them an "interlude" contains an analysis of Wilbye's contribution to *The Triumphes of Oriana*, and acts as a bridge between the two collections of madrigals. The conclusion mentions Wilbye's contribution to *The Teares and Lamentacions* "set foorth" in 1614 by William Leighton, and a few works, including a fantasia à 6, which survive in manuscript. The list of works includes sources.

704. Fellowes, Edmund H. "John Wilbye." *Proceedings of the Musical Association* 41 (1914-15): 55-86.

Comprehensive introduction to Wilbye's life and music.

705. Humphreys, David. "Philip van Wilder: a Study of his Work and its Sources." *Soundings* 9 [*recte* 8] (1979-80): 13-36.

Immaculate account of the Flemish musician who was active in England 1519-53 and who influenced the music of later English composers including Byrd.

APPENDIX

WILLIAM BYRD: A GUIDE TO RESEARCH SINCE 1986

In 1987 Garland published *WB153,* my Composer Resource Manual *William Byrd: a Guide to Research.* Its *terminus ad quem* was the end of 1986. The present appendix, which includes errata, updates the information in the Manual to the end of 1992.

Byrd stated in his will (1897Sw) dated 15 November 1622 that he was "now in the 80th yeare of myne age." This turn of phrase meant then what it means today: that he was 79 and that his next birthday was his eightieth. He was therefore born late in 1542 or during 1543. Both 1992 and, particularly, 1993 are being celebrated as the 450th anniversary of his birth. To this end, especially as the quatercentenary was overwhelmed by the Second World War, various publications, recordings and recitals are planned on a modest scale. (It is only fair to point out that the index to *The Musical Times* for 1943 reveals that commendable efforts on Byrd's behalf were made in difficult circumstances.) *Brio* proposes to publish during 1994 or 1995 an account of the activities celebrating Byrd's 450th anniversary. This will further update the information in this appendix to the end of 1993.

A reference prefixed *TM* indicates an item in the main sequence of the present guide to *Tudor Music.* The prefix *WB* indicates items either in the Bibliography (chapter III) of *WB153* (nos *WB1-WB140*) or in its continuation in section A-IV, below (*WB141* onwards). Items from the checklist alone are cited simply by their numbers. *WB153* was provided with its own catalogue of Byrd's complete authenticated works, plus appendix and apocrypha. Throughout that Manual, for consistency, individual works by Byrd were cited solely by catalogue number in the form of T plus numeral, e.g. T 191. (For historical reasons an exception was made in the case of the selective discography, chapter VI.) This system is continued in the present *Guide.* However, at the end of the appendix there is an index to Byrd's works cited by catalogue number, for readers without immediate access to the original Manual.

Articles that discuss Byrd in less detail than that which warrants inclusion in either the checklist or the bibliography may be traced by referring to the entries in the main sequence that are cited under Byrd's name in the musician index.

A-I

ERRATA

p.viii, l.2: delete.

p.xi: for "murmered" read "murmured".

p.xiii, l.28: after "ones" add "are".

l.30: for "1641" read "1616".

p.xiv: add extra line "*Gathering* (Newcastle upon Tyne: Bloodaxe, 1984), p.74."

p.9, l.2: delete "Vol. 16".

p.12, T 8: move first parenthesis down one line. T 11: insert as l.5 "C xi 80 no.12 (contrafact)". Insert as l.6 "D ii 262 (contrafact)".

p.37, T 188g: for "Apocrypha (b)" read "T A10".

p.69, T 438: for "Br." read "Mr."

T 442: for "2b" read "21b".

p.76, T 480: add "May be dedicated to Richard Farrant: see B ii 203."
T 483, L45: parenthesis should read "incipit: only three parts of *Pavan* survive, in partbooks "For the Flute" (*GB-HUu* DDHO/20/1) and "For the Base Viole" (*GB-HUu* DDHO/20/2) from a set of three, itself incomplete, in the Hotham Papers, and "For the Cittern" (Mills College, Oakland, California)."

p.77, T 489, l.6: add "of *Pavan*" at end, inside parenthesis.

p.85, T A10: insert as fourth line "D ii 89 (fragment)". T A12: add "May be contrafactum of T 204."

p.87, T A25, l.3 delete "p."

p.93, *Incola ego sum:* entry should read "*(see Retribue servo tuo)*".

p.97, *Piper's Galliard:* for "101" read "103".

p.99, *Spem in alium:* for "3" read "4".

p.100, *With Fragrant Flowers:* underline "101".

p.121, *O Praise Our Lord:* for "T 119 read "T 199".

p.148, 1923COOl: for "*11*" read "chapter VIII".

p.150, 1923HUm: for "1943" read "1543".

p.154, 1951Fw: add series "Festival of Britain 1951: London Season of the Arts."

p.169: add to end of first paragraph, within the parenthesis, "See also *70* pp.65-7."

p.171: delete last complete sentence.

p.174, para.5, l.3: after "*35*" add "and Monson in *96*".

p.196, ll.42-3: parenthesis should read "see the notes on *12* and *96*."

p.213, *63*: for "1984" read "1964".

p.234, *96*, para.2, l.15: after "See" insert "footnote to *10* and".

p.235, *97*: delete last line.

p.245, l.1: delete.

p.252, *124*: delete "*Early*".

p.265, *Conlon,* l.2: for "Health" read "Heath".

p.270, below *Humphries* insert: *King* See chapter IV."

p.272, *Bull,* l.5: add "*King*" within the parenthesis.

p.285, l.20: for "002" read "003".

p.287, ll.3-6: delete.

p.332, l.3: "T 199" and "T 204" should read "T 202" and "T 207".
Note on l.35: delete "2nd ed." Imprint should read "London: Brome, 1663." Delete last sentence: instead, see below, *WB161*.

A-II

GENERAL ADDENDA AND SUPPLEMENTARY INFORMATION

p.4, A: volume 2 published 1988.

p.5: volume 5 published 1989, entitled *Gradualia I (1605): the Marian Masses*. Volume 6 is divided into two volumes. Volume 6a was published in 1991, entitled *Gradualia I (1605): All Saints and Corpus Christi, with Hymns to the Blessed Sacrament and Other Motets*. The title of volume 6b is now *Gradualia I (1605): Other Feasts and Devotions*. Volume 7 is similarly divided. The title of volume 7a is now *Gradualia II (1607): Christmas, Epiphany and Easter*. The title of volume 7b is now *Gradualia II (1607): Ascension, Pentecost, Saints Peter & Paul, Saint Peter's Chains*. Volume 14 was published in 1987.

p.8, BMSJ: add "Errata, 9 (1987): 69. P *A Paven of Mr Byrds,* ed. by Richard Turbet. Lincoln: Lindum, 1993. Q *Five-Part Consorts*, ed. by George Hunter. Urbana: Northwood, 1986."
d: add "reprint eds, Shakespeare Association Facsimiles, 14.

London, Oxford University Press, 1937; Farnborough: Gregg, 1971."

e: add "reprint ed., Harrow Replicas, 3. Cambridge: Heffer, 1942."

p.9, EECM: add "Supplementary vol.2. Hofman, May *and* Morehen, John. *Latin Music in British Sources c1485-c1610.* 1987. MB XLIV-XLV: add "88.""

p.10, MB LV: volume number confirmed; published 1989. Add "TM Turbet, Richard. *Tudor Music: a Research and Information Guide.* New York: Garland, 1993."

p.11, under VV add "WI. Inglott, William. *The Short Service,* edited by Michael Walsh and Richard Turbet. Wyton: King's Music, 1989. 3v." *Tallis* & c.: add "reprint ed., Leeds: Boethius, 1976."

pp.14-16: paginations for T 19-34: 1 no.1, 15 no.2, 32 no.3, 42 no.4, 62 no.5, 73 no.6, 89 no.7, 124 no.8, 135 no.9, 150 no.10, 156 no.11, 169 no.12, 187 no.13 (also after "lv" add "140"), 202 no.14, 221 no.15, 229 no.16.

p.17, T 47: after "lv" add "172".

p.18, *Gradualia* & c.: add "2nd ed. Excudebat H.L. Impensis Richardi Redmeri,...1610; reprint ed., Wyton: King's Music, 1991."

pp.18-22: paginations for T 56-80: 2 no.1, 12 no.2, 16 no.3, 19 no.4, 31 no.5, 40 no.6, 50 no.7, 53 no.8, 56 no.9, 60 no.10, 65 no.11, 70 no.12, 78 no.13, 83 no.14, 87 no.15, 94 no. 16, 101 no.17, 108 no.18, 113 no.19, 117 no.20, 127 no.21, 136 no.22, 156 no.23, 166 no.24, 170 no.25.

p.22-4, T 81-95: now A vi a; paginations: 1 no.1, 4 no.2, 15 no.3, 27 no.4, 37 no.5, 48 no. 6, 53 no.7, 61 no.8, 67 no.9, 75 no.10, 77 no.11, 82 no.12, 87 no.13, 92 no.14. 97 no.15.

pp.24-7, T 96-118: now A vi b.

p.28, *Gradualia* & c.: add as p.18, above.

pp.28-31, T 119-42: now A vii a.

pp.31-4, T 143-64: now A vii b.

p.37, T 188: add "Benedictus arranged by Robert Shenton (c.1730-98) as Jubilate in *GB-DRc* A18, pp.18-22.""

p.42, T 223: after "lv" add "148".

p.44, T 238-41: after "lv" add "149", "150", "152" and "154".

p.48 T 275: add note: "The bass viol part that survives in GB-Cu Dd.5.20 is from an incomplete set for broken consort, not viols: see TM554."

pp.49-52: paginations for T 280-307: 1, 4, 6, 10, 13, 16, 18, 22, 27, 30, 33, 36, 39, 47, 51, 57, 64, 70, 84, 91, 97, 105, 128, 136, 144,

154, 165, 171.

p.55, T 326: after "lv" add "158".

p.59, T 375: insert first line "A xiv 42 no.15".

p.60, T 375: after "lv" add "161".

p.61, T 383: insert first line "A xiv 114 no.26". T 384, l.63; add "Q 28 (Pavan of Five Parts). Provides authentic tenor part found subsequent to A."

p.76, T 483: add "P (reconstruction)".

p.81, T 508-9: after "lv" add "2" and "3".

p.87, T A24, l.4: after "lv" add "83" and add at end "*or Piper's Galliard*".

Below T A25 add "T A26. *Pavan*. MB lv 50 no.15. See pp.xix and 179," and "T A27. *Pavan*. MB lv 52 no.16. See pp.xix and 179."

p.88: below *Ah Silly Poor Joas* add "*Air* (keyboard: see *Alman II*)".

Alman (keyboard) II: after "lv" add "90" and at end add "Entitled *Air* in *Fourteen Pieces for Keyed Instruments by William Byrd*, ed. by J.A. Fuller Maitland and W.Barclay Squire (London: Stainer & Bell, 1923), p.47, no.XIV, and *Pavan* in *Dances Grave and Gay* by Byrd, edited by Margaret H. Glyn (London: Rogers, 1923), p.5, no.1."

p.89: below *Bonny Sweet Robin* add "*Born is the Babe* à 1 + 5 viols, chorus à 5. MB xxii 74 no.46. Anonymous. Attributed to Byrd on BBC Radio 3 programme *Byrd at Ingatestone* 29 December 1989. See 1990Bm."

Below *The Burying of the Dead* add "*Captain(e) Piper's Pavan* (see *Piper's Pavan*)".

p.91: insert "*Dum transisset.* D vi 257. Attributed to Tallis and Byrd, Birmingham: Collins, 1918." Below *Fantasia* add "*Nine Fantasias à 4 (fragments). L A-4-5 (incipits only 2-9). TM*".

Galliard (keyboard): after "lv" add "13".

p.92, *In nomine* à 5: now published, so pagination is "59 no.152 *In nomine II*".

p.94, *Medley:* after "lv" add "103".

Below *Miserere* à 3-5 add "*Miserere nostri Domine* à 7. D vi 207. Attributed to Byrd and Tallis jointly in *GB-Lbl* Add. 5054 f.1v. and to Byrd alone in *GB-Lbl* Madrigal Society 710-14."

p.95: below *O Mistress Mine* add "*O Mortal Man* à 5. EECM Supplementary i 34 no. 318 (incipit), MM (b) MS Mus. 439 f.9. Attributed to Byrd in VV 149 and 354, but not in either MS source cited on 149."

p.96, *Pavan and Galliard* (keyboard) III: after "lv" add "22".

p.97: below *Pavan* IV add "*Pavan* (keyboard; see *Alman* (keyboard) II)" *Piper's Pavan:* add "Another setting in *The Byrd Organ Book,* edited by M.H. Glyn (London: Reeves, 1923), p.6, no.6. Anonymous in source. See *17* p.214."

p.98: Below *Quia illic* add "*Retribue servo tuo* à 5. *Incola ego sum* (2nd section). D ix 241, *Incola ego sum* only. By Robert Parsons. See J 109." *Salve Regina:* Here Kerman states that Dart never made public his reasons for attributing this piece to Byrd. Its unique but incomplete source is *US-Ws* V.a.405-7 which also contains *Ecce quam bonum* (T 96) and the two dubious fantasy quartets (T A18 and T A19). This is a Folger set from the Paston manuscripts (see *63*) and Philip Brett suggests that "Since the Folger set does have other Byrd, Dart probably thought that, by analogy with Harvard Mus 30 and Add 29401-5, the un-named pieces stood a good chance of being by Byrd." (Letter to author 28 August 1992.) *Short Service I:* delete 2nd line and insert "WI".

p.99, *Watkin's Ale:* after "Iv" add "118".

p.100: below *Ah Youthful Years* add "*Air* Apocrypha".

p.104: below *Bonny Sweet Robin* add "*Born is the Babe* Apocrypha".

p.105: below *Cantate Domino* add "*Captain(e) Piper's Pavan* Apocrypha".

p.108: insert "*Dum transisset*".

p.115, *Jubilate:* insert "T 188".

p.118: below *Miserere mihi* add "*Miserere nostri domine* Apocrypha".

p.120: below *O Lord Give Ear* add "*O Lord God* (contrafactum) T 92".

p.121: below *O Mistress Mine* add "*O Mortal Man* Apocrypha".

p.122, *Pavan*, T A25: add "-7".

p.126: below *The Retreat* add "*Retribue servo tuo* Apocrypha".

p.152: insert "1933Hw Howes, Frank. *William Byrd.* Popular ed. Masters of Music. London: Kegan Paul, Trench, Trubner, 1933. *12.* Note: Reissue of 1928Hw."

p.163, 1985To: add "and letter, 10 (1986): 132." 1986 Ti: after "11" add "and Errata, 9 (1987): 69."

p.241, *100*: add "In *Notes* 38 (1987): 825-8 Richard Taruskin suggests Kerman should have drawn attention to Byrd's debt in the style and idea of his *Gradualia* to Palestrina's *Offertoria totius anni* of 1593."

p.254, *129:* add third ISBN 0571100554.

p.261, *134*: delete "82" as index is still in progress. From instalment 5, 1989, published at York.

p.291, I.38: after "relations," add "a reading from *GB-Och* 979-83."
p.292: CRD 1147 not released.
p.302:delete final paragraph.

A-III

WRITINGS AND CRITICISM: ADDENDA TO 1986
AND SUPPLEMENT 1987-92

Since 1986 some more literary references to Byrd have come to light. "William Byrd" and "The Motetts of William Byrd" can be found in *Collected Poems of Ivor Gurney*, edited by P.J. Kavanagh (Oxford: Oxford University Press, 1982), pages 253-4 and 257-9. Although both are included by Leonard Clark in his edition of *Poems of Ivor Gurney, 1890-1937* (London: Chatto & Windus, 1973), the latter, retitled "The Motets of William Byrd," is given here in a truncated version of only the first 32 lines. Gurney, who in later life tragically lost his reason, is unusual in having achieved equal eminence as a composer and a poet. In 1991 John Pile won Diabolus in Musica's Sonnet Competition with "To Mr. William Byrd, Gentleman of the Chapel Royal," which was published in *Midlands Early Music Forum Newsletter* (December, 1991): 6. In the novel *English Music* by Peter Ackroyd (London: Hamilton, 1992), the modern hero Timothy meets Byrd in a vision. *The Viola da Gamba Society of Great Britain Newsletter* published Marjorie Wardles's *Fantasy for Five* (78 (1992): 10) which refers specifically to Byrd's surviving fantasia for five viols, T 378.

In *WB30* I noted that later composers based their own individual works on the music of Tallis, but tended only to arrange specific pieces by Byrd. Edward Harper has arranged T 34, the second section of T 32 and T 28 as the unpublished *Three Motets by William Byrd* for brass quintet composed to celebrate the quatercentenary of Byrd's first *Cantiones*. However, *pace* my own observation, he has used T 243 as the basis of his own *Fantasia III* (Glasgow: Scottish Music Information Centre, 1977), also for brass quintet. The second movement of Hans Werner Henze's *4th String Quartet (1976)* (Mainz: Schott, 1976) is based on "William Byrd Pavana," but this turns out to be the apocryphal *Pavan* (keyboard) IV known to be by

Holborne: see page 97 of *WB153.*

Checklist of Byrd Criticism: Addenda to 1986

1923HOt Add "Byrd and Weelkes." *Musical Times* 64 (1923): 199.

1936Br Byrd, William. *Reasons briefely set downe by th'auctor, to perswade every one to learne to sing.* Oxford: Venables, 1936.
Note: Single sheet with hand coloured illustration.

1937Ls Lee, E. Markham. "The Student-Interpreter. Old English Harpischord Pieces: Arne, Dupuis, Hayes and Byrd." *Musical Opinion* 60 (1937): 407-8.

1943Ce Colles, H.C. *Edmund H. Fellowes: Author and Musicologist: About the Author, by Dr. H.C. Colles, Tributes to the Author, His Books and Editions of Music - with Special Reference to the Quatercentenary of William Byrd, 1543-1623.* London: Oxford University Press, 1943.

1948Bp Byrd, William. *The pleasure of singing.* New York: Coq d'Or, 1948.
Note: Broadside.

1984Gw Gould, Glenn. "William Byrd and Orlando Gibbons." In *The Glenn Gould Reader,* ed. by Tim Page. New York: Knopf, 1984; London: Faber, 1987, pp.11-13.

1984Mt Morehen, John. "The Tallis/Byrd 'Cantiones sacrae' (1575): an Appraisal of Current Methodology in Computer-Assisted Analysis." In *Informatique et musique: session musicologique de l'International Computer Music Conference, Paris, 1984,* ed. by Hélène Charnasse. Publications Elmeratto. Ivry sur Seine: Eratto, 1984, pp.59-76.

1984Oc Owens, Jessie Ann. "Charles Butler: a Key to the Music of William Byrd." In *Abstracts of Papers Read at the Fiftieth Annual Meeting of the American Musicological Society Meeting Jointly with the Society for Music Theory,* ed. by Anne Dhu Shapiro and Peter Breslauer. Philadelphia: American Musicological Society, 1984, pp.40-1. *WB147.*

1985Be Brett, Philip. *Editing Renaissance Music: the Byrd Edition.*" Chicago: Renaissance English Text Society, 1985.

1986Ht Harris, D. "Two Elizabethan Lute Masterpieces by John Dowland & William Byrd." *Guitarra* 12.68 (1986): 4-9.

1986Sw Sargent, Brian. "William Byrd: Mass for Five Voices." *Music Teacher* 65 (April 1986): 19.

Checklist of Byrd Criticism: Supplement from 1987

1987Mt Moroney, Davitt. "'Thinking and Pondering' about Byrd...on Two Recent Books." *Musical Times* 128 (1987): 18-20.
Note: Review article on *WB100* and *WB129.*

1987Rw Reeve, Edward Henry Lisle. "The William Byrd Tercentenary." In 1987Tw, pp.303-16. *WB152.*

1987Tw Turbet, Richard. *William Byrd: A Guide to Research.* Garland Composer Resource Manuals, 7. Garland Reference Library of the Humanities, 759. New York: Garland, 1987. *WB153.*
Note: Includes items by Reeve and Wood: see above and below.

1987Ww Winch, Nicholas. "William Byrd." *Pastoral Music Newsletter* (June/July 1987): 3-5.

1987WOa Wood, Anthony. "Anthony Wood's Notes on William Byrd." In 1987Tw, pp.329-33. *WB154.*

1988Br [Beechey, Gwilym.] "Reasons Briefly Set Down....1588." *Consort* 44 (1988): 2-7.

1988Pb Patton, John *and* Turbet, Richard. "Byrd in British Cathedrals, 1986." *Musical Opinion* 111 (1988): 52-9. *WB157.*

1988Th Turbet, Richard. "Homage to Byrd in Tudor Verse Services." *Musical Times* 129 (1988): 485-90. *WB158.*

1989Bw [Beechey, Gwilym.] "William Byrd 1589." *Consort* 45 (1989): 1-3.

1989Hw Howard, Michael. "William Byrd: an Account of His Life and Work." In TM469, p.313.
Note: Abstract of talk, with note of source.

1989Tb Turbet, Richard. "Byrd, Birmingham and Elgar." *Elgar Society Journal* 6 (1989): 7-8.
Note: Reprint of 1986Tb, slightly revised.

1989Tw Turbet, Richard. "William Byrd: Lincoln Cathedral's Greatest Musician." *Lincolnshire Life* 29 (October 1989): 63.

1990Bm Banks, Janet. "Mr Byrd's Musical Feast." *Radio Times* 263 (23 December 1989-5 January 1990): 128.

1990Dm Duncan-Jones, Katherine. "'Melancholie times': Musical Recollections of Sidney by William Byrd and Thomas Watson." In *The Well Enchanting Skill* (see *TM192*), pp.171-80. *WB160.*

1990Ip Irving, John. "Penetrating the Preface to *Gradualia.*" *Music Review* 51 (1990): 157-66. *WB188.*

1990Tb Turbet, Richard. "A Byrd Miscellany." *Fontes artis musicae* 37 (1990): 299-302. *WB161.*

1990Tc Turbet, Richard. "Continuing Byrd." *Musical Times* 131 (1990): 544. *WB162.*

1990Tg Turbet, Richard. "The Great Service: Byrd, Tomkins and Their Contemporaries, and the Meaning of 'Great'." *Musical Times* 131 (1990): 275-7. *WB163.*

1990Tw Turbet, Richard. "William Byrd and the English Musical Renaissance." *British Music Society Newsletter* 45 (1990): 123-4. *WB164.*

1991Fp Fawkes, Richard. "Protest Songs: Were There Coded

Messages in Byrd's Sacred Works?" *Classical Music* (23 March 1991): 33.
Note: Preview of television programme and video: see below, section A-VI.

1991Fw Fulton, K. *and* McCord, D.H. "William Byrd's Music and its Use within the Anglican Rite." *American Organist* 25 (January 1991): 62-9.

1991Hw Harrison, Christopher. "William Byrd and the Pagets of Beaudesert: a Musical Connection." *Staffordshire Studies* 3 (1990-91): 51-63. *WB165.*

1991Nb Norris, David Owen. "Byrd's Alman." *Keyboard Classics* 11.5 (1991): 40-1.

1992Bb Brown, Alan *and* Turbet, Richard, *eds. Byrd Studies.* Cambridge: Cambridge University Press, 1992. *WB168.*
Note: Includes essays by le Huray, Rees, Morehen, Wulstan, Monson, Kerman, Bennett, Irving, Gaskin, Hunter, Neighbour and Greenhalgh: see below.

1992BEb Bennett, John. "Byrd and Jacobean Consort Music: a Look at Richard Mico." In 1992Bb, pp.129-40. *WB167.*

1992Gb Gaskin, Hilary. "Baldwin and the Nevell Hand." In 1992Bb, pp.159-73. *WB169.*

1992GRb. Greenhalgh, Michael. "A Byrd Discography." In 1992Bb, pp.202-64. *WB170.*

1992Hm Hunter, Desmond. "My Ladye Nevells Booke and the Art of Gracing." In 1992Bb, pp.174-92. *WB171.*

1992Ib Irving, John. "Byrd and Tomkins: the Instrumental Music." In 1992Bb, pp.141-58. *WB172.*

1992Iw Irving, John. "William Byrd and the Three-Part Ayres of Thomas Holmes." *Brio* 29 (1992): 71-7. *WB173.*

1992Kw Kerman, Joseph. "'Write all These Down': Notes on a Byrd Song." In 1992Bb, pp.12-28. *WB174.*

1992Ls le Huray, Peter. "Some Thoughts About Cantus firmus Composition; and a Plea for Byrd's Christus resurgens." In 1992Bb, pp.1-23. *WB175.*

1992Mt Monson, Craig. "'Throughout All Generations': Intimations of Influence in the Short Service Styles of Tallis, Byrd and Morley." In 1992Bb, pp.83-111. *WB176.*

1992MOb Morehen, John. "Byrd's Manuscript Motets: a New Perspective." In 1992Bb, pp.51-62. *WB177.*

1992Ns Neighbour, Oliver. "Some Anonymous Pieces Considered in Relation to Byrd." In 1992Bb, pp.193-201. *WB179.*

1992Pg Pike, Lionel. "The Great Service: Some Observations on Byrd and Tomkins." *Musical Times* 133 (1992): 421-2. *WB180.*

1992Re Rees, Owen. "The English Background to Byrd's Motets: Textual and Stylistic Models for Infelix ego." In 1992Bb, pp.24-50. *WB181.*

1992Sw Stern, David. "William Byrd: Mass for Five Voices." In *Music before 1600,* ed. by Mark Everist. (Models of Musical Analysis.) Oxford: Blackwell, 1992, pp.208-24.

1992Tb Turbet, Richard. "Byrd Throughout All Generations." *Cathedral Music* 35 (1992): 19-24. *WB182.*

1992Tg Turbet, Richard. "The Great Service: a Postscript." *Musical Times* 133 (1992): 206. *WB183.*

1992Th Turbet, Richard. "Horsley's 1842 Edition of Byrd and its Infamous Introduction." *British Music* 14 (1992): 36-46. *WB184.*

1992Tm Turbet, Richard. ""*Melodious Birde*": the Solo Songs of William Byrd." In *Aspects of British Song*, ed. by Brian Blyth Daubney. Upminster: British Music Society, 1992, pp.10-14.

WB189.

1992Wb Wulstan, David. "Birdus tantum natus decorare magistrum." In 1992Bb, pp.63-82. *WB187.*

A-IV

BIBLIOGRAPHY: ADDENDA TO 1986 AND SUPPLEMENT 1987-92

Everyone with any interest in Byrd should be acquainted with the editors' preface to the volumes of *The Byrd Edition*. In particular those prefaces written within the dates of this Appendix by Philip Brett for the *Gradualia* volumes are substantial essays in Byrd musicology and biography, often supplementing Kerman in *WB100*.

The numerical sequence continues the one established in *WB153*, although it is not practical to maintain the three broad subject categories. Late inclusions for 1992 are appended outwith the alphabetical sequence, after *WB187*.

Bibliography: Addenda to 1986

WB141 Mellers, Wilfrid. *Music and Society: England and the European Tradition*. 2nd ed. London: Dobson, 1950. ML3795.M4.

Attempts to describe the evolution of English musical styles in relation to the European tradition, and to relate this evolution to the social and philosophical concepts that went to produce it. There are many references to Byrd in chapters III-V, also in some later chapters. Moreover there are some, not indexed, in chapter II (pp.56, 62-4) and additional references, again not indexed, in chapter III (pp.65-7, 71-3 and 77).

WB142 Cooke, Deryck. *The Language of Music*. London: Oxford University Press, 1959. ML3800.C75.

Suggests that certain musical outlines possess specific expressive resonances. Many examples are taken from Byrd's music: see the index.

WB143 Smith, Alan. "The Gentlemen and Children of the Chapel Royal of Elizabeth I: an Annotated Register." *Research Chronicle* 5 (1965): 13-46.

See *TM136.*

WB144 Fellowes, Edmund H. [Two Letters.] In *Music and Friends: Seven Decades of Letters to Adrian Boult,* ed. by Jerrold Northrop Moore. London: Hamilton, 1979, pp.77-8.

Dated 26 November and 15 December 1926, concerning T 191, to be sung by the Birmingham Festival Choral Society, conducted by Boult, on 23 January 1927. The first concerns parts still missing from the original work, the more interesting second concerns interpretation.

WB145 Charteris, Richard. "Manuscript Additions of Music by John Dowland and His Contemporaries in Two Sixteenth-Century Prints." *Consort* 37 (1981): 399-401.

The additions consist of fragmentary secular vocal and instrumental pieces in the copy of the joint *Cantiones* of Tallis and Byrd, 1575, at *EIRE-Dtc* B.1.32, and songs from Dowland's *First Booke,* 1597, in a copy of Monte's *Primo libro,* 1570, at *EIRE-Dm* Z4.3.1-5.

WB146 Griffiths, David. "The Music in York Minster." *Musical Times* 123 (1982): 633-7.

Contains a brief biography of Jane Stainton who, during the seventeenth century, owned the only surviving set of the first edition of Byrd's first book of *Gradualia,* 1605.

WB147 Owens, Jessie Ann. "Charles Butler: a Key to the Music of William Byrd." (See 1984Oc.)

Suggests that Byrd did not think along traditionally modal lines, but used four principal scale types. The author finds support for these observations in *The Principles of Music* by Charles Butler (London, 1636); see especially chapter II of book I.

WB148 Doughtie, Edward. "'William Byrd and the Consort Song." In *TM180,* pp.62-79; "William Byrd," pp.68-79.

General introduction owing much to *TM166,* but including close analysis of T 212.

WB149 McCoy, Stewart. "Lost Lute Solos Revealed in a Paston Manuscript." *Lute* 26 (1986): 21-39.

Includes reconstruction as a lute solo of T 373 based on a study of cantus contamination - inconsistent inclusion of the cantus part in the intabulation - in Paston lute sources. See also *TM337.*

WB150 Popkin, J.M. *Musical Monuments.* London: Saur, 1986. 0862913896. DA650.

Contains descriptions of memorials to Byrd in English churches.

Bibliography: Supplement 1987-92

WB151 Murray, Sterling E. *Anthologies of Music: an Annotated Index.* Detroit Studies in Music Bibliography, 55. Detroit: Information Co-ordinators, 1987. 0899900313. ML128.A7M87.

Provides access to the contents of most modern historical anthologies of musical examples. Byrd has 23 entries.

WB152. Reeve, Edward Henry Lisle. "The William Byrd Tercentenary." In *WB153,* pp.303-16.

First hand descriptions of the main events of 1923 transcribed from a record kept by the Rector of Stondon Massey, where Byrd is buried, and where many of them took place. He provides the only surviving list of the members of the impressive Byrd Tercentenary Committee.

WB153 Turbet, Richard. *William Byrd: a Guide to Research.* Garland Composer Resource Manuals, 7. Garland Reference Library of the Humanities, 759. New York: Garland, 1987. 342pp. 0824083881. ML134.B96T9.

Contains a catalogue of Byrd's works, with references to modern complete editions, plus an appendix of dubia and an apocrypha of spuria all with references to printed editions, and an index of titles; an introductory survey and complete checklist of Byrd criticism; a broadly classified bibliography of 140 significant writings, many not in the checklist as they are not primarily about Byrd; a review of sources for Byrd's biography; a dictionary of people and places associated with him; and a selective critical discography. Of topics proposed for future research, see subsequent developments in *WB157, WB161, WB164, WB165, WB168, WB173,* and WI. The manual includes *WB152* and *WB154,* and the only published full original text of Queen Elizabeth's letters patent to Tallis and Byrd for printing music. There are author, conference, Festschrift and periodical indexes. The present appendix updates *WB153,* and is to be continued in *Brio,* volume 31 or 32, 1994 or 1995.

WB154 Wood, Anthony. "Anthony Wood's Notes on William Byrd." In *WB153,* pp.329-33.

Transcription, with introduction and editorial notes. The editor draws attention to differing opinions as to the date of Wood's writings, late in the seventeenth century. See also *TM609.*

WB155. Flanagan, David. "Some Aspects of the Sixteenth-Century Parody Mass in England." *Music Review* 48 (1988): 1-11.

See *TM72.*

WB156 Meier, Bernhard. *The Modes of Classical Vocal Polyphony, Described According to the Sources,* transl. by Ellen S. Beebe. New York: Broude, 1988. 0845070258. ML3811.M4313.

Translation of *Die Tonarten der klassischen Vokalpolyphonie* (Utrecht: Oosthoek, Scheltema & Holkema, 1974) after revisions by the author. Attempts to explain how composers went about the business of creating music within the modal system as they comprehended it in their own day. Byrd is the only English composer whose works appear in the tables of examples. Eight of his works are discussed by the author and six are included in his tables, including two not hitherto discussed. The topic of mode is controversial, but the author's comments on T 17 and T 86 are illuminating.

WB157 Patton, John *and* Turbet, Richard. "Byrd in British Cathedrals, 1986." *Musical Opinion* 111 (1988): 52-9.

Lists all works by Byrd sung in cathedrals and comparable establishments in the British Isles during 1986. Two complementary listings indicate which choirs sang the various works, listed alphabetically, and which works were in the repertories of the listed choirs. The relevant information concerning three choirs absent from this survey is included in *WB182*.

WB158 Turbet, Richard. "Homage to Byrd in Tudor Verse Services." *Musical Times* 129 (1988): 485-90.

Suggests that several of Byrd's younger contemporaries paid musical homage to him by basing the opening phrases of their own verse Services on that of T 189. See also the subsequent letter, "Byrd and Clemens non Papa," 130 (1989): 129.

WB159 Teo, Kian-Seng. "William Byrd and Chromaticism." In *TM253*, pp.163-9.

Places Byrd in the continuum of the development and assimilation of chromaticism into the English madrigal, noting his roots in Netherlandish polyphony and possible knowledge of the Italian madrigal. This section is basically factual and says nothing new, though it is good to have a study devoted to an aspect of compositional technique as important as chromaticism. The author notes Byrd's judicious use of it for expressive effect and to create an overall mood, commenting on Byrd's considerable influence on Morley and later madrigalists. See also *TM254* and *TM255*.

WB160 Duncan-Jones, Katherine. "'Melancholie Times': Musical Recollections of Sidney by William Byrd and Thomas Watson." (See 1990Dm).

Investigates the interrelationships between the three men. Byrd set Sidney's lyrics and two funeral songs for Sidney of which one or both may have been the work of Watson. The texts of those lyrics he set are in some cases different from the first published versions, but the author concludes that there is too little evidence to claim for Byrd either personal knowledge of Sidney or privileged access to his texts. Watson seems to have been closer, albeit subordinate, to Sidney. Byrd and Watson collaborated on T 313 and *Italian Madrigals Englished*, 1590, and she offers some speculations about the purpose of the latter, possibly a posthumous tribute to Sidney, and why Byrd made two settings of the same text addressed to the queen, T 287 and T 314.

WB161. Turbet, Richard. "A Byrd Miscellany." *Fontes artis musicae* 37 (1990): 299-302.

Offers a possible source for the baptism of the composer's son Thomas which, if confirmed, would shed light on Byrd's movements immediately after leaving Lincoln in 1572, and gives the source of Thomas's spell in Spain. It contains the first complete listing of those anthems by Byrd whose texts appear in either edition of James Clifford's *Divine Services and Anthems*, 1663-4. Finally it discusses problematical entries in the list of anthems by Byrd in *TM586*.

WB162. Turbet, Richard. "Continuing Byrd." *Musical Times* 13 (1990): 544.

Review article that identifies the transcribers, Overend and Danby, responsible for two eighteenth century scores of the elusive first edition of Byrd's first book of *Gradualia*. In fact the identity of the former had already been suggested by Harry Colin Miller in *Introductory Euing Lectures on Music Bibliography and History* (Glasgow: Bayley & Ferguson, 1914), p.30.

WB163. Turbet, Richard. "The Great Service: Byrd, Tomkins and Their Contemporaries, and the Meaning of "Great"." *Musical Times* 131 (1990): 275-7.

Provides contemporary Tudor definition of "great," argues that Tomkins's *Third Service* was mistitled "Great" in the source which also contained Byrd's *Great Service,* and concludes that Fellowes invented a category of "Great Services" whereas the only work ever known correctly as the *Great Service* was Byrd's. See also subsequent letter "Tidying Up," p.527, and *WB183*.

WB164. Turbet, Richard. "William Byrd and the English Musical Renaissance." *British Music Society Newsletter* 45 (1990): 123-4.

Lists several quotations by or about early twentieth century composers that testify to the influence of the music of Byrd throughout the English Musical Renaissance.

WB165. Harrison, Christopher. "William Byrd and the Pagets of Beaudesert: a Musical Connection." *Staffordshire Studies* 3 (1990-91): 51-63.

Investigates whether Byrd was dangerously linked to Catholic conspirators through his friendship with the Paget family. In pursuance of this, the author reproduces all or part of eight hitherto unpublished letters from the early Paget correspondence, 1573-81. Of these, one is from Byrd himself, offering further evidence of his movements after leaving Lincoln in 1572; five mention him; and one mentions music. The author concludes that Byrd was possibly more closely connected with active Catholic conspiracy than had previously been thought, but further evidence is necessary. For the letters alone, this is a most important article in Byrd biography.

WB166. Shaw, Watkins. *The Succession of Organists of the Chapter Royal and the Cathedrals of England and Wales from c.1538...* (See *TM133.)*

Important for establishing the date when Robert Parsons died (two years later than thought hitherto) and when Byrd left Lincoln and succeeded him, almost immediately rather than after a hiatus of two years, in the Chapel Royal.

WB167. Bennett, John. "Byrd and Jacobean Consort Music: a Look at Richard Mico." In *WB168*, pp.129-40.

Disagrees with the opinion expressed in *WB129* that Byrd's consort music exerted a minimal influence over later composers in the genre, and considers its effect on the small but excellent corpus of Byrd's younger contemporary, Richard Mico.

WB168. Brown, Alan *and* Turbet, Richard, *eds. Byrd Studies.* Cambridge: Cambridge University Press, 1992. 276pp. 0521401291. ML410.B996B9.

Consists of twelve essays covering all the genres of Byrd's output. The writers offer between them a wide variety of approaches to the music and some of the conclusions are controversial or revise earlier opinions. As a celebration of the 450th anniversary of his birth, the essays consolidate Byrd research to date and indicate its future direction. See *WB167, WB169, WB170, WB171, WB172, WB174, WB175, WB176, WB177, WB179, WB181* and *WB187.*

WB169. Gaskin, Hilary. "Baldwin and the Nevell Hand." In *WB168,* pp.159-73.

Examines the hand employed by the scribe John Baldwin in My Ladye Nevells Booke and discusses his copying procedures.

WB170. Greenhalgh, Michael. "A Byrd Discography." In *WB168,* pp.202-64.

Lists all recordings of Byrd's original music available commercially in the United Kingdom between 1923 and 1988. See also section A-VII.

WB171. Hunter, Desmond. "My Ladye Nevells Booke and the Art of Gracing." In *WB168,* pp.174-92.

Examines the application of grace signs in My Ladye Nevells Booke and reappraises keyboard gracing from evidence in the manuscript against the background of a more general discussion of virginalist ornamentation.

WB 172. Irving, John. "Byrd and Tomkins: the Instrumental Music." In *WB168,* pp.141-58.

Investigates the influence of Byrd's music for keyboard and consort on that of Tomkins. Since the author notes more in the case of the former, it has the lion's share of the essay.

WB173. Irving, John. "William Byrd and the Three-Part Ayres of Thomas Holmes." *Brio* 29 (1992): 71-7.

Concludes that, *pace* Meyer in *TM341*, p.172, Holmes's pieces owe little to comparable works by Byrd in terms of structure, and nothing in terms of intellectual depth. The article is carefully argued and well illustrated.

WB174. Kerman, Joseph. "'Write all these down'": Notes on a Byrd Song." In *TM168,* pp.112-28.

Close analysis of T 294, taking the reader through Byrd's compositional process, with a digression to T 242.

WB175. le Huray, Peter. "Some Thoughts About Cantus firmus Composition; and a Plea for Byrd's Christus resurgens." In *WB168*, pp.1-23.

Considers English cantus firmus composition in the sixteenth century, with special reference to *Christus resurgens* from the *Gradualia* of 1605. *Pace* Kerman in *WB100*, he suggests it is a relatively late work by Byrd. The essay is generously illustrated, especially with substantial excerpts from otherwise unpublished pieces by Byrd's senior contemporaries Parsons and Knight.

WB176. Monson, Craig. "'Throughout All Generations': Intimations of Influence in the Short Service Styles of Tallis, Byrd and Morley." In *WB168,* pp.83-111.

Considers Byrd's *Short (First)* and *Third Services* in respect of their debt to Tallis's *Short Service* and their influence on Morley's *Short Evening* and *Second Services.*

WB177. Morehen, John. "Byrd's Manuscript Motets: a New Perspective." In *WB168,* pp.51-62.

Describes a computer-assisted project to test the authenticity of eleven motets whose attributions to Byrd are dubious.

WB178. Morehen, John. "The English Anthem Text, 1549-1660."

Journal of the Royal Musical Association 117 (1992): 62-85.

Comprehensive account of the range and variety of texts set by English composers for use in Divine Service in the new Church of England between the Reformation and the Restoration. The author divides them into psalm, metrical, scriptural and unidentified texts, seasonal collects, prayers, and miscellaneous texts. He illustrates the broad distribution of anthem texts by percentages using these divisions, and tabulates contrafacta and seasonal collects set between 1549 and 1660. Byrd's anthems are therefore considered in the context of what other composers were writing at the same time.

WB179. Neighbour, Oliver. "Some Anonymous Keyboard Pieces Considered in Relation to Byrd." In *WB168,* pp.193-201.

Looks at pieces from the Forster and Weelkes virginal books, *GB-Lbl* R.M. 24.d.3 and Add.30485 respectively. Three are already established in the Byrd canon - T 432, T 508 and T 509 - and three are at least worth debating: T A24, T A26 and T A27 (see Addenda for p.87). He then considers whether Byrd was responsible for some keyboard arrangements of his own vocal music, and devotes his final section to an analysis of one particularly interesting example, T 31.

WB180. Pike, Lionel. "The Great Service: Some Observations on Byrd and Tomkins." *Musical Times* 133 (1992): 421-2.

Disagrees with the arguments advanced in *WB163* and maintains that there was indeed a category of great Services consisting, at the least, of Byrd's (T 191) and Tomkins's *Third Service.* The author makes some interesting analytical comparisons between the two works, suggesting that Tomkins was, in the musicological sense, parodying Byrd's piece, but he provides no new information or insights to disprove the contention in *WB163.*

WB181. Rees, Owen. "The English Background to Byrd's Motets: Textual and Stylistic Models for Infelix ego." In *WB168,* pp.24-50.

Querying received wisdom, argues that the English psalm motet was not so much a response to continental developments as a reflection of the content of Primers in use in English religious institutions.

WB182. Turbet, Richard. "Byrd Throughout all Generations." *Cathedral Music* 35 (1992): 19-24.

Traces the popularity or otherwise of Byrd's sacred music in English cathedrals from the seventeenth century to 1986. Includes a supplement to *WB157*.

WB183. Turbet, Richard. "The Great Service: a Postscript." *Musical Times* 133 (1992): 206.

Notes that Hooper's *Full Service* was also entitled "Great" in part of one source, and suggests that this was a mistake for Byrd's *Great Service* which is in the same manuscript. See also *WB163*.

WB184. Turbet, Richard. "Horsley's 1842 Edition of Byrd and Its Infamous Introduction." *British Music* 14 (1992): 36-46.

In 1842 the Musical Antiquarian Society published William Horsley's edition of Byrd's first *Cantiones* with an introduction by the editor that was dismissive of Byrd's music. The article traces Horsley's progress on his edition by quoting hitherto unpublished entries from his diary, and for the first time in 150 years reproduces in full his notorious introduction.

WB185. Turbet, Richard. "'Melodious Birde': the Solo Songs of William Byrd." In *Aspects of British Song,* ed. by Brian Blyth Daubney. Upminster: British Music Society, 1992, pp.10-14.

Assessment of Byrd's consort songs, using lesser known examples from the recorded repertory.

WB186. Turbet, Richard. "The Musical Antiquarian Society, 1840-1848." *Brio* 29 (1992): 13-20.

Three of the Society's nineteen publications (all fully listed) contained music by Byrd, and the Society can be credited with initiating the resurrection of William Byrd. (The final date on p.19 should read 1843.) See also *WB184* and section A-VII on further

Byrd research. A paper by the same author on "William Dyce and the Motett Society" which had similar aims is scheduled for publication in *Aberdeen University Review* 55 (1993).

WB187. Wulstan, David. "Birdus tantum natus decorare magistrum." In *WB168,* pp.63-82.

Partly assisted by computer analysis, describes Byrd's vocal scoring at different stages in his career, supporting the author's view that the performing pitch level of the Latin music was closely related to that of the Anglican music. This is the author's final statement on the question of pitch (see also *TM22*) and he is combative in disputing the points raised in *TM398* and *TM153.*

WB188. Irving, John. "Penetrating the Preface to *Gradualia.*" *Music Review* 51 (1990): 157-66.

Considers Byrd's comments, in the preface to the first *Gradualia*, about inspiration, and attempts to apply them to Byrd's own compositional process, using *Iustorum animae* (T 86) as a model. This paper was published late in 1992.

WB189. Stern, David. "William Byrd: Mass for Five Voices." (See 1992Sw.)

Schenkerian analysis of Kyrie.

A-V

BIOGRAPHY AND DICTIONARY: ADDENDA AND SUPPLEMENT

Biography

Since 1986 three important items relating to Byrd's biography have appeared, along with an addendum to chapter IV of *WB153.*

In *TM133* (p.3) Watkins Shaw announces he has found a discrepancy in the dating of contemporary Chapel Royal records which confirmed beyond reasonable doubt that Robert Parsons died in 1572, not 1570 (or even 1569) as previously thought. Byrd therefore replaced him as a Gentleman immediately and not after an inexplicable delay of over two years. This also clarifies the situation in Lincoln, where Thomas Butler's succession to Byrd can now be seen to have been straightforward and not anticipated two years in advance. Referring back to Shaw's definitive article on Byrd at Lincoln (WB20) he translates the fairly standard document appointing Byrd to the post of Organist and Master of the Choristers (p.52). This the Dean and Chapter did "for his good service already rendered." Probably this refers to a probationary period served beforehand, especially as his predecessor was last encountered in 1560, three years before Byrd's appointment (TM133, p.155). Nevertheless in view of the evidence that both Bull and Morley, pupils of Byrd, returned to be organists of cathedrals where they had been choristers (TM133, pp.132 and 198-9), it is tempting to wonder whether this phrase refers to a period Byrd might have spent as a treble in Lincoln Cathedral Choir, the more tempting in view of our almost total ignorance about his life before 1563, lightened only by Wood's passing remark in WB154. Any such discussion must bear in mind the existence of Thomas Byrd, a Gentleman of the Chapel Royal from 1526 to 1561 (TM436, p.418) about whom next to nothing is known (ibid., p.298): if Wood is right that Tallis taught Byrd, this was probably at the Chapel Royal, during Thomas Byrd's lifetime.

It is suggested in WB161 that the baptism of Byrd's second son Thomas may have taken place in Clerkenwell in 1578. In a most important article WB165, the historian Christopher Harrison transcribes a letter written by Byrd from Clerkenwell in 1573. It is documented that Byrd left Lincoln in 1572 and that his wife was living at Harlington in 1577, so any indications of his whereabouts during the mid 1570s are welcome. See section A-VII for some further research on Byrd's biography.

In The Progresses, Processions, and Magnificent Festivities, of King James the First (London: Nichols, 1828, vol.2), p.193, John Nichols records that at the Merchant Taylors' Hall, London, on 16 July 1607 "divers synging-men ... did sing melodious songs at the said dinner" including "William Byrd." See WB143 for which voice he probably sang.

Dictionary

Lownes, Humphrey (fl.1587-1629)
Printer of second editions of both books of *Gradualia,* 1610.
(*Humphries*)

Redmer, Richard (fl.1610-32)
Publisher of second editions of both books of *Gradualia.* (*Humphries*)

Key: *Humphries* See *TM473.*

Mary Brownlow died in 1680.

A-VI

SELECTIVE CRITICAL DISCOGRAPHY 1989-92, AND VIDEO

WB170 begins at 1923 and includes recordings commercially available in the United Kingdom to the end of 1988. Only one predates the Tercentenary, a rendering of the *Lullaby* (T 241), number CL2 on page 65 of *TM469.* To remain consistent with chapter VI of *WB153,* the present discography cites both title and catalogue number. It contains discussions of recordings released since the end of 1988, the terminal date of *WB170* (see above), and unless otherwise stated the numbers cited are for compact discs. Since the advent of the compact disc Byrd has fared well for recordings of pieces previously unrecorded, as well as his more familiar music. In response to the pleas of the editors of *WB168* (pp.xii-xiii) there have been some quasi-liturgical recordings of the mass ordinaries with propers. The intention of the present discography is to guide those interested towards the best or most useful recordings of Byrd's music, not to provide a complete listing. For information about a continuation of *WB170,* see section A-VII on future Byrd research.

Two cycles of recordings of propers using the three masses (T 1-3) have been initiated since 1988. One is complete. This is performed by The Choir of Christ Church Cathedral, Oxford on Nimbus. NI 5237 contains the *Mass for Five Voices with the Propers for All Saints'*

Day. Although the performance of the mass lacks the ultimate spirituality of the version by The Choir of St John's College, Cambridge, praised in *WB153* (p.289), it is the best interspersed with propers, T 84-7, amongst which *Iustorum animae* receives its finest rendition on disc. Three further motets act as fillers, of which *Laudate Dominum* (T 163) is recorded for the first time. (See *WB162* for a review as part of a longer article.) NI 5287 consists of the *Mass for Four Voices with the Propers for the Feast of Corpus Christi.* It is less successful than its predecessor, and regrettably omits *O sacrum convivium* (T 94) from the sequence of propers (T 88-95) while including a long plainsong sequence. On the side of the angels is the most distinguished recording of the familiar *Sacerdotes domini* (T 90), first recordings of *Quotiescunque manducabitis* and *O salutaris hostia* (T 91 and T 93), and a fine performance of *Pange lingua* (T 95) to replace the unpleasant rendition listed in *WB170.* NI 5320, *Mass for Three Voices with the Propers for the Nativity*, ranks among the best of Byrd recordings. The mass is performed uniquely for SAT, at a high pitch using trebles whereas all others use men's voices at ATB pitch. The performance is luminous but so is the interpretation. The propers (T 119-27) have all appeared on a disc discussed in *WB152* (pp.290-1). Christ Church's performances are everything for which one could hope, none more so than the sublime *O magnum misterium* (T 126).

The other cycle is still in progress at the time of writing. Performed by The Sixteen on Virgin, VC 7908022 contains the same repertory as NI 5237 above, though with different fillers: two motets in eight parts, *Diliges Dominum* and *Ad Dominum cum tribularer* (T 15 and T 179), neither of them first recordings. These are all fine performances with only the merest trace of blandness rendering them in any way inferior to those of Christ Church. VC 7911332 consists of the *Mass for 4 voices with Propers for the Feast of Saints Peter & Paul.* This is an eccentric collection for two reasons. First, it begins with Monte's *Super flumina Babylonis* (see *WB153,* p.276, for the reason) and Byrd's companion piece for eight voices, *Quomodo cantabimus* (T 180). In some respects the performance of the mass is better than Christ Church's, but the jewel of this disc is the presence of Byrd's wonderful (and only) propers for six voices, T 156-62. Amongst them is the second eccentricity. *Tu es Petrus* (T 159), the only proper recorded before, should be sung twice during the course of the mass, first with its concluding alleluia, later without. Here, only the alleluia is sung the first time, so listeners never hear the work in its entirety. Conversely, both the required differing manifestations of *Constitues eos principes* (T 157) are given in full. See section A-VII below for details of the proposed completion of this project.

Little needs to be written about *The Three Masses* sung by The Choir of Winchester Cathedral (Argo 4301642). This is the best recording with all three masses on one disc. Indeed, both the performance and the interpretation of the Mass à 4 approach as near to perfection as makes no difference. The Mass à 3 has been recorded competently by the Lay Vicars of Wells Cathedral on Alpha CDCA 924.

Gradualia volume 1: The Marian Masses by The William Byrd Choir (Hyperion CDA66451) is the first in a projected recording of all the music in both books. It covers T 56-80, though only T 56-60 and T 70-7 are unique recordings.

Ave verum corpus: Motets and Anthems of William Byrd (Collegium COLCD 110) is a fine anthology by The Cambridge Singers. Of eighteen items, three are unique recordings: *Plorans plorabit, Veni Sancte Spiritus et emitte* and *Christus resurgens* (T 83, T 154 and T 97), all most welcome additions to the Byrd discography. Indeed T 83 and T 97 are two of Byrd's most intense creations. Volume 1 of Tudor Church Music by Worcestor Cathedral Choir (Alpha CDCA 943) contains the first recording of *Cantate Domino.*

Compline with Anthems & Motets (Gamut GAM CD 531) includes three items by Byrd sung by Clare College Chapel Choir, Cambridge, all from the 1575 *Cantiones: O lux beata, Miserere mihi* (*sic,* not "mei" as on the insert) and *Memento homo* (T 9, T 16 and T 11), but the last mentioned is sung in its early seventeenth-century form (from a manuscript in Durham Cathedral) as a contrafactum *O Lord Give Ear,* containing some fascinating musical differences from the published Latin version.

Born is the Babe is an outstanding recital of songs and consort music by the boyish toned soprano Annabella Tysall and the Rose Consort of Viols (Woodmansterne WOODM 001-2). Two of the pieces for viols are by Byrd, as are three songs in a generous total of twenty items. Of the latter, two are unique recordings: *O God That Guides* and *Out of the Orient Crystal Skies* (the version listed in *WB170* and *TM469* - wrongly under ANON - is Thurston Dart's unnecessary arrangement for duet and continuo), T 303 and T 330. The latter appears anonymously in Peter Warlock's arrangement for five voices (published posthumously edited by W.G. Whittaker in 1932 before Dart and Brett established it was by Byrd: see *WB53*) on *The Frostbound Wood: Christmas Music by Peter Warlock* (Continuum CCD 1053) sung by the Allegri Singers. The disc also contains *My Little Sweet Darling* which, similarly in tune with the musicology of the day, is attributed in its original form to Byrd. Neither attribution is updated in the accompanying notes, dated 1992.

Night's Black Bird and *Goe Nightly Cares* are a pair of discs (Virgin 7907952 and 7911172) by Fretwork each comprising dances from Dowland's *Lachrimae* with consort music and, on the latter, also four of the finest songs by Byrd sung by the countertenor Michael Chance. The former disc contains a unique recording of Byrd's first fantasy trio (T 372) and the latter, unique recordings of the first and third In nomine quintets (T 388 and T 390). See section A-VII below for the proposed development of this project.

On *Renaissance Music for Recorders: the English & Franco-Flemish Schools* by Sesquitertia (Adda 581180) there are nine relatively unfamiliar items by Byrd (out of 27) including unique recordings of the second *Christe qui lux* and *Miserere* (T 398-400 and T 404-5).

Two anthologies devoted to Byrd's keyboard music have been released. *Pieces from the Fitzwilliam Virginal Book* (Claves CD 50-9001), played by Ursula Duetschler, have all been recorded before, but this is a well balanced programme including less familiar items, such as the Pavan and Galliard in g minor no. 3 (T 497) and Fantasia in G major no. 2 (T 448). On *Grounds and Variations* (Koch 370572H1), played by Elaine Thornburgh, there are only two pieces in common with the *Fitzwilliam* anthology - *Walsingham* and *The Carman's Whistle* (T 521 and T 439) - yet it too is replete with classic pieces, from the introspection of *Fortune* (T 451) through the profundity of *Hugh Aston's Ground* (T 463) to the dazzling virtuosity of the *Passamezzo* Pavan and Galliard (T 487) and the sparkle of *O Mistress Mine* (T 478).

An interesting "spuriosity" to find its way onto disc is the *Short Service* by William Inglott that is attributed in one source to Byrd (see above, section A-II, addenda for page 11). On Priory PRCD 396, Norwich Cathedral Choir sings the Venite and the Te Deum. The entire Service survives fragmentarily though reconstructably in two sources, but the Te Deum is the only movement to survive in three. The disc also contains music by Parsley and Morley, including the evening canticles of the latter's *First Service* which, as demonstrated in *WB158,* pay homage to Byrd's *Second Service.*

The anonymous *Salve regina* attributed to Byrd by Thurston Dart when his edition was published in 1955 is sung by The Festival Choir of the National Shrine of Our Lady on *Music from Walsingham* (Herald HAVPC 149, cassette only).

Video

On Sunday 31 March 1991, Channel Four Television broadcast *The Two Lives of William Byrd*, a Yorkshire Television production directed by Tony Scull. It is previewed, with an informative interview with the director, in 1991Fp. Of particular interest are the illustrative performances by the Nonsuch Consort of ten pieces, complete or in part, including the Easter propers (T 138-42 omitting T 140). Of equal interest are the Anglican contributions: Lincoln Cathedral Choir sings the Nunc dimittis from the *Short Service* (T 188g) and the choir of the Chapel Royal, St James's, sings the Benedictus (T 188c); neither canticle has been recorded on disc. Using hitherto unreproduced early sources, the programme emphasizes Byrd's perceived double role as a member of the Protestant Chapel Royal and as a practising Roman Catholic. The video can be purchased *for private use* from Programme Sales Department, Yorkshire Television, Kirkstall Road, Leeds LS3 1JS, England (telephone 0532 438283, extension 4060).

A-VII

BYRD RESEARCH AND INFORMATION: THE FUTURE

As stated in the introduction to this appendix, a review of the activities during the 450th anniversary of Byrd's birth, 1992-3, will appear in *Brio* during 1994 or 1995. Several of these activities will be in the form of writings or discs, and those known to be in progress are noted below, to be listed in *Brio* if and when completed.

Six volumes of *The Byrd Edition* with their indispensable introductions are still awaited, of which all but volume 9, unpublished Latin motets including the questionable attributions edited by Warwick Edwards, are the responsibility of Philip Brett. The remainder are volumes 6b, 7a and 7b to complete the *Gradulia* and 12 and 13 consisting of the secular vocal collections of 1588-9. (In volume 1, Craig Monson omitted from his list of surviving printed copies of the 1575 *Cantiones* a contratenor partbook in the Britten-Pears Library, Aldeburgh, Suffolk, England, call number 787.99 + 780.4.)

Joed Press of Carshalton Beeches is producing a complete edition of the *Gradualia*, with separate volumes for each set of propers, specifically for liturgical use, edited initially by Michael Proctor, then by Jon Dixon. The former has prepared an "introductory and companion booklet" awaiting publication.

Of continuing projects, *TM434* will provide three forthcoming volumes relevant to Tudor music: VI (1558-1603) and VII (1485-1558) plus a *A Biographical Dictionary of English Court Musicians, 1485-1714* by Andrew Ashbee, David Lasocki and Peter Holman. *The Songs, Services and Anthems of William Byrd* by Philip Brett, the second volume in the series *The Music of William Byrd*, will be the last to appear and is still awaited (see *WB129* and *WB100*). Michael Greenhalgh is maintaining his discography begun in *WB170* with a view to the possible publication after 1993 of an update from 1989. David Wulstan's computer statistics for *WB187* will appear in *Musicus* in due course.

Among new projects, four papers on Byrd are in a Festschrift entitled *Sundry Sorts of Music Books: Essays on the British Library Collections presented to O.W. Neighbour on his 70th Birthday*, edited by Chris Banks *et al,* scheduled to be published by the Library in April 1993: David Moroney writes about compass in the keyboard works, Alan Brown contributes a paper on *The Woods so Wild* (T 523), Philip Brett discusses the Paston manuscript, and Richard Turbet contributes "The Fall and Rise of William Byrd 1623-1901": in fact a study of how Byrd's reputation fared from his death in 1623 until the beginning of his revival in the middle of the nineteenth century, based on a study of the collections of printed music in the Library. This is continued into the twentieth century in a booklet about Byrd (Lincoln: Honywood Press), which will also consider how his music has fared in Lincoln since 1623, and will offer a new critical insight into his relationship with Sheppard, confirming the place of *Similes illis fiant* in the Byrd canon. This is scheduled for publication during May 1993.

Roger Bowers has accumulated enough material for a paper on Byrd's boyhood and early career. This derives from Bowers's research towards a chapter on music for *The History of Lincoln Cathedral* edited by Dorothy Owen to be published by Cambridge University Press. He has evidence that Byrd may after all have been a chorister at St Paul's Cathedral in London during the 1550s, a proposal first made by Rimbault in 1841 (see *WB5*) but rejected by recent historians since Fellowes in 1923Fw. Bowers surmises that the influences Byrd met as a choirboy seem to explain much about his subsequent life and career, especially his recusancy.

Warwick Edwards has reconstructed the Fantasia à 4 III (T 377) for performance by the Scottish Early Music Consort (premiered at The Queen's Hall, Edinburgh, 10 December 1992). Richard Turbet has reconstructed the fragmentary broken consort arrangement of *The Fifth Pavan* (T 483) for publication during 1993 (Lincoln: Lindum Desktop Music) and premiere at the Lincoln Society of Arts, Usher Gallery, 15 October 1993, by Bergamasca. It is proposed also to reconstruct the probable original version for a consort of viols.

There are important recording projects in hand, though these are always at the mercy of commercial vicissitudes. For Virgin, Fretwork are hoping to produce a disc of all Byrd's consort music that survives intact, which would include items on the discs mentioned in section in A-VI above.

For the same label The Sixteen intend to complete their cycle of Byrd's masses and propers with the Mass à 3, propers for Advent (T 67-70) and five substantial fillers including *Infelix ego* (T 50) and the unpublished and unrecorded *Petrus beatus* (T 174). Also for Virgin Davitt Moroney is recording Byrd's complete keyboard music. Meanwhile at the draft stage of *WB168* it was noticed in *WB170* that some of Byrd's keyboard pieces remained unrecorded. A selection of these are on the cassette released as a supplement to *WB168* (see p.264) and entitled *William Byrd: Organ Music* played by Mark Duthie (TD 0901), distributed by Top Note Music, 123 Crown Street, Aberdeen, Scotland (telephone 0224 210259). The remaining unrecorded pieces will be played by Alan Cuckston on *William Byrd: Harpsichord Music* (Swinsty FEW 127), a release scheduled to celebrate Byrd's 450th anniversary. For Hyperion The William Byrd Choir plans to record the complete *Gradualia*, four more discs to follow the first volume noted above in section A-VI. It is a matter for profound regret that John Rutter had to abandon a plan to record all of Byrd's sacred choral music with the Cambridge Singers on Collegium, after the one disc noted in the same section. Volume two of *Tudor Church Music* by Worcester Cathedral Choir on the Alpha label will include Byrd's Easter propers and two other motets. On the same label The Vicars Choral of Wells Cathedral include *Defecit in dolore* on their second compact disc (Alpha CDCA 944). The Byrd video is scheduled to be repeated during 1993.

A-VIII

WILLIAM BYRD MEMORIAL (OR ANNIVERSARY) CONCERTS 1987-92

These concerts have been given annually in Stondon Massey Parish Church since 1968 by the Stondon Singers, as near as possible to the date of Byrd's death, July 4. (See *WB153*, pp.315-6). The Byrd pieces performed, usually as part of a programme including music by other composers, since 1986 are as follows:

1987: T 1 (d-e)
1988: T 189, T 90, T 193, T 437, T 314

1989: T 55, T 304
1990: T 47, T 55
1991: T 50
1992: T 52, T 86

A-IX

INDEX OF BYRD'S WORKS CITED BY CATALOGUE NUMBER

T 1 (d-e): Mass à 4 (Sanctus and Agnus)
T 17: *Tribue Domine*
T 28: *In resurrectione*
T 31: *O quam gloriosum*
T 32: *Tribulationes civitatum*
T 34: *Laetentur coeli*
T 47: *Miserere mei*
T 50: *Infelix ego*
T 52: *Cantate Domino*
T 55: *Haec dies (à 6)*
T 86: *Iustorum animae*
T 90: *Sacerdotes Domini*
T 189: *Second Service*
T 191: *Great Service*
T 193: *Arise O Lord*
T 212: *My Soul Oppressed*
T 242: *Why do I Use*
T 243: *Come to Me Grief*
T 287: *This Sweet and Merry Month* (à 4)
T 294: *Retire my Soul*
T 304: *Praise our Lord*
T 313: *Let Others Praise*
T 314: *This Sweet and Merry Month (à 6)*
T 373: Fantasia à 3 II
T 432: Alman in C Major no.2
T 437: *The Carman's Whistle*
T 508: Prelude in F Major
T 509: Prelude in G Major
T A24: *Piper's Galliard*
T A26-7: Pavans: see Addenda for p.87, above.

A-X

ILLUSTRATIONS

(a) Plates 1-8: The tenors of nine anonymous pieces à 4, Viola da Gamba Society numbers 1361-9, reproduced from leaves sewn into the back of an isolated tenor partbook of Byrd's first book of *Cantiones Sacrae,* 1589, now in private hands. I am grateful for the owner's permission to reproduce these parts, of which only the first has previously been published.

Plate 1: *Tenor 4 parts 1* (Anon.)

Plate 2: *Tenor 4 parts 2* (Anon.)

Plate 3: *Tenor 4 parts 3* (Anon.)

Plate 4: *Tenor 4 parts 4* (Anon.)

Plate 5: *Tenor 4 parts 5* and Tenor no.9 transposed. (Anon.)

Plate 6: *Tenor 4 parts 6* (Anon.)

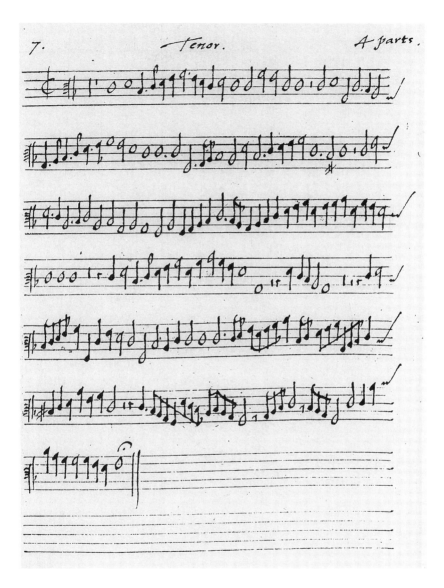

Plate 7: *Tenor 4 parts 7* (Anon.)

Plate 8: *Tenor 4 parts 8* and *9* (Anon.)

AUTHOR INDEX

References are to running numbers in the bibliographies: e.g. 705 (Tudor Music), 1986Sw (Checklist of Byrd Criticism), WB146 (Byrd Bibliography) or XI (introduction to specific chapter in Tudor Music section).

MUSICIAN INDEX

p. 6